COACHING SOCCER

10-15 Year Olds

Planning Technical and Tactical Training

**Library of Congress Cataloging
Publication Data**

Coaching Youth Soccer
by Stefano Bonaccorso

Original Title: Calcio - Allenare il settore giovanile
Original Printing - 1999 by Editoiale Sport Otalia Milan
Translated from Italian by Maura Modanesi
Eitorial coordination - Marco Marchei
Technical Director - Ferretto Ferretti

ISBN # 1-890946-63-X
Library of Congress Catalog Number 2001090053
Copyright © July 2001

Art Direction/Layout/Illustrations
Kimberly N. Bender

Editing and Proofing
Bryan R. Beaver

Printed by
DATA REPRODUCTIONS
Auburn, Michigan

REEDSWAIN Publishing
612 Pughtown Road
Spring City • Pennsylvania 19475
1-800-331-5191
www.reedswain.com
EMAIL:info@reedswain.com

COACHING SOCCER

10-15 Year Olds

Planning Technical and Tactical Training

by Stefano Bonaccorso

FOREWORD

In the last few years, soccer has gradually undergone several important changes inevitably resulting from the general cultural unrest that is characterizing the world of sport as a whole.

The figure and the role of the fitness coach have progressively become increasingly important and this has consequently improved specific training programs for physical skills, thus helping build and train increasingly powerful and fast athletes capable of physical endurance.

The evolution of both systems of play and tactics - characterized by an increasingly improved defensive arrangement - has emphasized the concept of "short team", aiming at re-gaining possession of the ball through pressing, double teaming and offside strategy. All this has dramatically reduced both space and time for players to think and act, thus often causing the rhythms of the competition to increase abruptly to the detriment of the quality of play. Fortunately, these exaggerated tactical movements are somehow nullified by exceptionally technically skillful players, whose creativeness and talent often upset the opposing defensive lines. Therefore, it would be desirable - in youth soccer, at least - to revive a soccer philosophy that concentrates less on pure competition and exaggerated tacticism, and focuses greater attention on all those creative and constructive aspects of playing soccer.

It is fundamental to encourage athletes to perform all the main technical movements during the course of a match, like dribbles, final passes or shots on goal that suitable programs specifically designed for youth soccer should constantly pursue as priority goals.

The content of this book - dealing with the most innovative methods for coaching and learning basic technique and individual tactical skills, which should always be considered the key component of youth soccer - can offer important suggestions and interesting inputs on the subject.

This work - resulting from the author's long experience as a youth soccer coach - intends to be a useful support to help enrich the knowledge of all those who work to train and educate youth through soccer.

Mino Favini
Head of the Youth Sector
at Atalanta Bergamasca Calcio

To Simona and Filippo

I wish to express my heartfelt thanks to Lucia Castelli
for she offered me her valuable support in writing this book
and the first chapter, in particular.
I would also like to thank Anna Ghilardi, Emanuele Sangalli,
Aida Zoppetti, Roberto Bellocci, Andrea Bacheroni, Davide
Colciaghi, Sonia Lanza, Massimiliano Donadoni, Roberto Radici, Eugenio Perico, Isa,
Carla and Paola.

INTRODUCTION

In our long tradition, soccer has always been handed down from generation to generation - rather than really coached - on the basis of all the personal experiences of the coaches who (with great passion and full knowledge of the facts, of course!) have often reduced general training plans specifically designed for adult athletes to a small scale, thus adapting them to suit youth players.

Training sessions in youth soccer have always been based on traditional coaching methods where the coach explains, demonstrates, has his players perform the exercise and finally corrects their bad movements, leaving the players little opportunity for creativity.

For years, soccer coaches have applied to exaggerated technical movements, with the intention of improving players' performances in competition.

Recent studies of training methodology and educational psychology clearly point out the importance of going beyond any ideal technical model that youth players are asked to imitate and avoiding all those exercises that are simply based on pure coaching methods where the solution to any difficult and problematic situation is anticipated, suggested and finally solved by the coach himself. By contrast, those studies mainly focus the attention on how activities and exercises are suggested, on the importance of "how one should do something" instead of "what one should do", in order to make coaching and educational suggestions much more effective.

Inductive coaching-and-learning methods – those that offer the player the opportunity to discover, perform, test, become aware of and reflect on the particular technical movement or the best tactical strategy in a given situation - are said to enhance extremely elastic sports skills that can be easily adapted to all the various situations of play, thus allowing players to make coordinated and effective movements peculiar to soccer. Furthermore, these particular methods positively influence the development of such important cerebral capacities as attention, concentration, perception and memory, while also favoring the development of tactical thinking.

Today, youth soccer coaches are heartily invited to enrich their competence beyond mere technical and tactical basic ideas and improve their knowledge in various fields, including methodology, physiology, educational psychology and so forth. I would say that the modern coach should work to make learning much easier and help players express the potential they have, rather than simply work to train his players' physical skills and coach specific soccer abilities.

In this way, the coach also becomes an educator whose attention is mainly directed at creating a positive atmosphere of stimulating mutual cooperation in training sessions and encouraging and exploiting the emotional dimension of his young players, consequently enhancing their motivation to learn soccer.

This is why it is absolutely fundamental for a competent coach to be able to plan, scheme, study and work out effective soccer suggestions and functional solutions for the activity of the whole team, while also focusing on the personal needs of every single athlete.

This book is not intended to be a simple technical and tactical handbook. The activities shown are not to be considered as strict guidelines to be followed literally. In fact, they can be used as useful instruments for the coach to enhance and exploit all the various aspects of his young athletes' personalities. This is possible only if both inductive and deductive coaching methods are properly combined according to the particular situations that the coach will have to deal with and in relation to educational goals.

The modern young soccer player is a person who is able to think reasonably, choose freely the best way to solve problems, control his own feelings and emotions, communicate to others, cooperate with others and finally act, being fully aware of his actions.

The Author

PREFACE

This book, specifically conceived for coaches, trainers, club managers, educators and all those who work to train and educate young people through sport, points out all the various educational potentialities of soccer in the period of pre-adolescence that can be developed by means of specific coaching methods and models, combining the traditional approach and both the cognitive and humanistic ideas of modern educational psychology.

The relevant coaching-and-learning methods are all illustrated both at a theoretical level and by means of concrete examples. When they are properly combined together and carried out in training sessions, this considerably helps the young soccer player become aware of all the various learning mechanisms involved in the process, thus favoring the optimum development of all those skills peculiar to soccer and of his general motor intelligence as well.

The whole sequence of coaching and training units suggested throughout the book which coaches can easily use to plan training sessions in a fairly elastic manner - transforms what can be defined as occasional coaching, based on contents exclusively, into a really innovative didactic method, properly planned according to specific goals and to the players' personal needs.

The movements focusing on both basic technical skills and individual tactical abilities are all explained and shown in a particularly detailed manner, in order to clearly point out all those main aspects of coordination that directly influence an effective performance of the movement itself. Furthermore, this also helps explain where, how, when and why one should make a particular soccer movement, thus gradually enhancing the coach's awareness, allowing him to plan well-aimed and differentiated didactic-coaching solutions for his players.

In particular, this work offers coaches and educators important suggestions, inputs, practical information and play solutions to plan and organize such basic activities as starting games, specific exercises, drills, play situations and conditioned games.

Moreover, this book also wants to point out that the final outcome of all the various learning situations and opportunities does not depend on the activities the coach suggests in training sessions exclusively, but is also significantly influenced by the relationship between the coach and the athlete himself. A good and positive relationship between the protagonists of this important coaching-and-learning process obviously favors the development of a highly positive and stimulating atmosphere and this condition is absolutely necessary to enhance personal motivations and improve not only one's sports performance, but also the qualities of one's character.

Lucia Castelli

LEGEND FOR FIELD DIAGRAMS

○ ◉ ●   players

A B C   players

P   goalkeepers

Ⓜ   the coach or trainer

⊛   the ball

〰→   dribble

──→   path of the ball

⌢→   path of the ball in air

- - -→   path of the player without the ball

∧↓   path of the player

⏢   footstall/plinth

△   cone

⬡   hoops

⊓   hurdles

👣   footsteps

EDUCATIONAL POTENTIAL OF SOCCER **1**

1.1 EDUCATIONAL VALUES IN SPORT

While sport is nothing but a pure abstraction in itself, in practice it has a number of meanings and results in several different experiences according to the way people approach and practice it. Its' contents should be checked regularly, since only in this way is it possible to decide whether that particular activity is truly effective and should be suggested to young people.

Sport in general - and soccer, in particular - are not simply educational instruments, but also mean entertainment, business, economic activity and a vehicle for advertising as well.

It is convenient to avoid the generic and groundless assumption that coaches and parents sometimes make, which is "*practicing sport is good in any case and always has an educational intent*".

In this sense, it is first of all necessary to re-define the concept of educational sport, since all its forms are not to be considered as suitable models that can be easily suggested to young people.

One possible re-definition of the concept of sport necessarily involves the athletes sharing basic requisites:

competition with:
- oneself (in order to improve oneself)
- others (in order to confront each other without causing physical damage)
- natural obstacles (in order to overcome them without causing damage to them)
- time

activity:
- disinterested (with no intent to make money)
- arranged with one's opponent
- on equal conditions
- that does not cause any physical or emotional damage to another.

In specific sports contexts the lack of just one of the above-mentioned key elements is enough for the activity not to be referable to the concept of educational sport.

Sport can have an educational value when it means culture and is included in the general development and training of the individual through a suitable suggestion of particular styles and models of living, enhanced awareness and spirit of aggregation and active participation; otherwise, sport is nothing but a simple way for an individual to follow a temporary fashion.

In order to pursue a specific educational intent it is fundamental to focus the attention on the main goals one wants to achieve through sport, the ways and the context where such discipline is practiced.

Sport can have an educational value when it is not an end in itself, but is essentially interpreted as a "means" for human advancement, a support for well-structured motor training and cognitive development of the young player, which generally tends to favor spontaneity and the authentic components of the individual's personality rather than passively imitating sports heroes (models that do not often correspond to the possibilities of most young players). Sport - considered as a useful educational tool - is based on constant activity conceived as learning, proof of one's own abilities, attempt and desire to change and improve oneself. This is why sport with an educational intent directly excludes: selection, extolling élite groups, fanatic championships, stardom and showing-off, exaggerated competition, sports consumerism, the need for increasingly competitive performances at the limits of one's possibilities and the spasmodic pursuit of immediate result.

These elements often characterize the unhappy picture of the general background in sport, a picture that significantly points out a negative evolution of this social phenomenon. As a matter of fact, it is evident that in our highly productive social and economic reality, sport is often seen as an opportunity to show off one's ability rather than as a real formative experience.

At this point, what kind of sport - and what kind of soccer, specifically - is it advisable and convenient to suggest to young athletes?

Although we all accept the concept of competitive and athletic sport – that which involves many different values such as constant improvement, will power, determination and cooperation - it is necessary to refer to a particular kind of sport that mainly focuses the attention on the individual qualities of every single athlete and works to develop and enhance them as much as possible. A sports activity that allows everybody to be himself, expressing himself as he really is, with no fears and doubts and without feeling he is not up to the task or completely excluded if his performances and prospects for the future are not like those of his "best" fellow athletes.

The modern idea of sport concentrates on the individual first, with all his individual and original characteristics and his potential abilities.

It is desirable to encourage all young boys and girls to approach the world of sport, since practicing sport considerably helps shape and improve the individual by developing and enhancing his potential, while always remembering that everybody is not destined to become a champion. This is why any sports activity should be properly "calibrated", adjusted, balanced and finally defined according to the athletes' personal qualities, their age and their individual aspirations as well.

It is possible to make the educational influence of sport on young players still more effective and efficient provided that all those who work to train and educate them (parents, teachers, coaches, trainers, educators and Local Organizations) are willing to develop open dialogue and mutual cooperation in order to find objectives, methods and solutions that they jointly agree upon to totally focus the attention on the individual they want to educate and train.

For this to be possible, it is fundamental to share all the basic aims underlying the concept of sports education, considered not only as technical learning but also as a truly important opportunity that young people are offered to enhance their self-esteem and develop suitable ethical behaviors specifically aimed at achieving their own wellbeing and improving social skills.

One of the main possible objectives that educational and formative organizations should specifically pursue and share is enhancing both the motor and cultural background of all young athletes, regardless of the position in the final rankings and excluding the principle of selectivity.[1] Actually, selectivity can undermine young athletes' personal motivations to practice sport in the long term and easily cause them to abandon the activity, in the process impairing their self-esteem and self-confidence.

Moreover, another common goal that all the people working in youth sectors should constantly pursue is educating and training young athletes to view competition as a test with others in order to improve one's skills, make progress, enjoy oneself and play, rather than as a struggle against others in order to dominate and win. This educational approach can help develop responsibility, encourage cooperation and enhance the capacity to enjoy sports in an absolutely civil manner.

---

1 There are coaches who mainly aim at achieving success immediately through a process of early specialization, encouraging the system of exclusion in reality: Hann points out that "the probability that the best young athletes will finally succeed at an international level some years later is only 10, 20%" (from L'allenamento infantile - Training in childhood, note of the translator - by Hahn E. - S.S.S., Roma 1986).

1.2 EDUCATING THROUGH MOTION AND SPORT

On the basis of the modern trends and ideas developing in the field of life sciences and in light of the studies carried out on physical and motor training[2], it is possible to say that, in the context of an educational approach to the human being, the body plays a key role in shaping the individual's personality at the cognitive, emotional and social level.

In this way, we clearly assert the close connection between the development of one's motor skills and the development of one's intelligence, sociability and affective components, thus confirming that motion and the body itself play a role of great importance in the general development and growth of the child.

Educating the body while moving and educating through the body while in motion considerably help to:
• develop intelligence as well as intuitive and creative logical capacities
• shape and consolidate the character
• develop positive relationships with others
• encourage cooperation
• develop and adopt specific habits specifically aiming at one's psychological and physical wellbeing.

Sport in general, and soccer in particular, can have an educational value provided that they are used as instruments for the development of the individual in all the following aspects:
• cognitive (knowledge)
• emotional and affective (behavior)
• social and relational (behavior in relation to others)
• motor (action).

While practicing any sport activity, the child should always be aware of what he is learning and progressively enhance his ability to know, behave, approach others and move.

In particular, since soccer is a sport discipline based on several different and specific situations, it inevitably stimulates young people to carry out rather complex cognitive and motor tasks, for instance solving particular difficulties of play by using and combining tactical thinking (see, understand and choose) and the relevant motor action (performance). Making the child reflect on all the various cognitive operations he is making considerably helps him enhance his awareness and therefore realize a much more coordinated movement.

---

2 A considerable support to the research on the role of the body in education and the educational value of sport was given by some important authors and their famous works; in particular, I would like to remember: Guido Giugni: I presupposti teoretici dell'educazione fisica - Theoretical assumptions of physical training - SEI, Torino, 1979 and Il corpo e il movimento nel processo educativo della persona - Body and motion in the educational process of the individual - SEI, Torino, 1986; Pier Seurin: Problemi fondamentali dell'educazione fisica e dello sport - The main problems in physical education and sport - Roma, Società Stampa Sportiva, 1981; Refrigeri G.: Scienza e pedagogia dell'educazione fisica - Science and padagogy in physical training - Giunti e Lisciani, Teramo, 1989; Jean Le Boulch: Lo Sport Educativo - Educational Sport - Armando, Roma, 1991.

The cognitive sphere (knowledge) is connected to:

- perception
- intuition
- attention
- power of observation
- understanding / intelligence
- memory
- analysis
- formulating hypotheses
- synthesis
- problem-solving

The emotional and affective sphere (behavior) is connected to:

- controlling one's emotions
- self-knowledge
- self-esteem (self-control and self-confidence)
- resolution and determination
- volition and perseverance
- disposition to endure effort (enduring the sense of fatigue)
- disposition to tolerate moderate risk
- making commitments
- consciousness of one's own responsibilities
- motivation
- independence
- setting a precise system of values

The social and relational sphere (behavior in relation to others) is connected to:

- capacity to comply with rules
- communication
- joint effort
- cooperation
- disposition to help others
- disposition to share responsibilities
- capability to work in group
- tolerance and understanding
- disposition to accept the decisions of others

The motor sphere (motor performance) is connected to:

- sensory perceptive capabilities
- motor patterns and postures
- motor skills
- technical skills
- tactical skills

Table 1

1.3 AN OUTLINE OF THE LEARNING THEORIES AND THE RELEVANT TEACHING MODELS

Some specific theories have been studied in the field of science which try to codify, systematize and explain how people learn. These theories can be summarized in three main currents as follows:

1. **Behaviorism** (Pavlov, 1940; Skinner, 1938)
2. **Cognitive psychology** (Piaget, Bruner, 1960; Vygotsky)
3. **Humanistic psychology** (Rogers, 1963; Maslow, 1968)

Since learning is a complex and non straightforward process, it is evident that the above-mentioned theories cannot exclude each other, but can be considered inter-connected and interdependent, even though each one plays a priority role compared to the others when one has to decide and choose the best teaching-training-coaching model to use (according to the particular context, the needs and all the various phases in the general educational process).

According to the classic definition of the term, **learning** is seen as the combination of all those processes whereby the learner reaches an increasingly higher level of competence in some specific fields of knowledge or in particular intellectual faculties (and sports skills, as well). However, each one of the above-mentioned learning theories starts from different convictions on how the human being's learning mechanisms develop and therefore gives its own definition as follows:

1. The **behavioral theories** (based on stimulus and response) maintain that learning is a change in one's behavior (observable and measurable), occurring when a situation acting as a stimulus affects the subject so as to bring about a change in his performance. This is the result of an external conditioning and occurs only when the individual reacts to a stimulus, giving a particular response in order to achieve a specific result. These theories completely focus the attention on **behavior** and performances, giving great importance to reinforcers (reward and punishment) intended as events or behaviors which can accelerate learning. It follows that human development is strongly conditioned by the environment and learning is brought about by a quantitative **accumulation** of knowledge, skills and competence.

The risk implicit in these theories is that the learner is considered a passive **receiver** of information, as an empty container that needs to be filled with new information. Actually, the abilities one can learn (at motor level, too) cannot be reduced to the sole observable and measurable components of the individual's performance, but also depend on the cognitive functions.

In fact, learning is the result of highly complex mechanisms and for these mechanisms to be somehow clearly understood it is first of all fundamental to analyze all the cognitive processes underlying and causing learning. This is why it is not possible to limit the attention to behavior and performance exclusively, but to understand all the **mental processes** through which the subject builds, refines and accumulates knowledge. This field of research has been largely investigated and developed by cognitive psychology.

2. In **cognitive psychology**, learning is a complex process that the human being uses to acquire, interpret and exploit information in order to achieve a competent performance. The cognitive theories shift the attention **from the final result of learning to all the internal mental processes** that influence learning (like perception, concentration, memory and so forth) to try to understand how the human mind structures and processes the information it gets.

The subject actively **builds** his own learning, acquiring fresh information and new ideas and combining them with those which are already stored in his memory, which are gradually re-structured and refined in their turn as time goes by. One of the main theories that concentrates on the development of the cognitive structures and mechanisms in a particularly exhaustive and comprehensive manner is psychologist Jean Piaget's theory[3]. Actually, Piaget's work focused on the attempt to understand the development and the meaning of cognitive functioning in the developmental age and is typically expressed in terms of his stage theory, in which the child is seen as passing through a series of cognitive periods, each displaying its characteristic modes of thinking.

---

3 Piaget (1960): His stage theory - or periods in the developmental age - distinguishes four main stages in the individual's cognitive development: 1) sensory-motor intelligence (from one's birth to the age of two); 2) preparatory thought or intuitive thinking (from the age of 2 to 7); 3) concrete operations (from the age of 7 to 11); 4) formal operations (from the age of 11 to 15).

The Swiss psychologist argued that thinking is organized in different mental structures, through which the child gradually builds his relation to the external environment. These structures change in time during the child's development: from elementary patterns of action to mental imaging, to logical and mathematical reasoning, and concrete experiences are gradually translated in abstract concepts.

The interaction between the subject and the environment results from mutual adaptation, which involves two complementary processes: assimilation and accommodation. In the first case, the child absorbs and assimilates the information coming from his body and the external world and unconsciously conveys it into his mental structures; in other words, the child includes new information and data or new situations in a similar mental pattern that he has previously built. By contrast, through the second process the child modifies internal schemes to fit a changing cognizance of the reality and according to the needs imposed by the reality itself. Accommodation occurs when the child's cognitive schemes available at the moment are no longer suitable and sufficient for the child to properly interpret an object or an event.

From the point of view of motion, the combination of all the sensorial functions is part of the process of assimilation, while the motor response the subject finally carries out is one of the most important aspects of accommodation[4].
In Piaget's theory, the individual's cognitive development occurs through an endless series of assimilation and accommodation processes repeatedly following and combining with each other[5].

For instance: a child tries to shoot at goal for the first time: he first needs to acquire the basic shooting technique, receiving helpful information from the contact with the ball, the distance and the size of the goal, the suggestions given by his coach, the presence of an opponent, and so forth. These elements are not enough by themselves to bring about effective motor responses, since they do not coincide with the internal schemes the child has previously stored in his memory. As a matter of fact, a truly effective motor performance results from a further process of accommodation whereby the subject makes a series of adjustments which will allow him or her to process and create new patterns of action in order to achieve the required objective: scoring a goal. In this perspective, learning is a process consequent upon the individual's cognitive development. Consequently, it is not possible to accelerate such a critical process through forced anticipation. A practical implication resulting from this concept is that it is heartily recommended to avoid teaching contents requiring cognitive structures that the learner has not yet developed in his mind and that he is not ready to handle. For this reason, it is fundamental that teaching programs and methods are carefully studied so as to adjust them to the different developmental stages.

The cognitive theories do not generally attach great importance to training, but set high value on learning by discovering and on the subject's capability to solve problems. Therefore, for the teaching-and-learning process to be effective it should have a constructive intent. This means that it should allow the subject to structure and create his own cultural and motor background.

---

4 Le Boulch
5 "In his or her interaction with the external environment, the child always tries to apply those cognitive structures he or she already has at his or her disposal and often has to face upsetting "failures", since the approach and the relation to the reality always offer new aspects to deal with. These failures in assimilating the object or the event inevitably result in frequent processes of cognitive adjustment and accommodation which raise the chil to a slightly higher cognitive level" - (Miller, 1983).

The cognitive theories on learning have been gradually revised and rethought by several authors belonging to the current school of humanistic psychology which attributes a significant part of human development to the emotional and affective relationship between the teacher and the learner, to the various mechanisms of communication and to human emotions as well.

3. In the field of **humanistic psychology** (specifically concerned with higher human motives, self-development, knowledge, understanding and esthetics), learning is an activity for self-development that the subject makes by freely experiencing and testing his own potentialities which gradually become specific skills if the teacher is able to discover and properly exploit them. The humanistic theories specifically focus the attention on the process of self-discovery of one's own potential and one's own latent energies in order to progress towards increasingly higher levels. They stimulate and enhance will, the sense of responsibility and independence of the subject. Moreover, they attach great importance to the relationship between the teacher and the learner (and to the behavior of mutual empathy[6]) and to the role of the emotional and affective sphere involved in the learning process. From this point of view, the coach-educator is motivated to develop a positive and stimulating atmosphere among his athletes based on mutual confidence, sympathy and cooperation. Learning should be aimed at encouraging self-realization (that is the fulfillment of one's potential), self-consciousness, self-esteem and open dialogue with others. The possibility to develop and experience positive relations in the situations where learning takes place obviously favors the general development and maturation of the subject. The reality is completely different if the communication that the coach regularly (and in an unconscious way, in some cases) develops with his athletes contains such messages as: "You are unable, you cannot understand!" or "Come on, you can do it, tell me what you cannot understand!"

The above-mentioned theories generally aim at not "*separating education from learning, the content from the process, the individual reality from the social one, emotional and*

---

6 Empathy: "*an effort todetach from oneself to plunge into the universe of the other and humanly understand him or her*" (Roger Mucchielli, 1983). This means adopting a sympathetic attitude towards the other which helps accepting him or her and avoid any form of judgement.

affective life from the cognitive sphere, thinking from performance, the truth from the error". (...). It is a challenge that goes far beyond the scientific concepts and educational intents of teaching and which finally plunges into the much wider sphere of existential choices and ethics (De Beni, 1994).

The coach will consequently apply to different teaching and coaching models and methods in relation to the learning theory which he will be referring to at that moment.

Learning theories	Learning mechanisms	Learning models	Learning methods	Purposes of teaching
B E H A V I O R I S M	**Adaptive** Stimulus-response • by imitation and modeling • by conditioning • trial-and-error learning	**Hierarchical and taxonomical** Systematically structured from the simple to the complex. • search for more effective and consistent teaching strategies • directive teaching (gives little room to creative-ness and self-realiza-tion)	**Deductive** • prescriptive • assigning tasks • accurately planning the activity • explaining, showing, asking to perform, making adjustments • training and directive method	• Encouraging and accelerating learning through reinforcers (reward and punishment)
C O G N I T I V E P S Y C H O L O G Y	**Gradual and constructive** The mental organization of the subject intervenes between the stimulus and the response. It is also conse-quence of his or her existen-tial and emotional-affective condition, as well as of his or her motivations and values. • by understanding • by intuition (insight) • by problem-solving	**Constructivist** Allows the learner to grad-ually build his or her learn-ing. • more open curricular strategies, focusing great attention on acquiring knowledge through "personal discovery" and not by transmission.	**Inductive** • free exploration • research to finally solve problems • guided discovery • didactic planning, not based on several teaching units divided in a number of different sequences, but based on much wider didactic programs, including various alternative choices, going far beyond predetermined developments, favoring interdisciplinary and omnisports opportunities	• helping actively build knowledge and skills • informing the learner about the didactic program, its education-al goals and strategies as well (the learner be-comes master of him- or herself) • developing metacogni-tion (consciousness) • enhancing the ability to transfer experiences • enhancing creative and critical capabilities and independence
H U M A N I S T I C P S Y C H O L O G Y	**Self-realization** Self-development of one's personality. • by discovering and using one's potential or resources.	**Exploiting the potential of the subject** focusing on the individual and his or her capacity of self-discovery. • planning situations (games and activities, frequently alternated with questions-stimuli) which help the learner discover his or her resources, limits and emotions.	**Clinical conversation** • dialogue, encouraging the learner to recognize, name and express his or her emotions. • non-judging attitude • creating a comfortable relational atmosphere, encouraging empathy, reciprocity, co-operation between learners and teachers themselves and learners and teachers.	• raising the level of awareness of one's own potential to a higher level • enhancing self-confi-dence • building a real image of oneself • discovering the role of emotions • discovering the value of one's will and the sense of responsibility • positively accepting and enduring changes.

Comparative synthesis of the three theoretical currents on learning; the synthesis underlines the consequences on the choice of the teaching models and the relevant teaching methods (by Castelli and Bonaccorso, 1999).

1.4 INTEGRATED TEACHING MODELS

In the field of teaching-coaching in sport, the three models are:

1. the model mainly based on training and education (taxonomical models, behaviorism)
2. the model that attaches greater attention to discovering and understanding problems at a conceptual and cultural level (cognitive or constructive models)
3. the model focusing on the individual

These do not exclude each other, but can be combined together effectively; rather, the main problem is to balance the choices of the teaching-coaching methods which may result from such a combination. In fact, the various methods favoring and enhancing learning should be accurately chosen in relation to the various skills one intends to develop.

Among all the theories explaining the teaching-and-learning process, both the cognitive and humanistic theories best meet the need to distinguish, characterize and personalize the didactic approach of training in sport, specifically concentrating on the constructive, strategic, interactive[7] and original aspects of learning.

Furthermore, it is also advisable to remember that learning to reply to a stimulus effectively is not an older or less appreciable kind of learning than discovering something by oneself independently of others. Every real learning process involves, at different levels of course, both discovering and receiving information.

It can thus be said that:

a) learning by receiving and accurately carrying out specific operational directions - involving connected and necessary training - enhances in the subject the development of a competence that can ensure him effectiveness and efficiency;

b) learning by discovering by oneself independently of others - involving the basic method of personal research - favors and enhances in the subject the ability to plan, innovate and manage oneself, which means encouraging self-control and independence.

When the coach has to choose which teaching-coaching methods he should use to approach his athletes, he needs to remember that independence and competence are two inseparable components in the critical process of developing dynamic, harmonious, creative and motivated personalities.

---

7 Interactive: acting in an interdependent way between individuals, the nature of the task, environmental situations, motivations, emotions; in short, with everything that somehow takes part in the learning process.

1.5 MOTOR LEARNING

Learning in soccer refers to any activity aimed at acquiring and improving specific knowledge, skills and capabilities, in order to master all those technical movements and situations that are peculiar to this particular sports discipline.

Two important researchers - Kurt Meinel and Jean Le Boulch - specifically concentrated their studies on motor learning in all its various facets, so they can be considered as helpful points of reference in this context.

Kurt Meinel[8]

In his works, Meinel argues that learning is a highly complex process, involving a number of subjective variables, requiring such basic general assumptions as a social environment, a language, strong motivations, the starting motor level of the subject, the feedback, and a perfect understanding of the assigned motor task. Coaches need to remember and consider all these elements when planning their didactic approach and coaching programs.

It is possible to say that motor learning means acquiring, internalizing, refining, reinforcing and using particular motor skills that allow the athlete to increase performance through constant training.

PHASES	CHARACTERISTICS
Phase of unrefined coordination	• Understanding one's learning task • Picturing the process of the movement in one's mind by receiving and processing information with the help of one's motor memory • Planning the movement • Regulatory behavior
Phase of refined coordination	• Reaching a higher level of coordination between forces, partial movements and phases of the movements • A much more harmonious and continuous development of the movement • Enhancing the control over one's motor performance (accurate and rational performance)
Phase of reinforcement of refined coordination and variable receptiveness	• Being aware of the control over one's performance • Making performance become automatic (internalization) • Using that motor skill also in difficult and uncommon conditions

Synthesis of the various phases in the learning process (Kurt Meinel).

8 "Teoria del Movimento" - "Theory of motion" , note of the translator - Società Stampa Sportiva, Roma, 1984.

Jean Le Boulch[9]

This author has always attached great importance to the cognitive aspect of motion. In fact, Le Boulch firmly supports the theory of learning by discovering, focusing on the awareness of one's motor positions and actions, on the importance of the mental components in structuring one's body image, on the conscious adjustment of one's postures and movements in order to bring about and enhance motor skills and automatic movements that can rapidly adapt to different mutable situations.

PHASES	CHARACTERISTICS
Phase of exploration	• Experiencing situations personally so as to understand the problem
Perceptive training	• Consciousness of one's body in static and dynamic situations • Mental imaging of one's body and movements • Xenoceptive (providing information from the outside reality) and proprioceptive feedback to regulate and adjust postural and motor patterns • Dissociating movements (in order to modify an automatic movement or a posture and make it more effective)
Internalizing and reinforcing automatic movements	• Motor patterns and postures are internalized as steady automatic elements, while always remaining flexible and adaptable to different situations (receptiveness)

Synthesis of motor learning by Le Boulch.

Le Boulch argues that for motor learning to be fruitful, it cannot neglect the use of an inductive teaching-coaching method, giving particular importance to the young player's conscious action.

Starting from the assumption that every individual learns as a whole entity - this means that learning affects the subject at many different levels - I would say that each learning process in sport is connected both to the development of motor skills and to the development of intellective and social capacities and other features of the individual's personality as well.

This means that the performance in sport is always an expression of the integrated development of all the various components that work to bring about such a performance.

---

9 Sport Educativo - "Educational Sport", note of the translator - Armando Editore, 1991 (original 1989)

Factors that influence the performance:
• Physical
• Technical
• Tactical
• Psychological

Only if all the above-mentioned factors are properly combined together, carefully considered and accurately educated is it possible to enhance the performance capacity in sport to higher levels. Such an enhanced performance capacity directly results in improved and optimized play skills.

In general, the coaching-and-learning programs of most sports aim at developing play skills intended as the possibility to combine together and use the physical and coordination capacities, psychological qualities and technical-tactical skills necessary to handle both defensive and offensive situations in order to deal with and solve all the various motor problems which typically arise during the course of a match. Consequently, the essence of the so-called "play skill" is the need to combine together the factors that influence the performance in soccer and make them interact with each other.

The diagram below represents the concept according to which developing technical and tactical skills - as well as play skills consequently resulting from this - is possible only when one starts from strong sensory perceptive motor bases. The larger and more various the motor base is, the better the quality of the performance one can achieve.

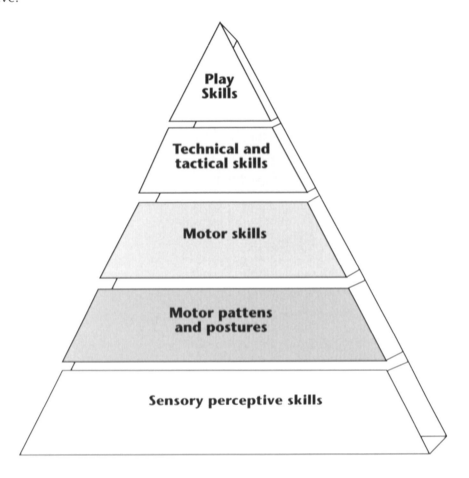

1.6 MOTOR LEARNING AND COGNITIVE THEORIES

In the field of motor activities, researchers are now giving greater and greater importance to studying all those mental processes that are somehow involved in carrying out given motor tasks. The attention is turned from the final movement to the factors that first prepare, influence and finally condition the performance.

Consequently, when referring to motion one cannot only speak of physical and coordination abilities, but also must deal with attention and concentration, mental processing, anticipation, planning, recalling situations, control, memory[10], motivations, emotions, and so forth.

Operative learning (i.e. manual, technical and motor learning) is not disconnected from cognitive learning (i.e. learning concepts) at all; rather, there is an important interconnection between "conceptual capabilities" and "knowledge" on one side, and operative skills on the other.

Such relations have positive effects on the possibility to choose suitable teaching-coaching methods, since the coach can apply to a large number of resources to favor the improvement of his players' motor skills. This means that for the coach to truly favor and enhance learning, he should specifically work on the various cognitive capacities that somehow influence and condition learning such as:
• enhancing concentration
• practicing memory
• stimulating the capacity to perceive one's body consciously
• encouraging players to express sensory information verbally
• practicing the ability to control one's actions
• carefully reflecting on the movements aimed at enhancing consciousness
• encouraging and practicing self-rating (or self-evaluation).

Using these cognitive functions helps in acquiring and enhancing refined coordination, an ability that is absolutely fundamental to make effective movements in sport.

Consequently, the coach should not limit himself to asking his players to perform and repeat sequences of movements mechanically, but must encourage the athlete to use and exploit the whole of his potential, informing and making him become aware of of the various phases of his learning process (that is learning to learn = metacognitive capacity).

---

10 In this field, it is particularly interesting to analyze the studies on memory in motion carried out by Cratty B., Espressioni fisiche dell'intelligenza - Physical expressions of intelligence - SSS Roma, 1985; By Janssen J., Memoria e tecnica sportiva - Memory and technique in sport - Rivista di cultura sportiva, SDS Roma, year 3, issue n.2, 1984; by Oserov V., Sviluppo psicomotorio degli atleti - Atheletes' psychomotor development - SSS Roma, 1984.

1.7 MOTIVATIONS AND LEARNING

The fact that every type of learning is possible only if the subject is truly motivated to learn is now commonplace. Kurt Meinel writes that "any kind of movement can be learned and internalized only if (...) one is willing to learn". In this case, "willing" is used as a synonym for "motivated".

Motivation is a significant driving force in our psychological life. It encourages the subject to act (thus bringing about motivated behaviors). Since it consists of different elements, it is usually defined as **motivational sequence**.
It includes:

- **physiological needs (basic needs) or a state of deprivation,** such as the need to move that young people generally feel when they experience situations of prolonged inactivity;
- **need for exploration,** conceived as a spontaneous disposition to discovering something new - from environmental to much more conceptual discovery - or as an inclination to solve problems (many games can be included in this group). Some affinities with the need for exploration can be found in the **need to control the environment**, connected to the so-called **motivation for competence**. Pleasure and satisfaction resulting from this are mainly centered on **doing**, performing actions and feeling able to do something rather than on the final outcome of the performance. In this case, people generally speak of intrinsic motivation - referring to the motivation of any behavior that is dependent on factors that are internal in origin, since it usually derives from feelings of satisfaction and fulfillment, not from external rewards - referred to the particular type of sports movement or training, for example, which find its expression in feelings of **control and effectiveness**;
- the needs that one learns from the environment and personal experiences; in psychology, they are defined as:
  a) **need for affiliation,** that is the desire to stay with other people and be accepted by one's teammates, as well as the need to have a coach who is able to ensure a sense of security, confidence, help and protection;
  b) **need for achievement,** which means accomplishment, self-fulfillment, the "actualization" of one's full personal potential, attaining some goals and gaining approval;
  c) **need for power,** which means the inclination to reach increasingly higher levels to gain more power and prestige than one's teammates, like in the case of the captain of a team. In this context, it is fundamental to distinguish two different manners of being a leader in a group: on one side there is an authoritarian figure who is intolerant, impatient and aggressive; on the other hand, there is an authoritative person who has all the peculiar qualities of a leader and is able to stake his own responsibility serenely, with no anxieties or fears;
- **rewards or incentives** (motivators of behavior): these elements do not originate directly in the child, but typically originate in factors outside the individual; in any case, they are particularly important in motivating young athletes. For instance, players could be easily encouraged and motivated through the extrinsic reward of receiving a new shirt, being awarded a small tip by one's parents or finding suitable accommodation when away for a period of training (extrinsic motivations

which bring about extrinsically motivated behaviors).

Some theorists argue that the motivations acquired from the external environment or through personal experiences have their own **functional autonomy** - a term which refers to the tendency for a motive or motivating force to become independent from the original, primary drive that initiated it. According to this theory, the need for affiliation would originate from a situation where the youth for the first time develops and experiences a positive relationship with a coach who welcomes him with enthusiasm, helps him and makes him feel good, for example. At the end of this experience, the youth would obviously feel as if something were missing in his life; this feeling would immediately trigger the need for affiliation once again as well as the need to be part of the environment and situation that he had experienced before.

This mechanism of repetition commonly occurs in many different situations, like in those experiences when one finally achieves success.

A recent theory - better known as "**attribution theory**" in social psychology - maintains that motivation to learn is conditioned by how the learner perceives the result he has achieved, which can be positive, negative or even totally unexpected.

The search for and analysis of the motives that have brought about the final outcome on the part of the young athlete concern either internal causes like his own skills, the effort he has made, the strategies he has used and so forth, or external causes such as the support and cooperation offered by his teammates, the level of difficulty of the task, good or bad luck.

The youth also looks for permanent motives like his own abilities, or temporary causes such as his health condition, his psychological state, his fears, his training level and so on.

Some of these driving forces can be controlled by the individual, like his effort, while some others cannot, like good or bad luck, for example.

The young person's way of thinking, his emotional and affective life and, consequently, his motivational approach to the performance are directly influenced by the particular type of motive (or driving cause) that he himself ascribes to the result he has achieved.

If a player fails in one of his soccer performances and attributes his failure and negative outcome to his poor abilities, which is one of the permanent causes, his expectations for the following performances decrease more than if the athlete ascribed his negative result to temporary causes like fear or his training level.

From this very short exposition, it is clear that the learning process is characterized by a highly intricate combination of cognitive factors, motivational aspects and emotional reactions.

1.8 THE ROLE OF THE COACH AS AN EDUCATOR

This brief introduction in the field of educational psychology - an introduction that does not pretend to be an exhaustive analysis of all the complex problems and mechanisms involved in both teaching-coaching and learning processes - clearly helps us understand that teaching and **coaching youth soccer** is a demanding task, a tough job full of difficulties and involving serious responsibilities.

The interrelations between the many different factors that are involved in this delicate and crucial process (like the personal characteristics of the learner, his own past experiences, his learning activities, the particular type of ability he wants to acquire, the goals he finally wants to achieve, and so on) should encourage the coach to enhance his knowledge on the matter in order to enrich and improve his didactic competence and therefore make his suggestions for training much more effective for his players.

Acquiring new awareness of the importance of the role of the coach in sport helps develop a new way of coaching which puts the coach " in systemic relation with both the athlete and the sports discipline", acting as a person who **encourages and makes learning much easier**; this means that the coach is no longer seen as a figure who trains his players simply by conveying contents and taking care of developing their physical features exclusively.

The coaches who are now awakened to these important problems will plan their coaching and didactic activities focusing greater attention on the individual they are training and on the best way to convey knowledge, new information and basic sports contents.

The starting point is key: it is absolutely fundamental to acknowledge that there are several different ways whereby one can learn and accept that every single person builds concepts and enhances his own motor skills in a different way according to his personal learning patterns.

For instance, one player can learn a particular technical movement more easily if he manages to decompose it in all its basic original parts and repeat it over and over again, while another athlete can learn and internalize the same motor ability more effectively if he is in the condition to experience and perform it as a whole movement.

The young player uses a correct and truly effective motor pattern if he can understand the importance of making such a movement in that particular context and situation and if he is motivated to do so.

The more a coach is able to identify the differences in the perceptive, cognitive, emotional and relational structures of every single athlete, the more he is able to plan suitable didactic programs and the relevant coaching methods to enhance, exploit and combine those differences.

1.9 PLANNING AN EDUCATIONAL SPORTS PROGRAM THROUGH SOCCER

Planning refers to the combination of all those decisions, activities and procedures that the sports club and the coaching staff study, agree upon and finally carry out together in light of the goals they intend to achieve, in order to accurately and effectively program the learning processes and opportunities of playing soccer, specifically designed for their players. Planning obviously considers all those components that are involved in the formative and educational process in sport (i.e.: the need for personal motivations, coaching and didactic methods, interaction between the coach and his athletes, cooperation between players themselves, the social reality of the area where one is operating, resources and bonds, and so forth).

The theory of planning - which is conceived and originates in the economic sector rather than in a pedagogic context - is also applied, and often successfully, in the **field**

of educational sport, since it allows a shift from purely occasional teaching-coaching to a well-structured organization of methods and activities, which are scheduled carefully and consistently, focusing the attention on the athletes one intends to educate and coach.

Planning one's coaching approach is an excellent instrument for coaches, since they can constantly monitor the outcome of their work whenever they want and in any situation.

Obviously, planning one's activity should not become something excessively rigorous and binding, which prevents the coach from modifying and adjusting his plans as time goes by in relation to contingent needs or unexpected situations (including inconvenience, mistakes and failures).

A flexible planning of one's coaching philosophy allows the coach and educator to take and exploit some unexpected opportunities which may also have a high educational, formative and cognitive value.

Consequently, it is advisable for a coach to take the opportunity to combine different coaching models together; even though this innovative method first starts from planning one's activity according to set (taxonomical) goals, it also leaves room to other teaching and learning patterns, like teaching "by problems"[11], which helps enhance the multiplicity of personal learning styles and individual differences while also favoring the conscious acquisition of new motor skills.

The traditional coaching perspective which necessarily needs to be structured in an economical manner, with all its elements properly organized in their right place in order to achieve the final goal in the shortest time possible can be combined with an innovative coaching approach which encourages the coach to mainly focus the attention on social relationships (interpersonal relations) and the need to consider the young person as the one who actively builds his learning, knowledge and skills in sport.

The didactic planning of training in sport includes different phases which develop as follows:
1. Analysis of the starting situation
2. Analysis of the needs
3. Setting general and specific goals
4. Selecting and planning contents
5. Building well-structured coaching units and setting definite periods of time
6. Choosing and planning coaching methods
7. Evaluating
8. Strategies for recovery and reinforcement

1. Analysis of the starting situation

Making a close analysis of the starting situation means making a diagnosis of the original condition, an instrument that is absolutely necessary for the coach to:
• understand the physical, motor, psychological, emotional and social conditions of his athletes;

---

11 For further details on teaching by problems see G. Petter in his work La valigetta delle sorprese. Saggio sulla motivazione ad apprendere. - "The suitcase of surprises. Essay on motivation to learn." (note of the translator) - La Nuova Italia, Firenze, 1994.

- identify the social and cultural background of every single player;
- know all the various resources he has at his disposal (the environmental condition, the way the club is structured and organized, the economic situation and so forth).

The first two components are generally analyzed by means of motor tests, questionnaires, interviews with both athletes and their parents and careful observation of their behaviors. The analysis of the third factor can be carried out through accurate researches and surveys at one's Sports Club and in the area where one is operating.

In general, entrance tests that athletes typically have to pass through at the beginning of the sports season are aimed at identifying:

Athletes' motor and cognitive prerequisites (that is their basic motor capacities as well as their technical and tactical skills)
a) knowledge of one's body
b) coordination capacities
c) physical capabilities
d) basic technical skills
e) individual tactical abilities.
a. Morphological and functional features:
   which means measuring and monitoring the athlete's weight, height, circumferences, postures and attitudes of the body in general (position of the backbone, position of the feet, knees and so on)
b. Emotional, affective and social behaviors which can be detected in situations of play; the coach should carefully analyze the various situations and then record his evaluations in special tables and forms (see paragraph 7. Evaluation).

2. Analysis of the needs
The analysis of the needs is absolutely fundamental for a coach to identify and understand the psychological and physical characteristics of the players in the age group in question and probe their requirements to set well-aimed goals.
The needs generally refer to:
a. morphological, functional, psychological features typical in children between 11 and 16 (including the structure and the functioning of the main systems: the locomotor apparatus, the cardiovascular, nervous and endocrine systems, the respiratory tract; the way their thinking is structured as well as their learning mechanisms, emotional life and so forth)
b. personal motivations (the reason a youth decides to play soccer)
c. personal expectations (what a youth really expects to gain from playing soccer).

In short, it is possible to summarize schematically a series of needs that preadolescents and adolescents typically feel that **playing soccer** could help satisfy:

1. motion
2. contact
3. affiliation
4. recreation
5. security
6. self-esteem
7. independence
8. self-actualization
9. competence (knowledge - consciousness)
10. knowledge exploration

Furthermore, it is also important to remember that when speaking of preadolescents and adolescents, one is not dealing with a category of persons characterized by codified behaviors and easily generalized attitudes. Actually, studies on psychology in the developmental age, focusing on the experiences connected to the changing body, show a complex and varied profile of adolescents, thus revealing that the situation is widely heterogeneous.

AGE GROUP	AVERAGE AUXOLOGICAL SITUATIONS	PSYCHOMOTOR CHARACTERISTICS	PHYSIOLOGICAL CHARACTERISTICS	PSYCHOLOGICAL CHARACTERISTICS
Primary school cycle 9 to 11 year olds	"TURGOR II" and beginning of "PROCERITAS II" phase, the second period of height development	Final enhancement of the body structures functional prerequisites. Motor exuberance gradually decreases and the youth is capable of greater self-control. Motor coordination is rather developed. Suitable enhancement of balance while in the air.	Excitement slightly prevails over cortical inhibition; muscle system is much more developed. The hypodermic layer of fat grows thicker; the stroke volume increases while the blood pressure decreases. The main ossification points begin to appear.	The real golden period when youths are particularly receptive to motor learning. Considerable improvement of learning. The rational approach to "space" favors interdisciplinary learning in the field of geometry and logical-concrete operations as well. The youth gradually begins to search for a group as a social instrument.
Junior high school cycle 11 to 14 year olds	"PROCERITAS II" prepuberal and puberal period	The development of the bony tissue (the bones grow longer) and the relevant stretching of muscles bring about a sort of regression of the whole body structure and pattern. Movements are less coordinated and rather clumsy. Balance suddenly diminishes. Joint mobility is further enhanced.	Maximum efficiency of the endocrine system. All the internal organs and systems develop at morphological level and increase in weight; such a critical development is not correlated with an equal enhancement of functions. Muscle tissue stretches while bones become longer. Final development of the most important ossification segments (elbow, shoulder, metacarpus, pelvis, knee, heel joints).	This period is characterized by considerable emotional instability and conflicts due to both physical growth and sexual maturation. Serious difficulties and problems with the family and at school (conflict with institutions and authorities) typically emerge in this period. The strong sense of insecurity leads the youth to search for a leader.
The first two years of the senior high school 15 to 16 year olds	End of "PRO-CERITAS II" and beginning of "TURGOR III" post-puberal period	Period of stabilization of values; coordination capacities gradually improve. This period is key for the individual to learn and internalize complex motor patterns. Improvement of balance while in the air. Divergent motor production, including high-level movements.	Excitement and cortical inhibition keep a certain balance, substantially. All the functional parameters generally improve. Good or excellent trophism of muscle tissue.	Once youths have overcome the so-called puberal crisis, they develop greater emotional balance and enhanced capacity to concentrate both in the field of study and physical exercise. Hypothetico-deductive behavior finally emerges completely. The youth now begins to consider the rule as an applicable point of reference. This is why any sports activity is seen as a model of activity and behavior.

Section of the table concerning "the different phases of the auxological, psychomotor, physiological and psychological development of youths between the age of 9 to 16", from "Perché? Come? Quando?" ("Why? How? When?") by Bin V. and Tosi R., S.S.S., Roma 1984.

The complex nature of our modern society, the various models of socialization, the cultural variables, one's social and family background, the individual differences in one's intrapsychic experiences as well as sex and age all contribute to make adolescence very diversified, particularly extended from the chronological point of view and in constant change. This is why the term "adolescence" is no longer sufficient and suitable to define a particular developmental period characterized by a number of individual differences.

Moreover, preadolescents and adolescents clearly show significant diversities also from the point of view of structural and physiological maturation, even though they may belong to the same chronological age group.

3. Setting general and specific goals

Goals are generally defined and classified in three different categories as follows:
- **general goals**, which refer to all those capacities and skills that constitute the basis for the development of every sports performance;
- **primary specific goals**[12], which include all the technical and tactical abilities that are peculiar to soccer;
- **secondary specific goals**, which refer to motor capacities.

All the goals must be:
- set in a very clear manner so as to be easily monitored;
- set only after an accurate reading, understanding and interpretation of the players' formative needs;
- in perfect harmony with all the various aspects of the individual: that is in harmony with his emotional and affective, cognitive and social-relational life.

Motor goals (motor performance)

General goals: *Enhancing sensory perceptive capacities*
  Secondary specific goals:
- Visual discrimination
- Auditory discrimination
- Kinesthetic discrimination
- Tactile discrimination

General goals: *Developing basic motor patterns and postures*
  Secondary specific goals:
- Walking, running, jumping, throwing, catching, shooting, rolling, climbing, sliding, and so on...
- Bending, tilting, folding, raising, stretching, abducting, abducting, rotating, swinging

General goals: *Enhancing motor skills*
  Secondary specific goals:
- Physical capacities:
  strength, endurance, resistance, speed, joint mobility

---

12 Primary specific goals can be further divided in operatory goals, each one representing one particular "motor skill" and describing the required performance in a much more detailed manner (see the coaching unit on Heading skills).

- Coordination capacities:
orientation, reaction, transformation, pairing, combination, differentiation, anticipation abilities, balance, rhythmicity, motor imagination

General goals: Developing technical skills
Primary specific goals:
- Basic technique:
ball possession, dribbling, controlling, heading, kicking the ball, taking throw-ins, goalkeeper's technique

General goals: Developing tactical abilities
Primary specific goals:
- Individual tactical skills:
- when in possession of the ball:
eluding the marking, defending and covering, passing, making feints and dribbles, shooting at goal
- when not in possession of the ball:
taking position, marking, intercepting the ball, tackling, defending the goal
- Team technical skills:
  - when in possession of the ball:
  maintaining possession of the ball, clearing space forward, shooting at goal
  - when not in possession of the ball:
  slowing down the opponents' offensive build up, preventing the opposition from shooting at goal, winning possession of the ball

The choice of the goals that best suit the psychological and physical features of the players can be schematically synthesized as follows; the table below shows the goals that should be attached greater importance and attention, even though it does not forget the combination of all those performance factors that must always be considered interdependent.

AGE GROUP	10 to 12	12 to 14	14 to 16
Goals that should be attached greater importance	• Starting youths off on playing soccer	• Starting soccer specialization (always from an omnisports point of view)	• Soccer specialization
General goal (concerning technical and tactical skills)	• Developing technical skills • Developing individual tactical abilities	• Refining technical abilities • Refining individual tactical skills • Coaching team tactical strategies	• Developing team tactical skills
General goal (concerning motor capacities)	• Enhancing coordination capacities • Training physical capacities	• Reinforcing coordination capacities • Enhancing physical capacities	• Refining physical capacities

Educational goals concerning all the various aspects of an individual

The goals one should struggle to achieve in the context of motor and sports learning are generally classified as in any other learning situation affecting all the various fields of knowledge and can be divided according to special indicators of behavior as is clearly shown in the following table:

COGNITIVE (knowledge)	EMOTIONAL-AFFECTIVE (behavior)	RELATIONAL-SOCIAL (behavior towards others)
• achieve a skillful performance • enhance the capacity to plan new coordinated replies • enhance the capacity to reflect upon and process one's motor experiences • enhance one's knowledge, not intended as simply filing information, but as the capacity to process and re-process information • properly handle one's learning, which means enhancing the awareness of and the control over one's performance • acquire new understanding and memory strategies • keep concentration • develop peripheral attention • make strategic choices in particular situations of play • analyze the real effectiveness of a movement (successful or unsuccessful performance) • enhance the capacity and ability to repeat movements • enhance one's problem-solving capacity • enhance one's transfer capacity (transfer actions and movements previously acquired in different fields and situations)	• understand the type and the intensity of one's emotions (fear and anxiety, anger, joy, boredom, envy and so forth) • enhance the capacity to control one's emotions • understand and accept one's qualities, capacities, aspirations, limits (personal image of oneself) • enhance self-esteem (self-control and self-confidence) • take decisions • act firmly and resolutely to finally achieve one's goal • enhance one's volitional capacities - persistence • willingness to accept effort (enduring the sense of fatigue) • willingness to accept controlled risk • take an active part in all the activities suggested • make proposals and suggestions • be able to undertake tasks • be conscious of one's own responsibilities • understand one's motivations • reach a certain independence • enhance the capacity to organize one's work • adopt behaviors aimed at enhancing one's psychological and physical condition	• consciously comply with established rules • accept and respect others • develop new relations with other people, taking care of their needs • be ready for mutual confrontation • communicate effectively • be able to listen to others • be able to work in group • cooperate with others sharing one's competence with them • cooperate for a common goal • be willing to help others • share responsibilities • be tolerant and sympathetic • overcome prejudices

The goals are schematically divided in three different columns simply because we want to be very clear in our exposition; in reality, many behaviors cannot be so easily and distinctly numbered in only one area of the whole human sphere.

4. Selecting and planning contents

In this case, the contents include all those motor and sports activities that the coach concretely suggests to his players whereby they achieve specific goals and acquire new motor behaviors (technical and tactical skills).

Carefully choosing and planning activities is a function of the final achievement of both the primary and secondary goals that are previously set in the training session or in each particular coaching unit. These coaching-and-learning methods are highly effective (as far as the ratio between the period of implementation and the result achieved is concerned) when the following experiences and situations finally occur:
• learning
• simulation of play conditions
• experiences of success
• transfer

Even though the classification below is not exhaustive at all, they could be possibly grouped as follows:
a. Starting games
b. Analytical exercises
c. Play situations
d. Conditioned games
e. Final game

When the coach selects the contents he wants to coach in that particular training session, apart from considering all the factors of the performance on which he intends to focus special attention, he should also be able to assess the "physical load" involved, that is the physical and athletic effort they require. In this way it is possible to combine both fitness training and technical and tactical practice, accurately evaluating the distance run, the time of the performance as well as the recovery period, the number of sets and repetitions (intensity of work loads) and so on.

However, it is also possible to train physical capacities by combining the contents of several sports disciplines together so as to enrich and enhance the young soccer player's motor patterns and personal experiences.

a) Starting games

Compared to the factors that directly condition the performance, starting games are typically planned in order to affect the psychological aspect in particular. They are aimed at creating a "positive atmosphere" inside the group, which means creating favorable emotional and relational conditions which the coach can specifically appeal to in order to enhance both the participation and the attention necessary for learning.

Playing activities can be accurately and suitably selected among **traditional games** and **games of introduction to the sports discipline** in relation to the specific goals peculiar to the training session.

Each game involves formative and educational values that are useful to achieve cognitive, emotional and social goals in addition to motor objects.

The coach will obviously choose the game according to the aspects of the athlete's personality which he intends to specifically concentrate on:
• mainly strategic games, specifically based on problem-solving and understanding

of rules, which favor the development of cognitive functions;
- games specifically involving decision-making and courage: they help enhance emotional and affective functions;
- games specifically based on joint effort, team work, cooperation and role-playing, which favor the development of relational and social functions.

While playing starting games, athletes can gradually become familiar with the technical and tactical abilities included in the particular coaching unit (how to dribble the ball when given a fixed rhythm).

These games can become part of the warm-up phase in the training session, so as to enhance and make traditional motor practice much more effective (jogging, accelerating, sprinting, joint mobility, stretching).

b) Analytical exercises

Compared to all the factors that directly affect the performance, analytical exercises are specifically used to enhance both technical skills and coordination capacities. The young player can measure himself and test his capacities in basic technical movements of soccer, which means that he can gradually experience the relationship between his body and the soccer tool - the ball - in order to develop the ability to "handle the ball", that is the capacity to touch, master, dribble, control, strike, kick and shoot it in a particularly economical, fruitful and profitable manner.

Learning and refining basic soccer skills actually depends on the number of times the athlete repeats the same exercises in variable conditions, requiring the subject to enhance the capacity to "handle his body and the development of its movements" in relation to the different paths and speeds of the ball. In short, analytical exercises do not require the athlete to adapt and adjust his movements to the behavior of another player (either the opponent or the teammate).

While practicing these activities - which can be carried out individually, in pairs, in groups of three players or in small groups - a player does not only enhance the kinesthetic sensibility that is necessary for the contact between the body and the ball, but also improves his capacities to run, slow down, restart, change direction and jump in order to finally make effective technical movements.

c) Play situations

Among all the factors that condition and result in the final performance, play situations are generally used to enhance individual tactical skills in particular.

Among all the various coaching-and-learning methods the coach has at his disposal to plan a training session, play situations play a key role in the training of the young soccer player, since they constitute the basic units of the match and involve at least one opponent and one or more teammates to take an active part in the situation. From the coaching and didactic point of view, they can vary from simple game situations (from 1 v 1 to 3 v 3) to more complex situations (from 4 v 4 to 11 v 11).

SITUATION	AREA WHERE THE ACTION DEVELOPS	PURPOSES OF THE SITUATION	
		Attacking Players	**Defending Players**
1 > P	goal area	Maintain possession of the ball moving towards the goal to shoot	Defend the goal slowing the opponents' path and trying to win the ball
1 > 1	penalty area		
1 > 1 + P	central third of the field		
2 > P	side third of the field		
2 > 1	central midfield	**How**	**How**
		Elude the marking, control the ball, pass, feint, dribble	Take possession, mark, expect anticipation, tackle

Following one of the possible solutions suggested in the table and accurately combining the exercise chosen, the area where the action should develop (topographical location of the play situation), the purposes of the situation and all the possible variables that the coach may suggest on the basis of his personal experiences and special needs (like in the diagram below), these activities reproducing real game situations can be reasonably planned following the coaching progression from 1 v the goalkeeper to 11 v 11.

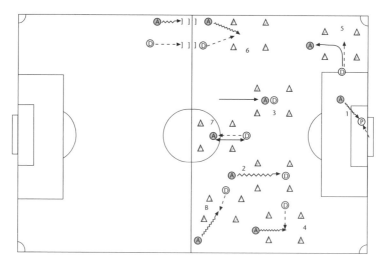

Real game situations are multifunctional exercises, in the sense that they favor a combination of solutions and stimuli having a training effect on all the various factors of the performance. For example: from the point of view of fitness practice, exercise number 6 in the diagram above first aims at helping solve problems concerning individual tactical solutions and then develop speed force in the first part of the drill while moving through the hurdles, and moving and performance speed in the second part while approaching the square.

As far as the technical aspect is concerned, youth players gradually learn how to use and apply the basic motor patterns they have previously acquired as a means to solve the problems resulting from the active challenge of the opposition as well as from the behavior of their teammates, choosing the most effective solutions that best suit the situation and solve the problem in the wide range of motor abilities they have progressively enhanced in training sessions.

In this way, the young player gradually gets accustomed to adjusting his technical abilities to contingent needs, specifically when the situation is new and unexpected so as to require him to find new solutions, invent movements, and carry out new motor actions, which means enhancing the capacity to handle and use his soccer technical skills in a variable and flexible manner.

From the tactical point of view, the player should first learn to read and understand the various contexts of play, collecting and storing information and working out suitable solutions in very short periods of time.

It is possible to train the young athlete to properly read the tactical situation in matches by planning simple game situations in training sessions and suggesting well-aimed, simple and gradual contents. At the beginning, it is advisable for a coach to simplify the exercises by reducing the number of variable factors and/or helping players to achieve the final goal. The variable elements include: the playing area, the attitude of both defenders and attackers, the technical condition, the numerical superiority or inferiority of a group, time pressure and psychological pressure.

The playing area can refer either to the topographical location of the action of play or to the size of the area where the action develops; other important elements are indissolubly connected to this aspect, they are: the time the athlete has to read and understand the situation, choose and perform the technical and tactical movements that best suit the situation of play and, consequently, the promptness of the performance and the accuracy of the movements. At the beginning, it is better to play in large playing areas, which can be gradually reduced as players progressively enhance their skills.

The attitude of the defenders: it would be advisable to accustom youth players to adopt and maintain realistic attitudes, thus avoiding semi-active or even passive opposition. This does not exclude that, in order to make practice much easier or more complex at a coaching and didactic level, the coach can work to control the attitude of the defenders by making suitable adjustments such as:
- making them start with a handicap in terms of space compared to the attackers or delay their action in time;
- making them start with a handicap (for instance: hold a ball in both hands or keep a ball under each arm);
- changing their starting position compared to that of the attackers (in front, on the right or the left or behind them), coaching and training a defensive line as aggressively and realistically as possible.

The attitude of the attackers: in principle, what has just been said for the defenders is also true for the behavior of the attacking players, while always considering two important variables that are key for the action to start:
- attacker in possession of the ball (facing, on the right or on the left of, turning one's back to the goal and/or to the defender);
- the attacker receives the ball at different speeds and along different paths.

The technical condition or bond: this means playing the ball at free, conditioned, limited or forced touches, using only one foot or specific anatomical areas for the contact with the ball.

Numerical superiority or inferiority on attack or on defense.

Time pressure: suggesting exercises to be performed in a given period of time.

Psychological pressure: including traditional training sessions, individual competitions, in pairs, with a score or penalties so as to enhance emotional involvement.

Position of the exercises on the playing field
When coaching 1 v 1 situations, it is fundamental to concentrate on the different starting positions of the attacker compared to the goal and the starting position of the defender compared to the player in possession of the ball. The most common and significant are:

> 1 v G (goalkeeper) from the left;
> 1 v 1 with the defender standing motionless
> 1 v 1 with the attacker turning his back to the goal and the defender in a marking position
> 1 v 1 with the defender coming from the left
> 1 v 1 with the defender coming from the right
> 1 v 1 with the defender coming later from behind
> 1 v 1 with the defender coming from in front
> 1 v 1 with the defender coming diagonally

Variable equipment: which means using balls of different weight, shape and size, or irregular playing areas - soft or hard - and goals of variable size.

Final purposes of the situation: all the various situations of play are always aimed at achieving specific primary goals. For the attackers, they include:
- maintaining ball possession
- clearing and gaining space forward
- shooting at goal.

While exercises specifically designed for defenders are aimed at:
- defending the goal (preventing the attackers from shooting at goal)
- slowing down the opposition's build up
- winning possession of the ball.

These goals can be achieved through specific individual tactical behaviors and movements as shown in the table on page 96.

By changing and adjusting the variable elements of each exercise, the coach can act on the final purposes of the game by concentrating either on the defensive or the offensive phase in relation to the needs of the situation, or even focusing the attention on shifting from defense to attack and vice-versa according to the principle of transition.

The psychological aspect
In real game situations it is possible to reproduce the pressures and the moods that typically characterize official matches, recreating such psychological conditions through competitions involving scores, given periods of time, direct confrontation or rewards so as to encourage those emotional dynamics that often cause serious

differences in the performance between official matches and training sessions. Moreover, these situations also offer the coach the opportunity to educate players in the principles of communication, joint effort, cooperation and decision-making which are obviously the key elements of team play together with mutual support and help.

In short, real game situations are the link between exercises focusing on basic technical skills and individual tactical abilities and the real match and therefore help to successfully transfer what is coached in training sessions to the competition, since they stimulate and maintain all the various peculiar elements of play.

d) Conditioned games

Among all the factors that influence and determine the performance, conditioned games are generally planned in training to work on the tactical aspect of the team. They can be played on the whole field or in smaller playing areas, between two teams that compete in a practice match and are forced to comply with specific technical rules (for instance: play the ball with one's less skillful foot or head the ball to score) and tactical directions (for example: score a goal after a cross coming from the flank of the field or after a one-two pass).

Two teams compete for ball possession, alternating in the defensive and the offensive phase, struggling to finally win the competition while always complying with the rules and the theme set for the game.

These games involve more or less complex technical and tactical tasks in particular contexts of play that constantly change, where the players have to learn to read and understand the situation, using all the technical movements and strategies they have learned in training to solve problems (comply with the condition and the rules of the game, score goals).

Conditioned games - which are particularly useful in enhancing communication and improving the relational aspect of team play - also help the coach check which athletes have learned from the activities carried out in the previous coaching phases.

e) Final game

The practice match generally played at the end of the training session is commonly used as a "free game" in which players are totally free to act, move and interpret the competition, though they always need to respect their positions, their tasks and the general organization of play.

This is the moment when young people can enjoy themselves, freely expressing their potential, impulse, imagination and creativeness, while always remembering that the practice match at the end of training - in view of championship official matches - cannot be reduced to a mere recreational activity, but must be played with suitable intensity and concentration. The coach should avoid constantly interrupting the game to provide suggestions and directions in order to make play much more coherent; this means that he should encourage his players, specifically individually, to freeze the match only in particularly important situations that could be helpful for the whole team. The coach should concentrate on both the behavior of every single player and on the play of the team as a whole, so as to make general evaluations that will help him plan the following coaching and didactic activities.

In the same way that players typically warm up at the beginning of the training session - actually, warming up is fundamental for athletes to progressively get accustomed to physical effort - they should also warm down at the end of training - warm down is intended as an activity whereby the athlete can gradually restore the original condition of peace. Warming down includes jogging and muscle stretching.

5. Building well-structured coaching units and setting definite periods of time

The operational aspect of general planning is the practical development of each training session, which should always be subject to specific principles of organization that are aimed at exploiting in the best way possible:
- spaces
- equipment
- practice time

The way in which the various coaching units are planned out helps optimize the periods of time dedicated to real motor practice, thus reducing dead periods such as:
- long lines of players waiting to kick the ball
- long pauses before making any other technical movement
- players seldom in possession of the ball.

In fact, these dead periods reduce the possibilities for players to practice and learn and players are likely to lose concentration.

For each goal, special temporal coaching units are suitably planned (they may include one or more training sessions) following the same principle that was first used for the general planning of the season, and following the program below.

COACHING UNIT

Age group for which the activity is specifically designed
Primary specific goal
Secondary specific goal
Instruments
Equipment
Contents
Methods
Test and check
Suggestions for the next session
Starting game
Analytical exercises
Play situations
Conditioned game
Final game

(by prof. Seno and modified by Bonfanti)

Setting specific periods of time, that is the duration of the activities concerning:
- coaching units
- training sessions

Every single phase of the training session should be quantified by the coach personally and subjectively in relation to several factors such as: the goal to achieve, the level of achievement of such a goal, the level of the performances finally achieved, players' learning capacities and motivations. Setting a priory specific periods of time for every single activity is therefore fundamental, since the development of every single learning situation cannot be predicted in advance.

In other words, the starting game may occupy the whole training session if the coach understands that such a game has considerable training effects and the players are highly motivated and respond enthusiastically to such an activity; in the same way, the time the coach has at his disposal to manage the whole coaching session may be suitably divided in relation to the different phases of the session.

In short, the coach should use the planning of contents as a flexible instrument, changing them accordingly as the situation dictates.

6. Choosing and planning coaching methods

The term "method" refers to the systematic procedure, a plan or system of conduct or action that the coach should follow to achieve specific didactic goals, in other words how the coach plans, arranges and carries out coaching-and-learning procedures.

It is based on a number of sequences following a special order and progression and therefore represents the antithesis of fortuity and improvisation.

The choice of the best coaching methods that the coach should apply depends on:

1) **The needs of the players**
   a) The need for personal experience and the importance of "doing"
   b) The need to combine different sports disciplines
   c) The quality of the relationship
2) **The learning theories to which the coach applies**
   a) Methods of research to solve problems
   b) Procedures used to actively build a game starting from semi-structured situations
3) **Purposes of motor activity** (educational, physical, technical and tactical objectives)

1) The needs of the players

The need for personal experience and the importance of "doing": young players often prefer personal experience, free exploration, a practical approach to the reality, direct tests and control of facts intended as basic instruments to acquire and enhance knowledge. They typically use **action as a means to experiment with the possibilities**, and choose to act directly and immediately without knowing the final outcome.

For players to acquire experience and learn from it, they need to feel particular sensations, be totally aware of them and able to place and control them inside their bodies. *When coaching or teaching young children, the adult tries to mediate his or her personal experience and feel for the child, in preadolescence the youth experiences the reality by himself* [1].

The youth gradually frees himself from the support of adults; his cognitive capacities progressively develop and he has more opportunities to deal with the external world, so that he can personally test his own skills, experience his competence and knowledge, work out a more personal style of action, become seriously conscious of his limits and weaknesses as well as of his strengths and skills, and apply his skills practically.

In this period, players need to be constantly stimulated to consciously listen to all the various sensations coming from their bodies (like states of mental strain, fatigue, weakness, well-being, self-control, and so forth) in order to understand the underlying messages and therefore act in a way so as to satisfy all the many and various desires and needs (not only physical needs, but also those concerning social relations, self-esteem and self-actualization)[14]. Consequently, the quality of the approach to and the relation with one's body is key at this age. The possibility to develop a positive contact with the sensations coming from inside is fundamental for the gradual development of personal experience itself.

Preadolescents are constantly and more and more actively searching for new situations that can offer them the possibility to test themselves and understand their newly acquired abilities.

The importance of "doing" to learn is also supported by neurophysiological mechanisms; in fact, motor learning leaves a trace of its effects in the central nervous system only if the movement is made, experienced and tested (a player cannot learn how to shoot at goal if he never tries to shoot). This predominance of "doing" results from the intrinsic nature of both body and motion. We cannot ignore, however, the fact that the individual also applies to verbal languages to revise, adjust, re-process, internalize and finally store the sports movement in his memory.

This brings about the opportunity for coaches to use inductive coaching methods which allow the athlete to personally experience and try what he is suggested, in order to favor the development of truly effective and fruitful learning in sport.

The need to combine several sports disciplines: in the period of preadolescence, it is advisable to introduce players to activities having a non-specific connotation, combining several sports disciplines[15], and therefore polyvalent and multilateral, in order to avoid early specialization that may result in a sort of crystallization (impoverishment and weakening) of acquired motor skills, thus preventing any future improvement and lowering the degree of personal motivation; this may even cause the youth to abandon the sports activity very early on because of physical and psychological overload.

People often believe that the sooner athletes practice highly specialized training, the more likely they are to enhance their performances to high levels. This is not always true; actually, the wider the range of skills that youths acquire and enhance in

---

13 By Fabbrini A. and Melucci A. in "L'età dell'oro. Adolescenti tra sogno e esperienza" - The golden age. Adolescents between dream and experience. (note of the translator) - Ed. Feltrinelli, Milano, 1992.
14 Fabbrini and Melucci argue that the emotional sphere can hinder the decoding and the clear understanding of sensory messages thus preventing the development of clear needs.
15 Combining several sports disciplines means involving a wide range of motor experiences, peculiar to different sports in order to finally enrich the motor background of the youth, so as to give him the opportunity to best express his personal potential.

training, the more likely they are to develop flexible behaviors and abilities that may be transferred to various learning situations.

Various kinds of sports experiences properly combined together increase the capacity to transfer acquired motor patterns to new and unusual situations of motion.

Several studies[16] confirm this: actually, research clearly shows that polyvalent athletes (decathletes, in particular) considerably enhance their mechanisms of motor memory compared to other athletes who are highly specialized in one sports discipline.

All the movements made in sport are a result of mainly rigid motor maps and essentially elastic motor patterns. The former permit internalization of the movement and make it automatic, which means avoiding fatigue, also at an intellectual level, but prevent the capacity to reply to a new and unexpected situation effectively. On the other hand, elastic motor maps correspond to motor patterns that have not undergone any process of early specialization and allow for easier adaptation to new situations in various contexts[17]. In short, training combining elements of different sports disciplines and practicing sports involving specific situations help the subject develop elastic motor maps.

The quality of the relationship[18]. Great attention should be focused on the emotional, affective and relational aspect as a way to effectively convey knowledge and information in the fields of motion and sport.

Sometimes, performances do not correspond to the athletes' real motor skills and, in many cases, the coach may fail to provide a suitable reason to justify such a poor performance.

The reasons for this can often be found in the action of the coaches themselves, in the way they approach their players, in the methods they use to plan and organize learning situations as well as in the relational dynamics developing between the players themselves.

In practice, the coach should work to help his athletes learn more rapidly and easily, and for this to be possible he should specifically:
- be willing to adjust his own behavior to the way in which every single player approaches the activity and the relationship[19]
- be willing and able to listen to his players
- frequently ask his players about the sensations they feel, their doubts, opinions and suggestions
- be willing to dialogue

---

16 By Oserov (1983), and Janssen (1983)

17 By Gori M. and Marzi F. in Educazione e allenamento. Ricerca pedagogica. Medicina sportiva" – "Training and education. Pedagocial research. Sport medicine." (note of the translator) – SSS, Roma, 1988.

18 For further details on the importance of social relations in learning read "L'arte dell'incoraggiamento" – "The art of encouraging" (note of the translator) – by Franta H. and Colasanti A., La Nuova Italia Scientifica, Roma, 1991, 1993. It is a novel formative itinerary for teachers to enhance their art of encouraging , that is the "process of cooperation between teachers and learners that aims at creating a positive psychological disposition – courage – favoring the possibility to handle and overcome any possible situation and achieve the final goals one had previously set".

19 "Il muro del pregiudizio. Letture in tema di ecologia della mente" – "The wall of prejudice. Readings on ecology of the mind" (note of the translator) – by Calegari P.; Ed. Liguori Napoli, 1994

- be able to accept and acknowledge unexpected situations as important opportunities for learning
- be rather authoritative in some cases
- be a guide for his players
- constantly encourage and stimulate his players
- cooperate with his players
- be assertive, that is show a strong and confident personality while always focusing great attention on positive aspects
- work to create a confident and relaxed atmosphere in the group.

2) Learning theories to which the coach typically applies

For many years, the coaching methods to introduce young athletes to playing soccer have been conditioned by exaggerated technique that pretended to build skillful players by coaching basic technical principles and movements a priory. In that way, the coach left no room for the creative potential of his athletes, but dictated the best solutions, preventing players from freely expressing their creativeness. Basically, that methodological strategy involved the coach explaining, asking his players to imitate and practically reproduce a model that was commonly thought to be valid, internalizing and reinforcing such a model through regular and constant performances and finally correcting and adjusting bad movements. (Behavioral theories – deductive methods: directive and training mechanisms).

Today, most coaches are more inclined to suggest to their players particular learning situations that stimulate the active processing and internalization of the experience through activities involving **semi-structured play**. In this case, players need to create rules and technical solutions by themselves in order to improve the development of the game while also enhancing their sports skills. In this way, greater attention is focused on how athletes develop and handle different play situations – always followed and directed by the coach – rather than on the final outcome of an activity previously planned and set by the coach himself. Through personal experiences players can build and enhance their motor learning mechanisms actively and consciously so that they are constantly encouraged to be creative, inventive and enterprising. (Constructive – cognitive- humanistic theories – Inductive methods: research and problem-solving).

For further details on this matter, read the suggestions and examples shown at paragraph 1.10 in this chapter and titled "Examples for planning games using the inductive method".

3) Purposes of motor learning
(educational, physical, technical and tactical goals)

The coach can use several different methods to carry out his job, which also depend on the final goals he wants to achieve by suggesting a specific motor task. In the same training session a coach can combine, in a complementary way, various coaching methods, like those that are shown in the table on the following page.

Type of Goal	Coaching Methods Used
E - F	Comply with the theory of increasing work loads very gradually.
E	Method of research aimed at respecting the time for perception, internalization, adjustment, adaptation and refinement.
E-TT	Mutual discussion on personal solutions (solutions to problem-solving, working out strategies and so on), without giving personal judgements of value on the adaptability and functionality of the motor responses suggested by the young players.
E - TT	The whole group discuss the development of the activity, the possible adjustments, the best suggestions to improve the method; open dialogue must be stimulated by suitable questions.
E	Reflecting on the gestures and activities carried out through verbal communication, written explanations or diagrams.
T-F	Frontal, expository and directive coaching session.

(by Castelli and Bonaccorso, 1999)
E=educational; F=physical; T=technical; TT=tactical

In other words, if the coach bases his coaching philosophy on mutual confrontation and open dialogue in group to find the best solutions to solve problems, he will certainly work to achieve educational and tactical goals; on the other hand, if the coaching strategy specifically concentrates on directive methods, it will mainly aim at refining technical gestures and enhance physical-athletic capacities.

The coaching methods mentioned in the table above can be divided into two important groups resulting from the different learning theories: the inductive method and the deductive one. Nevertheless, they cannot be distinguished and applied so strictly in the operative reality.

7. Evaluating[20]

By evaluating we refer to all the procedures and systems to gather information in order to finally make decisions concerning the best activities and solutions to suggest to the group. The main purpose of evaluation is improving the whole coaching-and-learning process and concerns both the athletes' learning level and the accuracy and effectiveness of the coaching-didactic choices that the coach has made.

Evaluation is a function of the theoretical coaching-and-learning model which the coach adheres to. If the coach refers to the cognitive model and to the method that focuses the attention on the individual, evaluation should be made on the whole

---

20 For further detail on the subject read: A.A.V.V. "La valutazione nello sport dei giovani" – "Evaluating in youth sport" (note of the translator), Società Stampa Sportiva, Roma, 1988; and "La valutazione in educazione fisica" – "Evaluating in physical training" (note of the translator) – by Dispenza A., S.S.S. Roma, 1992.

Inductive Method	Deductive Method
• The player-learner is the protagonist in the whole coaching-and-learning process • The player is the key subject whose potential needs to be discovered and exploited • Educating = drawing out • The coach does not suggest how, when, where, why; consequently, he does not suggest solutions that players need to remember, but only problems that they need to solve. • Active attitude of the player-learner • It encourages motivation to learn based on the need for competence and success (personal ability) • Experience – observe – compare – abstract – generalize (focuses the attention on personal suggestions, ideas, intuitions of the player-learner, consequently attaching great importance to his needs and desires, from which he starts to find personal solutions and alternative performances on his own) • The coach suggests semi-structured activities or even situations lacking any structure at all, where space, time, manners, roles, rules, purposes and strategies can be set by players-learners spontaneously in relation to their own needs and experiences • It approaches the principle of polyvalence: the learner is involved not only at motor level but also from the emotional-social-cognitive point of view • It enhances awareness of learning.	• The coach-teacher is the real protagonist in the whole coaching-and-learning process • The coach is the person who knows How, When, Where, Why? • Educating = putting inside • This is a directive method that teaches, trains and suggests solutions that the learner has to remember • Passive attitude of the player-learner. He must be always attentive and concentrated to understand, imitate and perform • It encourages motivation to learn based on external reward or approval by others • Explain – show – perform – correct – adjust • The player-learner is subject to constant tests, evaluation and judgement: "your movement was bad, you cannot move like that, you should do it this way, why don't you do what I tell you?". The coach dictates how the player should solve problems and make suitable gestures • The coach suggests structured activities of which he sets a priory: time, space, manners, roles, rules, goals and strategies • It somehow detaches from the principle of polyvalence: the player is considerably involved from the motor point of view; poor involvement at emotional-social-cognitive level • The awareness of one's learning is poorly stimulated

Comparative table of inductive and deductive coaching methods (by Bonaccorso and Castelli, 1999)

training process and not on the learner exclusively. It follows that this complex procedure is a formative opportunity - and not a punitive mechanism – aiming at helping the learner improve and not at humbling, excluding or punishing him. Rather, the learner is the subject of the coach's evaluation and not the object (the object is the coaching process, in fact), from whom the coach gets useful information to improve and optimize training.

In this perspective, the role of error acquires a different meaning compared to the meaning it would have in a more traditional coaching method. In fact, when the coach realizes that the reply he gets from his player is wrong, he does not promptly act to correct it, but carefully observes the mistake as an instrument to understand the player's competence and manner of learning, as an indicator that suggests at what level in the whole mental process or in the final motor performance the interference may have appeared, which prevents the subject from carrying out the task accurately. For example, a bad shot on goal may result from an inability to control anxiety in particular situations of intense emotional stress on the part of a very insecure player, or from his inability to make coordinated movements when shooting at goal.

It is fundamental for a coach to accustom the player-learner to observing himself so as to be able to make self-evaluation, thus becoming increasingly aware of his learning.

Evaluating is not simply a final process but should be constant and regular so as to characterize all the different phases of coaching. It includes three main stages:

COACH	PARTNER/LEARNER
Evaluation a priory (beforehand): aims at evaluating whether the acitivites he intends to suggest are important, pertinent and adaptable to his coaching plan, his players and his own competence.	**Starting formative evaluation:** the coach tests the starting conditions of his players on the basis of given purposes that are considered key (prerequisites): what the athlete can do.
Progressive evaluation (during): allows the coach to evaluate whether his suggestions are really effective and well-aimed. It also helps the coach promptly adjust his plans according to the replies given by his players. It allows him to carry out prompt supporting procedures.	**Intermediate formative evaluation:** allows the coach to collect information during the process of acquiring abilities, and helps him understand the rhythm and personal motivation to learn of every single player.
Final evaluation (at the end): the coach gathers and synthesizes all the possible data and information concerning the final outcome of the whole coaching process so as to assess its real effectiveness.	**Final cumulative evaluation:** allows the coach to ascertain to what extent one can master one's learning and the goals one has achieved at the end of a significant stage in the general coaching and didactic process.

The instruments the coach can use to make evaluations include:

1. **Objective experiences:**
   - standard motor tests
   - field tests on specific abilities peculiar to soccer
   - written tests (answer true or false; multiple choice; fill in the blanks and so on)

2. **Subjective experiences:**
   - direct observation both during play situations and while discussing in group (using prepared grids and forms)
   - personal interviews
   - verbal reports
   - special forms and tables

---

21 Evaluating the learning level achieved by every single player concerns: his motor performances, levels of capacity, goals finally achieved, improvements, attributes of his behavior and personality, acquired theoretical knowledge, awareness of his learning, his personal motivations.

Full Name	Takes the initiative spontaneously	Is aggressive	Is tolerant	Is a leader	Is a follower	Secludes himself Is passive	Is Creative

Observation form to record affective and social behaviors during particular situations of play:

OBSERVATION FORM - SCOUTING REPORT
GUIDELINES TO DRAW UP PLAYERS' EVALUATION FORMS

PHYSICAL ASPECT -- FITNESS
- Physical Structure
  - Height: (tall – short) - short-limbed - normotype - long-limbed
  - Weight: fat - slim
  - Muscle Tissue: poor - normal - developed
  - General Condition: early development - late maturation
- Athletic Attributes
  - Is capable of endurance – strength – rapidity – speed – power

TECHNICAL ASPECT
Relation with the Ball
- Favorite Foot
  - Right foot - left foot
  - Can use his non-favorite foot
- First Control (stop)
  - Can read the path of the ball – kinesthetic sensibility – muscular sensibility
  - Controlling skills
- Shooting Skills
  - Technique for kicking the ball
- Heading Skills
  - Technique for heading the ball both in the offensive and the defensive phase

TECHNICAL AND TACTICAL ASPECTS OFFENSIVE PHASE (OFFENSIVE BUILD-UP)
- Can Often Win Possession of the Ball
  - Sense of position (space and time orientation)
  - Eluding the marking
- Can Handle the Ball While Pressured by the Opponent
- Can Maintain Possession of the Ball

- Ball technique - control - ball possession
- Dribble the Ball too Much
  - Cannot read the situation of play. Peripheral vision.
- Can Play Easily
- Makes the Action Easier and Builds up Play
  - Can read the game. Peripheral vision.
- Quality of the Pass
- Time
  - When?
  - Time for the pass
- Space
  - Where?
    - In depth (through pass - pass to elude the marking)
    - Clearing pass (cross-over play) and back pass
    - Pass to one's teammate
    - Zone pass
- Accuracy of the Pass
  - How?
    - Which part of the foot? Inside – outside
    - Measuring the power of the pass (differentiation ability)
- Can Dribble
  - Creativeness - imagination

OFFENSIVE PHASE (FINALIZE THE OFFENSIVE BUILD UP)
- Positioning to Shoot at Goal
- Often Tries to shoot at Goal
- Often Moves to the Penalty Box
  - In the scoring area he prefers
    - to pass the ball
    - to shoot at goal

DEFENSIVE PHASE
- Can Mark His Opponent
  - Take position
- Can Challenge His Opponent
  - Anticipation action - intercepting

PSYCHOLOGICAL ASPECT
- Personality in Particular Play Situations
  - Temperament - grit
  - Communication
  - Cooperation
  - Sense of competition

by Bonaccorso – Perico – Favini

Field tests involving specific situations

Using field tests involving specific situations of play (as shown in the following pages) can help the coach evaluate both the technical and tactical skills of his players, since real game situations-problems include all the main elements that typically characterize the context of official matches:

- the ball
- the opposition
- the goal
- the goalkeeper

These elements, combined together, contribute to create those psychological pressures that characterize competition, where every single player is asked to solve specific tactical problems and make suitable technical movements and gestures in particular conditions of severe emotional stress (which is too often responsible for the most common mistakes).

Compared to analytical tests, in this case the control over the variable elements of play is less accurate also because the subjects in question enjoy complete freedom to make decisions and perform, since the main intent of the coach is to evaluate their real abilities. In order to adjust the activities to the various age groups and to the different levels of ability, the coach should properly change playing areas and distances. Each test will allow the coach to:

- identify those elements that clearly suggest that the goals have been achieved
- assess the level of effectiveness
- measure the speed of the performance.

The model of evaluation we will use in the following pages is based on direct observation of the athletes' behaviors through special grids, including those behaviors that are intended as standard indicators of the final goals to be achieved. The coach shall fill in the blanks, writing yes or no and his personal notes. The information he gathers will help him plan not only general activities for team training, but also special training and coaching suggestions for individual players in order to correct their weaknesses and fully exploit their potential.

The degree of effectiveness of each activity results from the ratio between the total number of attempts and the number of successful performances, which means from calculating the percentage of success and failure. The result the coach finally gets can help establish correlations and comparisons between the various age groups or between the same categories but in different contexts (amateur and professional athletes, for example), constantly monitoring the situation year by year.

Moreover, it is also important to underline that educating players to self-evaluate and enjoy successful experiences considerably enhances and feeds their personal motivations to practice sport. The speed of the performance – or better, the speed at which one finally manages to achieve set goals – measured in seconds is an indicator of the quality of the manner in which one expresses one's own potential and represents a significant target that, successful performances being equal, finally sublimates the result.

1 v goalkeeper. While focusing the attention on the relation between the player in possession of the ball and the goalkeeper, the coach should first concentrate on the behaviors shown in the grid and then analyze them in detail directly on the field, trying to answer a series of questions (**diagram 1 - table 1**).

- Why isn't the player skillful at shooting at goal?
- Doesn't he read the position of the goalkeeper?
- Can't he handle his emotions?
  Can't he kick the ball while moving?
- How does he shoot at goal? Does he take powerful shots before entering the goal-keeper's playing area? Does he take accurate shots? Does he dribble the ball straight to the goalkeeper because he always shoots from the right side?

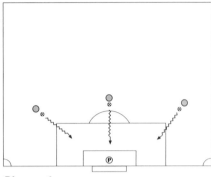

Diagram 1

The following variations could be introduced at a didactic level:

- the player has to dribble the ball either with his favorite or his less skillful foot;
- the player cannot enter the goal-area, so as to prevent him from dribbling to beat the goalkeeper and therefore increase the number of powerful shots on goal.

TABLE 1

A player in possession of the ball at the edge of the penalty box takes 10 shots on goal from each one of the three positions shown in diagram 1; the purpose of this exercise is to score as many goals possible in the shortest time possible. Each shot ends when:

- the ball goes into the goal;
- the goalkeeper manages to save the shot and wins possession of the ball;
- the ball moves out of the penalty area.

SCOUTING REPORT	
Player	
Can shoot at goal	
Can take effective and successful shots on goal	
Can take powerful shots	
Can take accurate shots	

	% OF GOALS SCORED	
from the left	from the central position	from the right
	Best scoring time in seconds	
from the left	from the central position	from the right

1 v 1 + goalkeeper. In this exercise, the coach can assess the player's ability in 1 v 1 situations both in the offensive and the defensive phase (**diagram 2 – table 2**).

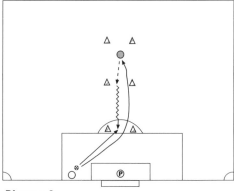

Diagram 2

- Does the player dribble on the right or on the left?
- Is the defender always beaten on the weak side of the ball?
- Does the defender always win the challenge on the strong side?

Apart from purely technical considerations, the coach can also make careful evaluations of his players' coordination capacities.

TABLE 2

A defender is standing at the edge of the goal-area on the goal-line near one of the two posts, takes an accurate shot into the far (second) square (8 by 8 yards); an attacking player is standing in this square area, controls the ball and then starts the offensive build up (1 v 1 situation) dribbling the ball through the lane marked out with cones and finally shoots at goal. Each player can repeat the exercise 10 times; the competition ends when:
- the ball rolls out of the lane or the penalty box;
- the ball passes through the goal;
- the goalkeeper wins possession of the ball;
- the defender manages to win possession of the ball after three touches.

EVALUATION FORM FOR ATTACKING PLAYERS	
Player.........................	
Can control the ball	
Can dribble the ball	
Can dribble and beat the opposition	
Can shoot at goal	
EVALUATION FORM FOR DEFENDERS	
Player.........................	
Can kick the ball	
Can approach and challenge the attacker	
Can mark the opponent	
Can tackle	
Can defend the goal	

For the attacking player: can he assess the speed and read the direction of the defender's run?
- Can he read the speed and the path of the ball?
- Can he adjust and modify his gestures and movements in relation to the defender's behavior?
- Can he change pace while running, dribbling the ball or in order to beat the opposition?

- Can he anticipate what the defender is going to do?
- Can he change the solution he has previously chosen?
- Can he make feints?

From the physical and athletic point of view, the coach could also make important evaluations on the player's force of acceleration and slowing down. Serious evaluation should also concern the defender, specifically focusing the attention on his real abilities in the defensive phase.

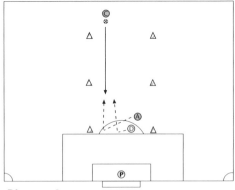

1 v 1 + support + goalkeeper.
The basic element the coach can evaluate in this test is the attacker's ability to elude the opponent's marking while clearing space to receive the ball (**diagram 3 - table 3**).

Diagram 3

TABLE 3

The attacker A, marked by a defender D, moves freely inside a playing area 10 yards long and wide like the goal-area previously marked at the edge of the penalty box; he tries to clear space in order to receive the ball from his midfield teammate C. Player C can only play as a support at a distance of about 10 yards from the playing area. The purpose of this test is to score the most goals in the ten different performances each player is allowed.

N.B.: When attacker A receives the ball, he can play it back to his midfield teammate just once in order to achieve the final goal of the test in the same performance. Each competition ends when:
- the ball moves out of the playing field;
- the goalkeeper wins possession of the ball;
- the defender manages to win possession of the ball touching it three times.

EVALUATION FORM FOR ATTACKING PLAYERS	
Player............................	
Can clear space to get free from the marking	
Can shield the ball	
Can make a return pass	
Can turn around while dribbling the ball	
Can shoot at goal	
EVALUATION FORM FOR DEFENDERS	
Player............................	
Can take suitable positions	
Can mark	
Can challenge the opponent, making him stand with his back to the goal	
Can intercept the pass	
Can challenge the opponent	
Can defend the goal	
EVALUATION FORM FOR MIDFIELDERS	
Player............................	
Can communicate with the attacker	
Can play the ball in relation to the movements of both the attacker and the defender	

- Does the attacker receive the ball in front of or behind the defender?
- Is the defender able to reduce the space for the attacker to move?
- Can the attacker maintain possession of the ball and shield it?
- Does the attacker show great creativeness and imagination while turning about with the ball?
- Can the defender anticipate the attacker's movement?

In order to highlight the didactic intent while also enhancing personal motivations, this test could also involve awarding set scores to the protagonists in relation to whether they have partially or fully achieved the final goal.

Attacking player: 1 point is awarded if he manages to receive, control the ball and make a pass back to his midfield teammate; 2 points if he manages to shoot at goal; 3 points if he can score a goal.

Defender: 1 point is awarded if he plays the ball out of the playing area; 2 points if he succeeds in winning possession of the ball with at least three touches; 3 points if he wins possession of the ball and counter attacks.

2 v 1. In this basic situation – which should be considered as the atom of collective play, as the real foundation of team play – the attention is focused on enhancing passing skills, (the player's ability to play the ball). (**diagram 4 - table 4**).

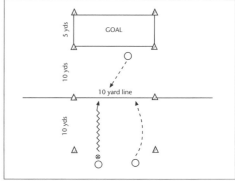

Diagram 4

The quality of the pass clearly indicates the level of communication developing between the two attacking players.
- Can they communicate with each other?
- Is the choice of the development of the offensive maneuver up to the player in pos-   session of the ball or to his teammate without the ball?
- Can they adjust their motor plans (alternative solution) if the opponent does not play as one would have expected?

Moreover, this test also helps evaluate the capacity of the attacking players to cooperate with each other.
- Can they develop positive relations of mutual support to achieve common final goals?
- Can they take their own responsibilities?
- Is the player without the ball conscious of his role of support?
- Is the success of the attacking pair more important than the successful performance of just one of the two players?
- Does the analysis of the defender's performance also concern his ability to handle the numerical disadvantage?
- Does the defender suffer in the situation?
- Can he take the initiative?
- Does he have a competent and suitable defensive attitude?

TABLE 4

In the playing area previously marked out by means of cones, the two attacking players in possession of the ball endeavor to gain space forward by dribbling the ball towards the target area, while the defender tries to challenge them. Both the attackers and the defender start from their respective goal-lines; ten competitions for each group of three players. The offside rule is applied from the 10-yard line. Each competition ends when:

- the ball rolls out of the playing area;
- the defender manages to win possession of the ball with three touches at least;
- the attackers run offside.

EVALUATION FORM FOR THE ATTACKER IN POSSESSION OF THE BALL
Player...........................
Can dribble the ball
Can dribble and beat the opponent
Can play the ball
Can choose a really effective solution of play
EVALUATION FORM FOR THE ATTACKER WITHOUT THE BALL
Player...........................
Can control the ball
Can play for his teammate in possession of the ball
Can make suitable cutting movements
Can make successful screens on the opponent
Can make overlapping movements
Can support his teammate in possession of the ball
Can adjust his play to the movements of his teammate in possession of the ball
Can clear space to freely move towards the target area
EVALUATION FOR FOR THE DEFENDER
Player...........................
Can take suitable positions
Can mark the opponent
Can challenge the opponent
Can intercept the pass
Can apply the offside trap
Can force the player in possession of the ball to move in a given direction

2 v 2. In this situation, mutual communication and cooperation play a role of critical importance also in the defensive phase, where the players need to work together following the principle of marking the player in possession of the ball while also covering the near space (**diagram 5**). They can apply both the offside trap and double teaming when it is necessary. Analyzing the offensive phase, the coach should specifically focus attention on the players' capacity to cooperate to solve a problem; moreover, in addition to evaluating the means whereby the two players finally achieve the goal, the coach should also concentrate on the time of their play actions; in particular: the time of the pass and the time of the movement made without the ball (to elude the marking).

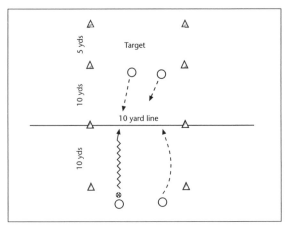

Diagram 5

TABLE 5

In a playing area marked out as in the diagram above, two attacking players try to gain space forward in order to reach the target area; meanwhile, two defenders endeavor to challenge them and prevent them from moving forward. The two pairs of players start from their respective goal-lines and are allowed ten different performances. Considering that the offside rule is applied starting from the 10-yard line, the test ends when:

- the ball moves out of the playing area;
- the defenders manage to win possession of the ball with three touches at least or passing the ball to each other;
- the attackers move offside.

EVALUATION FORM FOR THE DEFENDER WITHOUT OF THE BALL
Player...........................
Individual skills
Can dribble
Movements in cooperation with his teammate
Can play the ball
Can attack making overlapping movements
Can attack making cutting (diagonal) movements
Can attack making wall-passes
EVALUATION FORM FOR THE DEFENDER
Player...........................
Individual skills
Can challenge
Can intercept the pass
Movements in cooperation with his teammate
Can cover space
Can defend overlapping movements
Can defend cutting movements
Can defend wall-passes

3 v 3 + goalkeeper. Among all the situations suggested in these pages, this is the exercise that most approaches real-game situations and can therefore offer useful and convincing information. **(diagram 6 - table 6)**

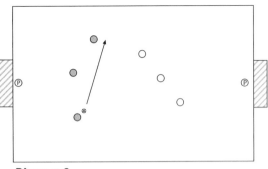

Diagram 6

The ratio between marking movements and the movements to elude the opponent's marking can offer important suggestions on the player's offensive or defensive attitude. The coach can focus his attention on how the player plays the ball.

- Does he make short or long passes?
- Can he choose between short or long passes in relation to the particular situation of play?
- Can he dribble the ball and beat the opponent in the right space and at the right time in competitions?
- Does he try to beat the opponent while dribbling the ball?
- Can he dribble past the opponent successfully?
- Does he try to shoot at goal?
- Can he take successful shots on goal?

The player's performance can be successful either because he shoots at the goal-mouth or because he manages to score a goal. The ratio between the player's attempts to shoot at goal and the number of successful shots could be an interesting element of evaluation. In this situation, great value is given to scoring headed goals, since this helps assess the players' crossing skills and, consequently, the ability to head the ball in the offensive and defensive phase.

In the end, this small-sided game also offers the coach the possibility to analyze the players' ability to read the situation of play and play in relation to the information they get at the moment; in this way, the coach can also understand if the game consists of a combination of individual and independent actions or develops as team play.

TABLE 6

A 3 v 3 game is played on a 20-by-30–yard area with small-sized goals (4 by 2 yards, for example) defended by the two goalkeeper. Two periods of 10 minutes each. Two points are awarded for each goal scored by heading the ball.

EVALUATION FORM	
Player...........................	
Individual skills	
Can mark	
Can elude the marking	
Can pass the ball	
Can head the ball	
Can shoot at goal	
Can dribble	
Can cooperate	

8. Strategies for recovery and reinforcement

The main strategies for recovery are specifically designed for those athletes who have not achieved set goals, while the strategies for reinforcement concern those who have already achieved such goals.

After careful evaluation of his players' skills, the coach should work on the results to plan and differentiate his coaching methods in relation to the athletes' individual abilities, so as to adjust his coaching suggestions and activities to the peculiarities and personal potential of every single player.

At this point, it is fundamental for a coach to offer several individualized opportunities which carefully consider the differences and distinctive features of the athletes as well as their different ways of learning, in order to:
- enhance and exploit the peculiar attributes of every single player
- help everybody live successful experiences in the context of differentiated and personalized activities
- encourage players to fully exploit their potential and achieve their own goals.

This means that those who are not truly skillful should not feel humiliated by constant failures; on the other hand, talented athletes should always be encouraged to try their best: this is why the coach should carefully plan training sessions so as to attract players' attention and make them feel stimulated and actively involved in all the activities.

All the various motor activities structured according to flexible didactic methods, accurate strategies of differentiation and personalization and suitable coaching techniques – obviously involving the presence of favorable learning conditions – are specifically aimed at enhancing individual abilities and inclinations. The final purpose is to help every single athlete improve to optimum levels, in relation to the potential that he can gradually express in time.

The coach should plan his coaching suggestions so as to distinguish several homogeneous groups on the basis of the athletes' individual skills (groups of equal level):
- using special training circuits
- assigning different tasks
- suggesting special activities for small groups of players.

1.10 COMPARING DIFFERENT METHODS: EXAMPLES FOR PLANNING GAMES USING THE INDUCTIVE AND DEDUCTIVE METHOD

A) *Example for planning a soccer game by means of the inductive method using integrated coaching models*

Procedure to plan a semi-structured game: "the sparrow-hawk".
Specific goals: dribbling the ball, defending and covering, making feints and beating the opponent.
Method: Method of research combined with basic training to enhance technical skills.

This coaching method involves the player as the subject, the protagonist in the whole learning process. The coach clearly arranges and explains the situation-problem (for instance, the player must dribble the ball with his feet up to the goal-line, trying to prevent the sparrow-hawk from touching him before getting to the target line) without previously telling his athletes how, why, where and when the activity is carried out. The players are guided to discover new solutions through suitable exercises, questions and careful consideration; in this way, not only are they involved at the physical level, but they also take an active part in the situation from the cognitive, emotional and relational point of view.

Phase 1

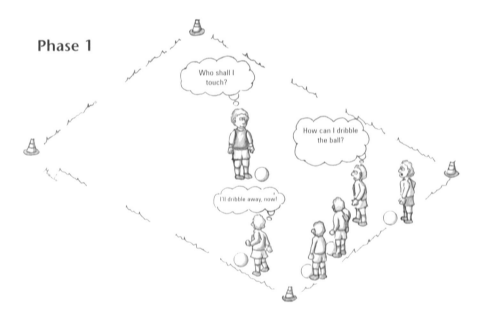

1. Development of the game. The players in possession of the ball dribble the ball through the playing area so as to reach the opposite target line; meanwhile, an opponent (the sparrow-hawk) hinders their movements, trying to prevent them from getting to the goal-line. The coach gives clear, concise and short orders and suggestions (verbal, gestural and iconic communication).

2. Play – action (period of chaos): during the first phase of the game, the players' motor behaviors will certainly be chaotic, utterly spontaneous and will obviously lack strategic organization both at the technical and tactical level.

3. Freeze the game – everybody is standing in a ring. The coach freezes the game and the players promptly position in a ring; this disposition helps communication (the athletes and the coach can see and listen to each other much better), exchange of information and considerations on the activities previously experienced, identifying personal needs, making suitable decisions and clearly understanding one's individual tasks.

a) The need to set rules.
- What are the boundaries of the playing area?
- Where can the sparrow-hawk move and operate?
- Does the sparrow-hawk play with or without the ball?
- What shall the sparrow-hawk do to touch the player? Shall he touch the body of the player or the ball the player is dribbling or even win possession of the ball?
- What shall a player do when he is touched by the sparrow-hawk? Is he directly excluded from the game or does he become a sparrow-hawk in his turn?
- What shall he do if he becomes a sparrow-hawk?
- How long does the game last?
- Are the starting and finishing signals established beforehand or are they decided freely by means of different signs chosen by the players themselves?
- Do the sparrow-hawks need to have special identification marks?

b) The need to improve the coordination of one's motor patterns (technical aspect)
- How can one dribble the ball forward while changing direction and speed or while turning about?
- How can a player dribble the ball and control the sparrow-hawk's movements at the same time?
- How can a player dribble the ball?
- How can a player dribble past the sparrow-hawk so as to elude his challenge?

c) The need to set definite strategies of play (tactical aspect)
- Why must a player run and keep his head up?
- Is it important to consider and control the sparrow-hawk's movements?
- Is it necessary to control the position of the sparrow-hawk and carefully assess his running speed?
- Is it better to dribble or kick the ball in order to beat the sparrow-hawk?
- While moving inside the playing area and challenging the opponents, should the sparrow-hawk concentrate on one player exclusively or can he focus his attention on different players?
- Should the sparrow-hawk make feints?
- Can the players cooperate to help each other?
- Should the sparrow-hawks cooperate and play together for a common goal?

These needs and demands emerge from combining playing and discussing while standing in a circle; the coach decides the best moment to freeze the game and discuss the situation during the course of one or more training sessions (Coaching Unit).

In this phase, the coach should avoid telling his players the solutions he has in his mind in advance; actually, his job is to allow his athletes to work out new possibilities by themselves and experience their own solutions to solve problems.
For this to be possible the coach can choose between two different didactic methods:

1. Either he can wisely guide and direct his players by means of suitable questions-stimuli to find right solutions (guided discovery);
2. Or he can exploit the suggestions, ideas and actions of every single player and consider them as starting points to build and develop the game. In this case, it is fundamental that the coach and the teammates refrain from judging the value and effectiveness of the suggestions given. The sentence recurring most often in this case should be: "Let's try!" Moreover, it is advisable for a coach to highlight and clearly confirm the suggestions of his players.

This didactic method may cause feelings of anxiety, since the coach is not absolutely certain of how the game is going to develop (as a matter of fact, it may develop in a completely different way than he had previously planned) and may feel as if he may not be ready and prepared to promptly choose suitable didactic suggestions. Nevertheless, this important competence (at an affective and relational level) can be acquired and enhanced like any other methodological competence. For example, mutual recognition[22], the capacity to surprise and feel surprised, the conviction that nothing is strictly pre-arranged (the game must fit the player and not vice-versa) are important capacities that can be trained and enhanced, considering that coaching and learning cannot be considered as two separate processes but always influence each other.

Phase 2

1. The first syntheses. The coach synthesizes all the coordination, technical and tactical problems that emerged in the first phase. This synthesis can be done orally or using special chalkboards, boards, diagrams, tables and forms to help his athletes better assimilate the rules of the game and internalize technical and tactical solutions.

2. The activities. The coach identifies and plans the activities that are necessary to achieve specific goals, for instance enhancing the coordination of technical moves through the following coaching-didactic progression:
• **Turn** - dribble the ball straight ahead and then change direction (**diagram 1**).

---

22 Mutual recognition is the capacity to understand and acknowledge that the athlete can have competence, sensations, significant emotions and self-educating potential of his own; it is the capacity to accept the possibility to change the roles of those who teach and those who learn, in a dynamic process of mutual teaching and mutual adaptation where the roles of teachers and learners alternate with each other, even though the necessary asymmetrical positions of the relation between teacher and learner remain unchanged (without excluding the role of authoritative leader and guide).

- **Turn through 360°** - dribble the ball straight ahead, turn around the cone and then change direction (**diagram 2**).
- **Slalom** - dribble the ball ahead changing direction and pace (**diagram 3**).
- **Dribble back** - dribble the ball straight ahead or backward by changing direction (**diagram 4**).
- **Dribble, look and speak** - dribble the ball upward and look ahead, while saying the number that the teammate is showing with his hands (**diagram 5**).
- **Chase** - the "chaser" without the ball runs after the runaway player in possession of the ball who is dribbling and shielding the ball while running at full speed (**diagram 6**).
- **Turn around the opponent** - dribble the ball ahead and then change direction turning round an opponent. The opponent is standing with his non-kicking foot in a hoop, but is allowed to touch the ball with the other foot. The player in possession of the ball tries to turn round the opponent shielding the ball (**diagram 7**).

In this phase, the coach can use a deductive coaching method (this means that he explains, shows, asks his players to perform the exercises and finally corrects them) even though it is always possible to apply to a purely inductive didactic method, which allows the players to personally experience solutions and adjust the models of the technical moves shown. For example, the coach could ask: "*With what part of the foot is it better to dribble the ball? Try to dribble the ball in different ways. Who can..........?*"

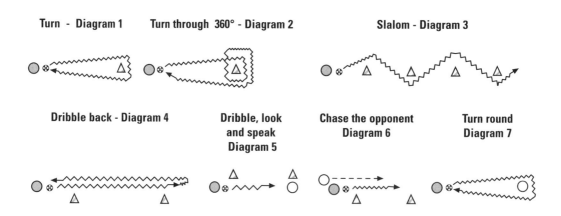

Turn - Diagram 1   **Turn through 360° - Diagram 2**   **Slalom - Diagram 3**

Dribble back - Diagram 4   **Dribble, look and speak Diagram 5**   **Chase the opponent Diagram 6**   **Turn round Diagram 7**

Phase 3
1. Action – the game is being structured. The athletes are playing.
2. Freeze the game – the players are standing in a circle. In this phase the coach underlines and confirms the suggestions given by his players, encourages them to check the competence and abilities they have acquired through open discussion and invites them to consciously examine their improvements both at a technical (enhanced coordination of their movements, for example) and tactical level (better solutions to the problems arising in the game). Consequently, the need to set new rules and work out innovative techniques and strategies is further pointed out.
3. The game goes on...and develops towards effective movements and strategies.

DIDACTIC PROCESS TO PLAN A GAME:

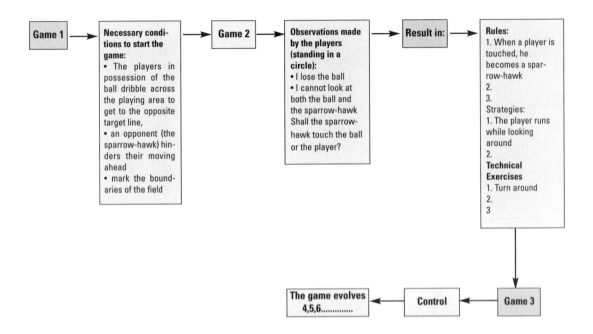

Example of planning by goals using the inductive method of research players solve problem-situations

The method of research is also pursued as a goal, since it helps to learn the necessary procedure to solve problems, independently in various contexts.

EDUCATIONAL GOALS	SPECIFIC MOTOR GOALS	SPECIFIC GOALS FOR RESEARCH	CONTENTS
• ability to plan activities • evaluate one's own job and that of others • use the resources of the environment and one's own resources • work in an independent and responsible manner • work in a group • solve problems • react to difficulties in a constructive manner • capacity to discuss with one's teammates • capacity to plan a game in a group, setting the necessary rules to carry out such a game • acquire the concept of role in a team game	• occupy space in a way that is functional to the purpose of the game • enhance the capacity to move on the playing area in relation to the opposition and one's teammates • dribble the ball, shield, defend and cover the ball, make feints and beat the opponent • assess the speed at which the opponent is moving	• identify and select the problem • examine experiences critically • form hypotheses • plan activities • collect information and data • tabulate and analyze data • process and interpret data and information • fix the results achieved so that they can be easily communicated • evaluate the results	**Game:** *the sparrow-hawk*

COACHING UNIT
PURPOSE: enhance the capacity to understand and select a problem

1.The coach suggests some basic conditions and rules to start the game	1.The athlete starts playing a) he promptly starts practicing b) he respects materials and equipment c) he does not get angry with his teammates d) he does not give up playing when faced with some difficulties e) he looks for his teammates' help f) he looks for his coach's support
2. The coach freezes the game	2.The athlete discusses while standing in a circle a) he can make pertinent remarks b) he takes an active part in the discussion c) he waits for his turn to speak d) he can listen to his teammates e) he can make suggestions f) he accepts his teammates' suggestions g) he sets the necessary rules and strategies to play
3. The coach invites his players to restart the game, making the adjustments they have suggested	3.The athlete restarts playing a) he can make the adjustments that have been suggested b) he can completely carry out the activity that was previously planned
4. The coach encourages his players to make helpful remarks and check how the game is developing	4.The athlete discusses while standing in a circle a) can make comparisons b) can make suitable evaluations c) can make detailed reports
The coach's analysis	**The athlete's analysis**
• He focuses the attention on the players' behaviors and motor performances • He draws up special forms and tables to record his players' behaviors • He evaluates the real effectiveness of the game • He assesses the awareness his players have acquired while absorbing the method of research	• He makes accurate self-evaluation, encouraged by the dialogue with both the coach and his teammates • He completes a questionnaire for self-evaluation • He fills in special forms where he writes down rules and strategies

B) Example for the development of the game: "the sparrow-hawk", structured by the coach using the deductive method exclusively.

THE SPARROW-HAWK

A group of players position along the starting line and dribble the balls forward trying to cross the opposite line marked out at a distance of 18 yards. Another player (the sparrow-hawk) is standing in the playing area between the two lines: he hinders the opponents' movements, trying to intercept or win possession of their balls so as to make them become sparrow-hawks in their turn. The last player who manages to maintain possession of the ball without being touched by the sparrow-hawk is the winner of the competition.

At the very beginning of the training session the coach sets:

1. **the goal:** enhance the ability to gain space forward while dribbling the ball
2. **the playing area:** an 18-by-9-yard playing field
3. **the time:** it can vary, since it depends on the ability of the sparrow-hawk
4. **the rules:**
   - the sparrow-hawk's behavior: he can move without the ball within a 5-by-9-yard playing area previously marked out and tries to touch the ball of a prey-player, who will immediately become a sparrow-hawk in his turn.
     Purposes: intercepting, challenging and winning possession of the ball.
   - the prey-player's behavior: he tries to cross the playing area from the starting line to the opposite target line while dribbling the ball forward (he cannot kick the ball). The coach gives the starting signal for the players to start dribbling.
     Purposes: dribbling, shielding and defending the ball, beating the opponent
   - the last prey-player who manages to maintain possession of the ball is the winner of the game
   - the coach explains a priory how, when and why the players should adopt certain technical and tactical attitudes
5. **the strategies:**
   - of the sparrow-hawk:
     - focus attention on one prey-player at a time
     - make feints so as to deceive the opponent
     - and so forth…
   - of the prey-player:
     - play within the boundaries of the playing area
     - dribble the ball considering the movements and attitudes of the sparrow-hawk
     - assess the running speed of the sparrow-hawk
     - and so on…

The coach has a directive approach to his players, since he assigns tasks and roles, explains the game, shows, invites them to perform the exercise, makes suitable adjustments, anticipates and imagines the development of particular problem-situations and suggests the possible solutions in advance.

COORDINATION SKILLS

2

Since soccer is a sports discipline characterized by unexpected and sudden situations, it obviously requires youth players to develop good coordination skills in order to handle the many variable elements of play in a truly effective manner offering creative, original and personal solutions.

Definition: Coordination skills can be defined as the ability to plan, control and regulate one's movements properly in view of a certain objective or aim[1]; they depend on the functional nature of both sense organs and the central nervous system. Coordination skills, together with sensory perceptive and physical-athletic capacities, constitute the basis of learning and of motor and sports performances as well.

Coordination skills combined together and interacting in a complex and synergetic manner allow the subject to carry out effective movements, gestures and sports actions and constitute the foundations on which technical and tactical abilities peculiar to soccer are gradually built. Several studies have clearly pointed out that learning and enhancing coordination skills is highly effective and profitable in a particular developmental period in the life of every individual. In fact, the development of one's coordination capacities is supposed to be further enhanced and therefore become much easier in the so-called "phases of enhanced sensibility". Although it is advisable to regularly suggest exercises aimed at improving coordination skills also out of the most "fertile" periods, accurate researches have definitely shown that the best periods for an individual to enhance such important capacities are included between childhood and preadolescence.

Classification: Considering that every form of classification is only aimed at explaining and making a method or a process much clearer, I would like to underline that the whole coordination process is always taken into proper account in motor performances (in this context the process is divided into several fragments simply because we want to be clear in our explanation) and the attention is not focused on one of its parts exclusively. Various authors[2] who have carried out important studies on motor learning have classified coordination skills in different ways, but the common classification most generally accepted can be synthesized as follows:

General coordination skills	• motor learning capacities • direction and control capacities • adaptation capacities
Special coordination skills	• they are generally classified in different ways by different authors

1 The sentence in italic is drawn from Meinel (work previously quoted) and helps complete the definition.
2 Meinel (1977), Hirtz (1974), Schnabel (1974), Harre (1977), Blume (1981).

2.1 GENERAL COORDINATION SKILLS

Meinel states that general coordination capacities are the basic skills in any sports discipline, have a highly universal character and can concern the whole field of motor performances in sport.
They can be classified as follows:

Motor leaning capacity:
This is the capacity to learn new movements that are progressively internalized and reinforced through constant practice and repetition.

Direction and control capacity:
This refers to the capacity to control one's movements during the motor performance in relation to a previously set objective and plan of action.

Adaptation capacity:
This is the capacity to change a particular motor plan or pattern, suitably adjusting it in relation to a sudden and unexpected situation, without jeopardizing the final expected outcome.

Every athlete unconsciously applies to these general coordination capacities every time he has to learn a new movement or needs to modify a special motor pattern he had previously acquired to adjust it to new situations of play.

2.2 SPECIAL COORDINATION SKILLS

Special coordination skills are strictly connected to general coordination capacities and develop in an interdependent way. The correlations between the two groups of coordination capacities are perfectly illustrated in the following diagram:

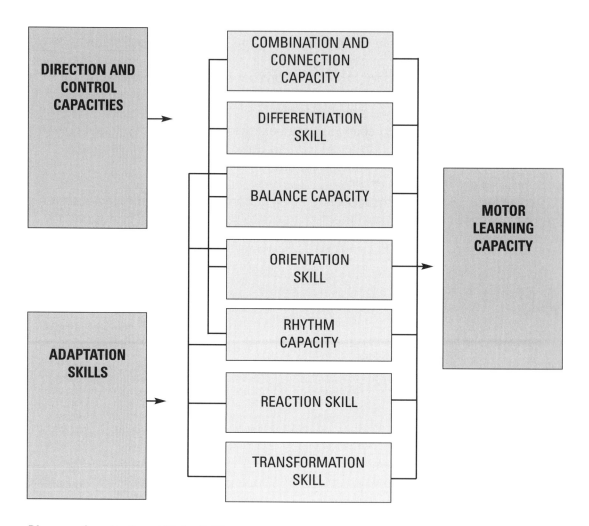

Diagram: Coordination skills by D. Blume.

In addition to the coordination skills classified by D. Blume as shown in the diagram above, this chapter will also focus on other important coordination capacities that further enhance and complete the wide range of abilities required in such a varied and unpredictable situation as playing soccer.

Specifically, coordination skills can be enumerated as follows:
2.2.1 Balance
2.2.2 Space and time perception
2.2.3 Combination and connection of movements
2.2.4 Differentiation

2.2.5 Space and time orientation
2.2.6 Anticipation
2.2.7 Reaction
2.2.8 Rhythm
2.2.9 Transformation
2.2.10 Motor imagination

2.2.1 BALANCE

Among all the various special coordination skills that a soccer player needs to plan, organize, regulate and control his movements, balance – which refers to maintaining the body "in a steady position" or restoring this original condition while making movements – plays a role of critical importance. The basic condition whereby the body manages to keep its balance can be visualized by a perpendicular line drawn from the center of gravity in the body (in the pelvis) directly into the base on which the body is resting. Soccer players play keeping unipodalic balance, that is on the foot on which one is standing with the weight of the body evenly distributed (this is often the sensory dominant foot), while the playing foot (which is often the motor favorite foot) is controlling, dribbling, passing, kicking...the ball (making those movements peculiar to soccer). During the course of a match, soccer players need to properly handle different aspects of balance (see **table 1**), from the static component while changing direction or turning about to the dynamic one when making any technical movement with the ball, from the flight aspect typical of scissor kicks and overhead kicks to diving headers, challenges in the air and sliding tackles.

BALANCE IN ALL ITS DIFFERENT COMPONENTS			
STATIC	**DYNAMIC**	**STATIC-DYNAMIC**	**IN THE AIR**
Maintain or restore the original condition of perfect balance in a position of relative peace or while making very slow movements.	Maintain or restore the original condition of perfect balance while making wide and/or rapid movements.	Balance while making movements where the subject also tries to properly and constantly control his posture.	Try to maintain a balanced control over one's postures while making movements in the air.
Kinesthetic and tactile-pressor analyzer as well as visual vestibular analyzer (but only in part)	Vestibular analyzer, helped by the kinesthetic, tactile-pressor and visual analyzers.	All the analyzers characterizing the previous aspects combine together.	Vestibular and optic analyzers.
Examples: • static positions, with the body standing on one foot both on the ground and on a high base • straight standing position or with the body resting on three supports	Examples: • walking, running and moving from one side to the other on a piece of gymnastic apparatus whose leaning surface is narrow or mobile • varied running	Examples: • moving forward and backward on the ground or on a high support while carrying objects and keeping them in steady balance (on the head, in the hands)	Examples: • jumping downward • jumping over hurdles after suitable run-up • springing on a small trampoline

Table 1 (by Cilia, Ceciliani, Dugnani and Monti, 1996)

Between the age of one to the age of three or four a child gradually shifts from the horizontal age, that is the period when his body typically lies in flat positions, to the vertical age when he can stand on his legs by progressively controlling different postures: prone, supine, upright trunk, sitting position, moving on four limbs, walking with a support until he can stand in a perfectly upright position and finally walking about. Improving the balance of one's standing posture depends on the ability of the body to suitably react to sensorial, visual, tactile-pressor and kinesthetic stimuli through enhanced and diversified motor experiences. Learning how to walk, run, jump, go up and down, turn about, roll on the ground, fall and kick is fundamental for a child to acquire and internalize those basic motor skills that are necessary in acquiring and enhancing coordination, of which balance is one of the key components. Only when walking and running have become perfectly automatic can the child try new movements and acrobatic acts that involve increasingly enhanced and refined balance.

Once again we have pointed out that basic motor patterns and coordination skills are not only interdependent in the period of development, but also constitute a very important prerequisite for the individual to learn specific technical movements peculiar to each sports discipline. The cerebellum is the nerve center that controls balance; its action is carried out automatically and is not subject to the control of one's conscience and will. At any moment it receives:

❏ information from the inner ear where the circular canals lie, which, through the movement of the fluid they contain, constantly record the position and orientation of the head in space (vestibular apparatus or analyzer)
❏ information from foot muscles that support the whole body about the pressure and load of the body weight on those supports (tactile-pressor analyzer)
❏ information from muscles, tendons and joints (kinesthetic analyzer)
❏ information from the eyes (visual analyzer).

The cerebellum processes all the information it gets and immediately activates a series of reactions better known as balance reflexes, causing those muscle groups that are necessary to keep the person in a standing position to contract. Its functioning is generally very accurate and allows constant adjustment of one's position to keep in perfect balance. Researches on the model theory of sensible phases (by Hirtz, 1979 and Martin, 1982) state that the period of maximum development – that is when balance capacities can be enhanced most – is between the age of 9 to 12, with significant peaks between the age of 10 to 11.

This means that the coaches who deal with 10 to 12 year olds should accurately plan their coaching programs so as to include activities that specifically stimulate and enhance such important capacities. The coaching progression suggested in the following pages seriously considers the possibility of carrying out polyvalent and multilateral motor experiences that can also have a non-specific character - which means that they are not necessarily connected to the typical aspects of soccer – in a natural or artificial environment (specifically in gymnasiums) using small or large pieces of apparatus and even including balance and sliding sports disciplines such as riding a bicycle, a scooter, roller skating, skateboarding and skiing, in order to gradually shift to increasingly specific motor experiences that aim at developing soccer skills and movements in a condition of perfect balance.

The coaching progression starts with basic activities (see **diagram 1**) to make the supporting parts of the body (contact between the foot and the ground) become more sensible and therefore help the player to consciously become aware of them; these parts constantly inform the cerebellum on how the weight of the body is distributed or concentrated. Then, swinging exercises (oscillation) follow where the weight of the body is slightly displaced to and fro. The players will certainly perceive automatic balance reflexes such as contracting muscles, the toes keeping a firm hold, and the calves and the knee joints stretching out, which are necessary for maintaining a perfectly upright standing position. Furthermore, if the players practice with their eyes closed, their capacity to perceive tactile and pressor information from the soles of their feet is further enhanced since they lack any visual reference and information.

The player also experiences the difference between maintaining balance with his legs fully stretched out and when they are in a more relaxed position (legs slightly bent). Players learn quickly that it is more economic and profitable to maintain any posture when one is relaxed rather than when one's legs are rigid and contracted. The player can gradually reduce and eliminate unnecessary muscle contraction through regular exercise and become increasingly aware of his body. This will certainly help him to better control his balance and the various parts of his body. Furthermore, he will internalize the stability factors of balance (that is the factors whereby he can easily keep his balance) which is obviously much easier to maintain or restore if the supporting base on which the body is resting is large, the center of gravity is low, the perpendicular line drawn from the center of gravity of the body falls into the supporting base and, finally, the area of the body that is in contact with the ground is wider. These concepts, for instance, should be assimilated by the defender who is marking his opponent when he needs to delay while standing in a position that allows him to keep his balance while in motion.

When the player consciously controls the positions of the body suggested in dia- **grams 2 to 5**, he inevitably experiences the importance of getting kinesthetic information when his eyes are closed. Using small or large pieces of gymnastic apparatus and equipment, wearing suitable shoes or moving barefoot on different surfaces means making the supporting part of the foot increasingly sensitive. For example, the coach can suggest different competitions involving given periods of time or penalties played in special training circuits or tracks, using several tools and various sports equipment suitable for enhancing balance. All the exercises focusing on ball possession will serve as special and practical application of balance skills – emphasized in a non-specific manner in the previous exercises – and as a sort of examination to the players' capacities. As far as the activities focused on dynamic balance are concerned, once again I would like to underline that they should be suggested in a light and ludic form, while also considering that starting to walk, run and jump standing in perfect balance on a high support often causes serious problems at a psychological level: actually, children are somehow inhibited from moving naturally since they fear they can fall and get hurt, and their fear and inhibition will further increase when they have to practice balance in air.

For this reason, it is advisable - at a preventive level, at least – to suggest these activities when the players still feel fresh both at a physical and psychological level, after intense warm up, using suitable equipment, involving the support and help of both the coach and teammates, avoiding any form of distraction and carefully watching for lapses of concentration since coaching and learning soccer acrobatic movements in particular may cause inexperienced and careless players to get hurt.

When coaching and practicing exercises using the elastic spring board, it would be advisable – for those who cannot have a special trainer in their coaching staff – to ask for the assistance of a competent and specialized trainer who can accurately educate players in how to take off, control the movements of their body while in the air, land and monitor isolated positions in order to avoid injuries and pain in their backs. When athletes do exercises where they need to move their bodies in the air, make rotations and twisting movements or roll forward, backward and so forth (pre-acrobatic practice), they considerably stimulate the vestibular analyzer to work and adjust to the situation perceiving labyrinthine information which he needs to control his body in a position of balance in the air and orientate in space and time after making an acrobatic technical movement.

EXERCISES

Static balance
Master one's supporting bases (diagrams 1 – 2 – 3):

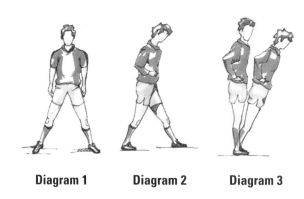

Diagram 1   **Diagram 2**   **Diagram 3**

❏ divide the weight of the body equally on both feet
❏ oscillate the body forward and backward, transferring the weight of the body on the heels, on the front part of the feet and finally on tiptoe
❏ tilt the body slightly to one side and then to the other so as to transfer the weight respectively on the inner and outer part of the sole
❏ transfer the weight of the body from one foot to the other (unipodalic balance) on the sole, on the front part of the foot, on the heel

Control the positions of the body maintaining the following postures for several seconds as shown in the following diagrams 4 to 7.

Diagram 4   Diagram 5   Diagram 6   Diagram 7

Use small and large tools and pieces of equipment as supporting bases on which the player moves trying to keep his balance diagrams 8 to 14.

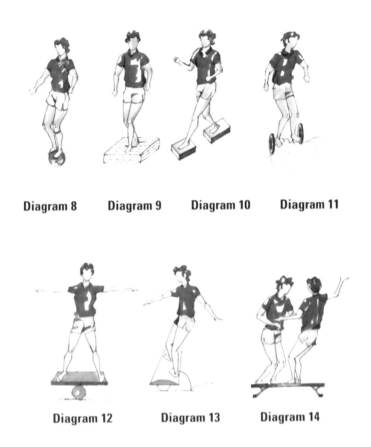

Diagram 8   Diagram 9   Diagram 10   Diagram 11

Diagram 12   Diagram 13   Diagram 14

Mastering the ball in a condition of static balance

❏ the player keeps one foot on the ball and tries to move it as far as possible from the supporting foot in the various directions (forward and backward, to the right and to the left)

❏ the player makes the ball roll so as to turn both clockwise and counterclockwise around his supporting foot one or more times

One-two-three... stop: the players in possession of the ball line up near each other along a straight line and, when the coach gives the starting signal, they sprint dribble up to the opposite target line. The coach is standing with his back to the players while they are dribbling and counts aloud: "one, two, three...stop". Afterwards, he turns about to look at them: they must stand motionless keeping one foot on the ball. Those who cannot stand motionless in a position of perfect balance must take three steps backward. The player who manages to cross the target line first wins the competition.

Kick the ball in a condition of static balance

Goal-kick by the goalkeeper: using the posture shown in **diagram 5** the player-goalkeeper – who is standing with the ball in his hands – kicks the ball towards a fixed target (for example: the goal is divided in different sectors for score competition) or a mobile target (a teammate who is moving) maintaining a position of balance both before and after kicking the ball, without the kicking foot touching the ground.

Kick the ball from a stationary position: using the posture shown in **diagram 7** the players compete with each other in a target-shooting competition, kicking the stationary ball from a stationary position after swinging the kicking leg forward and backward once or twice.

Receive the ball in a condition of static balance: using the posture shown in **diagram 6** the player practices controlling the ball with the instep – the balls come from different directions with varying trajectories – maintaining a position of perfect balance both before and after controlling the ball.

Dynamic balance

❏ Walk, march, run, run and stop and restart forward and backward following a straight or a curved line, moving along the boundaries of the playing field or in a special circuit made with several obstacles. Possible variations: walk, run, march... moving on the heels, on the front part of the feet, with the toes converging on or diverging from each other, crossing the legs while moving ahead and coordinating different positions of the arms

❏ Jump freely with both feet together, on one foot, forward and backward, to the right or to the left, clockwise and counterclockwise

❏ Skip using a skipping rope while also moving in different directions

❏ Control the starting and finishing positions of forward and backward rolls

Game: jump over the streams. Mark out a rectangular playing area and divide it in three parts (the streams) by means of free areas (banks). Every player starts from one end of the field and tries to get from one bank to the other by throwing or placing 3 or 4 hoops at a time in the various zones and jumping into them (as if they were stones lying in the stream). The second player tries to cross the stream on his turn and the game progressively develops in zones 2 and 3. The player who first manages to reach the bank of zone 3 wins the competition.

Game: jump on shore or into the pond. Consider a straight line as a point of reference: if a player moves to the right, he falls into "the pond"; if he goes to the left, he is "on shore". The players move from the left to the right, unless the coach tries to mislead them by saying "on shore" or "into the ponds"; in this case, the players who obey the coach's order are promptly eliminated from the competition.

Variation: the players can jump from one side to the other of the reference line holding a ball between their feet.

Dribble the ball in a condition of dynamic balance

Competition in pairs, relay competition, within a given time, with penalties
- ❏ dribbling the ball along the boundaries of the playing field
- ❏ making a slalom through 4 or 5 cones placed one yard apart, jumping on the supporting foot without letting the playing foot touch the ground
- ❏ every player has three supporting blocks. The players walk on these supporting bases, moving them alternatively forward and one after the other, trying to move through a given playing area. Those who put one foot on the ground must restart the game from the beginning. The player who first manages to cross the playing area without touching the ground with his feet wins the competition.
  Variation: the game develops in the same way, but the players have to dribble the ball to the target line.

Play hunter and prey on high supports

The hunter runs after the prey to catch them; the prey can save themselves by jumping and maintaining a position of perfect balance on bases, bricks, benches or other objects and supports previously placed in the playing area. The player who is touched before jumping on the supports immediately becomes the hunter.
Variation: the same as above, but this time the players also dribble the ball while moving in the playing area. The prey who is fleeing the hunter runs from one object to the other while dribbling the ball; before jumping on the support he must touch it with the ball.

Technical skills in a condition of dynamic balance

- ❏ Two players are standing on a balance board throwing the ball to each other; at the beginning, they can pass the ball freely, then they play the ball so as to take throw-ins and head it
- ❏ After making some passes while walking on the balance board, the two players get close to each other, cross each other trying to keep their balance and take their positions at the opposite ends of the board respectively
- ❏ A player is walking on the ground while also throwing the ball to his teammate who is moving on the balance board; the player walking on the board receives the ball with his hands, or heads the ball, or kicks or hits the ball with his thigh or chest.

Static and dynamic balance

Walk, run, skip and restart while holding balls of various weight, size and shape in a position of perfect balance on different parts of the body.

Handle the ball in a condition of static and dynamic balance

Competition in pairs, relay and penalty competition
- ❏ running 10 to 15 yards keeping the ball in balance on one's head
- ❏ walking 10 to 15 yards keeping the ball in balance on the nape
- ❏ skipping 5 to 10 yards with the ball in balance on the instep

❏ skipping 5 to 10 yards keeping the ball in balance between the thigh and the abdomen.

❏ skipping 5 to 10 yards in pairs keeping the ball in perfect balance between various parts of the body (for example: between the inner or outer parts of the feet).

Balance in the air
The high jump:
❏ jump over a hurdle with both feet or with one foot

❏ jump over a hurdle with the body taking different postures while in the air (for example: touching the knees or the tip of the toes)

❏ jump making a quarter of a rotation, half of a rotation or a complete twisting movement

❏ jump high (Fosbury flop - front jump)

The long jump:
❏ make a long jump with both feet and with one foot using a spring board

Jump and bounce on the elastic spring board:
❏ vertical bounces on the spot with both feet close together, with the legs wide apart, joining and opening the legs wide while in the air, coordinating different positions of the arms

❏ bounce making a quarter of a rotation, half a rotation or a complete twisting movement while in the air

❏ bounce on the carpet moving forward and backward, to the right and to the left

Jump down:
❏ jump down from a high support (a bench, a footstool, a balance board) monitoring the movements of the body while in the air and the position of the body when it lands on the ground (absorb the shock); for example: jump and stop into a hoop with the legs wide apart in a vertical or horizontal direction

❏ making a quarter of a rotation, half a rotation, a complete twisting movement or twisting as many times as possible while in the air.

Variation: increase the height of the supports from which the player jumps, modify the path of the flight, change the starting and the landing positions.

Head the ball in a condition of balance while in the air
Coaching progression to enhance heading skills, maintaining balance while in the air after take-off.

The players play in pairs: one player throws the ball while the other heads it; he can take off with both feet together, with one foot, from a stationary position, after skipping several times on the spot, after suitable run up, letting the body fall ahead, while diving, jumping over a hurdle, making a quarter of a rotation, half a rotation or a complete twisting movement while in the air.

Most of these exercises can be performed on the ground or using a spring board where the player takes off with one foot or both feet together so as to increase the period of time spent flying in the air, enhancing his capacity to control and master his body and the technical movement as well.

2.2.2 PERCEPTION OF SPACE AND TIME RELATION

Analysis of the paths

If a coach wants to plan the training session in a way so that training is truly effective, choosing the activities he intends to suggest to achieve set goals in an accurate manner is absolutely fundamental. The coach who knows a wide range of activities and exercises (quantity of the contents) can obviously benefit since he can work out a number of useful and diversified coaching and didactic progressions in relation to individual needs (quality of the contents). In this sense, using various training and conditioning methods typical of other sports disciplines – peculiar to volleyball, in this case – could be highly exciting, stimulating, motivating and profitable for coaches to teach and for players to learn soccer technique and skills.

The fact that soccer frequently involves sudden events and unexpected situations is also strictly connected to the use of a spherical object – the ball – that rolls, bounces and flies in various directions, at different speeds and following various paths, so as to influence the development of play and make it rather uncertain and unpredictable. Learning and carrying out most technical movements peculiar to soccer depends on the player's ability to read and assess the paths that the ball is following while moving.

In the dynamic development of any soccer match the players constantly need to perceive, read and assess the paths of the ball:
• to meet a cross, control and shoot at goal
• to volley
• to head the ball
• to intercept a pass made by the opponent
• to save a shot.
In short, every player should be able to anticipate , while playing, the point in space where he is going to contact the ball.

Reading the paths of the ball

Studying, coaching and training the paths of the ball in volleyball have now attained a higher and more advanced level than in soccer. Our coaching and didactic suggestions in the following pages aim at giving directions and showing particular exercises that are peculiar to volleyball in order to enhance the perception, the reading and the assessment of the paths of the ball. In fact, these elements are of critical importance for athletes to receive the ball successfully. In fact, controlling the ball is the technical movement and skill on which the following didactic sequence is focused; the whole coaching progression deals with the three movements characteristic of the ball: rolling, flying and bouncing (each one is then divided in three specific coaching units and training activities).

The first coaching unit includes conditioning exercises without the ball which involve the player imitating the movements of the ball so as to learn, acquire and enhance some basic motor patterns while also improving some physical and athletic capacities. The second coaching progression involves the player repeating the same exercises with the ball in order to enhance and internalize rolling, jumping, flying and bouncing movements and make them become completely automatic. The exercises suggested in the third coaching unit (focusing on playing with the ball) are specifically designed to develop those coordination skills that are necessary to handle the ball. The experiences and activities concerning these three didactic progressions can all be applied in the coaching section dealing with soccer technique (exercises to enhance controlling and passing skills).

The ball... rolls

These activities not only help reinforce and enhance such basic motor patterns as rolling sideways, forward and backward, sliding and crawling, but also improve the knowledge and the capacity to master the body through constant contact between the body itself, the ball, the ground and the wall. The exercise shown in **diagram 33** is a clear example of this: player **A** has to make a zone pass into the path of the run of his teammate B; for this to be possible he needs to quickly process several pieces of information on space and time. In particular, he needs to:
1. assess the running direction and the distance of his teammate **B** (space)
2. assess the speed at which **B** is running (space and time)
3. decide the exact point in space where he is going to play the ball (space and time)
4. choose the path of the ball and, in relation to this, he needs to balance the power (sensorial differentiation) with which he needs to kick the ball to make it roll at the correct speed (space and time)

The ball... flies

The coaching progression suggested helps enhance such abilities as jumping with suitable flight period, landing on the ground and recovering a position of perfect balance, and improving speed force. All the exercises with the ball help the players become aware of the various characteristic points of the path of a ball in flight; in particular:
• the starting point
• the point of stall, where the path of the ball reaches its peak and promptly shifts from the rising to the descending phase
• the point where the ball arrives or lands
Moreover, they also allow the players to distinguish and identify the three different types of path:
• with a large vertical component (skied ball)
• with a large horizontal component (flat path)
• with the two components that are equal (lobbed path - parabola).

In particular, in addition to common space-and-time evaluation capacities, players also need to constantly train their motor anticipation abilities, referring to those capacities that allow them to anticipate and read the path of the ball in advance or, better, fix the right coordinates in space for the impact with the ball (so as to take the suitable body position).

The ball... bounces

The coaching progression is further enriched with other exercises to enhance such basic motor skills as running, jumping, keeping one's balance and speed force at a physical and athletic level; meanwhile, they also help improve coordination: in particular, they enhance the natural sense of rhythm and the capacity to move and act rhythmically, another important prerequisite for the player to accurately half volley the ball.

CLASSIFYING THE PATHS OF THE BALL

GROUND PATH
The ball rolls on the ground...

FLAT PATH IN THE AIR at different heights:
The ball flies in the air...
• Head
• Chest
• Pelvis
• Knee
• Ankle

LOBBED PATH IN THE AIR
The ball flies in the air...
• High and long
• High and short
• Low and long
• Low and short

BOUNCING PATH
The ball bounces on the ground...

This table shows a clear classification of the various paths of the ball, while the **diagrams 1 and 2** on page 76 show the 8 different directions that players need to consider when they receive, play or hit the ball in relation to the posture and orientation of their body. **Diagrams 15 – 16 – 17 – 18 and 19** schematically illustrate the vertical and horizontal components of some paths. **Diagrams 20** and **21** correspond with the written descriptions in the box on page 82.

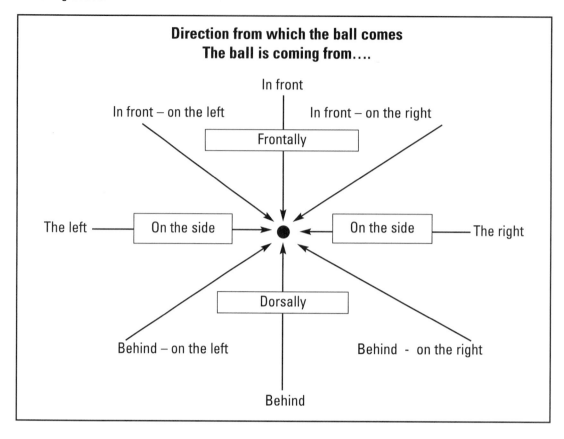

Direction from which the ball comes
The ball is coming from....

In front

In front – on the left   In front – on the right

Frontally

The left — On the side   On the side — The right

Dorsally

Behind – on the left   Behind - on the right

Behind

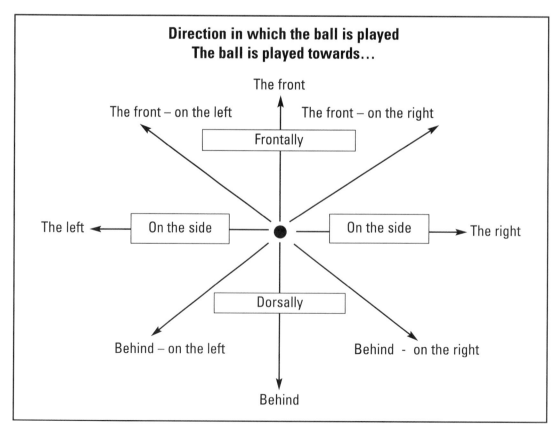

Direction in which the ball is played
The ball is played towards...

The front

The front – on the left   The front – on the right

Frontally

The left ← On the side   On the side → The right

Dorsally

Behind – on the left   Behind - on the right

Behind

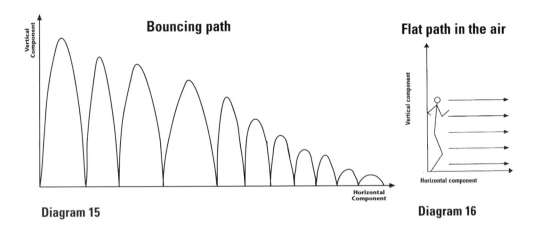

Bouncing path

Flat path in the air

Diagram 15

Diagram 16

Various Trajectories

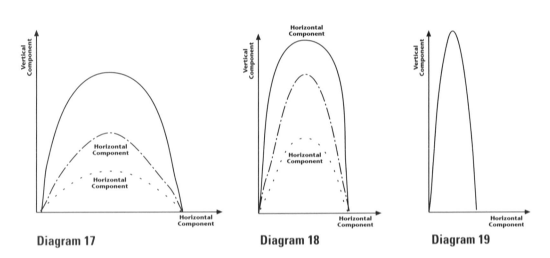

Diagram 17

Diagram 18

Diagram 19

Cross to head at goal

Action of play involving three players

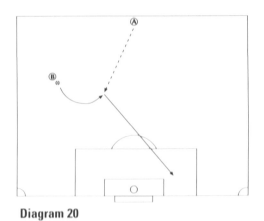

Diagram 20

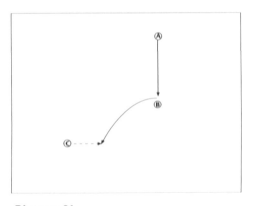

Diagram 21

COACHING PROGRESSION

The ball... rolls
Can you roll like a ball? On a soft surface (a mattress or a grassy ground, for example) every player rolls forward **(diagram 22)**, backward **(diagram 23)** and sideways – on the right and on the left – **(diagram 24)** several times while the coach is carefully observing and is ready to help if necessary.

| Diagram 22 | Diagram 23 | Diagram 24 |

Can you roll with the ball? In this case, the athlete rolls forward and backward while firmly holding a ball between his ankles, his knees, his thighs and the abdomen; then he rolls to the right and to the left holding two balls at the same time (one in his hands and the other between his ankles).
Can you roll the ball on your body? Make the ball roll from your feet up to your chest and viceversa **(diagram 25)**, from your back down to your feet **(diagram 26)**, from one hand to the other with the ball moving on your chest **(diagram 27)**, from one hand to the other with the ball moving on your back **(diagram 28)**.

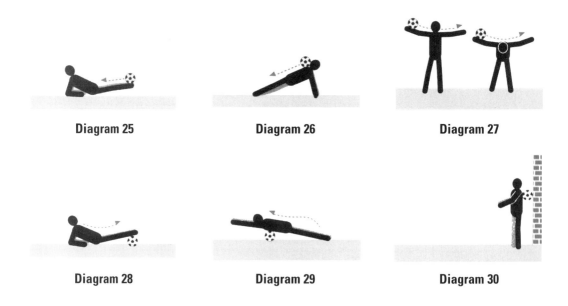

| Diagram 25 | Diagram 26 | Diagram 27 |

| Diagram 28 | Diagram 29 | Diagram 30 |

Can you roll and slide on the ball? Slide on the ball after pushing with your hands frontally **(diagram 29)** and on your back **(diagram 30)**. Make twisting, rolling and shifting movements while always maintaining the contact between your body, the ball and the wall **(diagram 31)**.

Play with a rolling ball

1. Player A makes a ground pass to his teammate; the ball is first played with the hands and then kicked with the foot into a 5-by-5-yard square area where his teammate B is standing. This player receives and controls the ball within the playing area he is assigned (control the ball on the spot).

Variation: player A changes the distance, the direction from which the ball is played and the speed of the pass so that his teammate B gets used to considering these important variable components while receiving the ball. Player B controls the ball and follows so as to play the ball out of the square, touching it only once **(diagram 32)**.

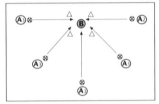

Diagram 32

2. Player A plays the ball on the ground (pass made to the teammate).

The ball is first played with the hands and then with the foot into the 5-by-5-yard playing area from a distance of 15 to 30 yards from the square. Player B starts when his teammate is delivering the pass: he needs to accurately assess the speed of the ball so as to run into the square (in sequence) before, after and at the same time that the ball arrives into that area **(diagram 33)**.

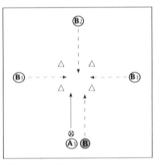

Diagram 33

Purpose: player B needs to monitor his running speed and adjust it to the speed of the ball.

Variations:
• Player A passes the ball at different speeds and from different distances;
• Player B runs to meet the ball in various ways (he can run backward or run lifting his heels towards his buttocks so that his knees are perpendicular to the ground);
• Player B comes from different directions (B1 – B2 – B3);
• Player B starts from different positions (on his knees, from a sitting position, lying prone on the ground and so on...);
• Player B meets and stops the ball inside the square (controls the ball on the spot) with various parts of his body (the sole of the foot, the heel, the inner part of the foot, the knee, the buttocks, the head, the back, the hands and so on...) facing or turning his back to his teammate A;
• Player B controls the ball and follows so as to play the ball out of the playing square touching it only once;
• Player B runs towards the square at different speeds and player A needs to adjust the speed of the pass to his teammate's running pace.

Final goal: monitor the movements of your teammate very carefully and adjust the speed of the pass to his running speed.

The ball...flies

Can you "fly" like a ball? Such global experiences as high jump, long jump and low jump should be given particular attention when the coach wants to plan a series of activities aimed at educating and training jumping skills. These activities should be practiced in gymnasiums, maybe using special pieces of apparatus – both small and large – like the springboard and the springy carpet which help prolong the flight period while also using thin or thick mattresses and suitable sandy or foam-rubber landing areas in order to prevent possible injuries.

Can you "fly" with a ball? Repeat some of the exercises mentioned above but with the ball. For instance: jump on the elastic carpet holding a ball in your hands or catching a ball thrown by one of your teammates while flying in the air after take-off.

Can you identify the characteristic points of a path?

Individual activities: throw the ball high in the air and:
- clap your hands or stamp your foot when the ball reaches its peak (the point of stall)
- catch the ball at the highest point possible
- catch the ball at the lowest point possible
- clap your hands or stamp your foot as soon as the ball lands on the ground (point of arrival)
- throw the ball so that it falls on your hand, on your foot, on your buttocks, on your back and on your chest (the player positions so as to wait for the ball to bounce on his body; this is possible only if he dives to the ground after anticipating the point where the ball is going to land).

Exercises in pairs:
1. Player A throws the ball in the air while his teammate B claps his hands or stamps his foot when the ball reaches its peak (point of stall) or its landing point.
2. Player A throws the ball towards his teammate B so as to force him to move away. Player B moves during the rising phase of the path of the ball; this means that he first moves away from his starting position, then claps his hands so as to identify the peak of the ball and finally catches the ball. From the moment when he claps his hands he can no longer move from his position.
3. Player A throws the ball to his teammate B who has to (**diagram 34**):
   - jump over it freely
   - jump over it with his legs wide apart
   - get into position with his legs wide apart so that the ball bounces between his legs.
   - anticipate the exact point where the ball is going to land and catch it with his hands at the level of his chest (**diagram 35**).

Diagram 34   Diagram 35   Diagram 36

Final goals: take a suitable position so as to face the ball
Soccer technique with the ball flying in the air: the coach suggests the exercises shown in **diagrams 32 and 33** so that player A can train and enhance his technique in passing the ball: in particular, he concentrates on making lobbed passes either to space or directly to his teammate; consequently, player B can practice his technique in receiving the ball on the spot or control the ball and follow the pass.

Diagram 37   Diagram 38   Diagram 39

The ball... bounces
Can you "bounce" like a ball? This coaching unit includes exercises to educate and train jumping skills, like jumping and skipping with both feet together, with one foot forward and backward, to the right and to the left, high and low, long and short, making a quarter of a rotation, half a rotation and a complete twisting movement while jumping, using soft surfaces and small pieces of apparatus (like hurdles, skipping ropes and footstools).

Can you bounce with a ball? Arrange several competitions in pairs or different heats where the athletes have to cover distances of about 10 yards while jumping:
❑ with both feet together holding a ball between the ankles or thighs
   (diagram 36).
❑ with one foot holding a ball between the back of the thigh and the calf
   (diagram 37).
❑ with one foot holding a ball between the other foot and the shin (**diagram 38**).
❑ with one foot holding a ball between the thigh and the abdomen (**diagram 39**).
Play with a bouncing ball
❑ Throw the ball in the air and let it bounce on the ground:
❑ clap your hands every time the ball reaches its peak (point of stall).
❑ stamp your foot every time the ball touches the ground.

- alternate rhythmically the clapping of your hands when the path of the ball reaches its peak and the stamping of your foot when it lands on the ground
- reproduce the same movements of the ball by bouncing on the ground stamping your feet or skipping with both feet together or on tiptoe
- let the ball bounce on the ground and then throw yourself on the ground, anticipating the exact point where the ball is going to bounce the second time so as to make it bounce on your buttocks, on your back or on your side.

❏ Throw the ball in the air and promptly move below the ball without touching it every time it bounces on the ground. Count how many times you have managed to pass without touching the ball.

❏ Throw the ball high in the air and alternate your passing below it and over it keeping your legs wide open every time it bounces.

❏ Throw the ball high in the air and roll forward, or jump over a hurdle or turn round a cone or dive to the ground and catch the ball again after it bounces the first time.

❏ Throw the ball in the air and stop it between the inner parts of your feet, your ankles or your thighs on the first bounce.

❏ Juggle the ball letting it land on the ground, which means alternating one touch of the ball with one bounce of the ball on the ground.

Soccer technique with the ball bouncing on the ground. Once again the coach suggests the exercises shown in **diagrams 32 and 33** so as to help player A practice his technique in making bouncing and dropkicked passes (for example: he can start the exercise juggling or holding a ball in his hands), and help player B practice receiving dropkicked balls (control the ball and follow).

Cross to head at goal (diagram 20). Player A – who is running towards the goal to meet the pass by his teammate – heads the ball coming from the right with a lobbed path (long and low) so as to aim it forward towards the left and make it follow a flat path (at the level of his head).

Action of play involving three players (diagram 21). Player A, coming from........ plays the ball with.............., aiming it towards.............. so as to make it follow a ....path
The player B, coming from........, hits with .... the ball coming from .... with a .... path, aiming it towards........... so as to make it follow a .... path
The player C, in .... receives with........... the ball coming from .... and following a .... path

---

2.2.3 COMBINATION AND CONNECTION OF MOVEMENTS

Definition: The capacity to combine and coordinate the movements of the various segments of the body, sequences or single phases of movements to finally carry out a well-aimed movement or gesture.

Description: During the course of a soccer match, the players often have to handle special situations of play where they need to connect and combine simple or complex motor patterns one after the other or simultaneously.

Combining motor patterns

When a player tries to elude the opponent's marking he sprints in different directions and at different speeds and, for his movements to be really effective and achieve the final goal, he needs to properly combine, control and harmonize all the movements of the various segments of his body. This means that, in training sessions, the players should be given the opportunity to practice different styles of running and combine the movements of the upper and lower limbs at different levels; running and skipping in various manners including run-up and take-off, take-off and sprint, run up – stop - take-off and restart, for example.

Combining motor patterns and technical skills

On the other hand, when a player runs to shoot at goal he needs to combine a cyclic movement such as running with an acyclic one, that is shooting at goal, one after the other in a short period of time. Another typical movement of soccer, such as taking off to head the ball, involves the player simultaneously combining the typical motor pattern of jumping with the technical ability to head the ball. Consequently, it is advisable for a player to practice such movements as running after the ball and stoping it; running and throwing in; diving and heading the ball; sliding and tackling; running and crossing; feinting and dribbling past the opponent.

Combining technical skills

It is evident that a player in possession of the ball can only solve the motor problems that he typically deals with during the course of a match if he is able to properly combine different technical movements such as: dribbling the ball and crossing; dribbling past an opponent and shooting at goal; controlling the ball and passing; controlling the ball, dribbling past an opponent and passing.

At a didactic level it is advisable and helpful to introduce special training circuits and activities focusing on these aspects in the traditional training session.

2.2.4 DIFFERENTIATION

Definition: the capacity to express great accuracy and economy in making movements, between the single phases of a movement or between movements of the various parts of the body (in relation to the perception of muscle strength involved, space and time).

Description: Sensorial differentiation capacity is also defined as "sense of motion", since it allows us to receive and perceive, in a particularly detailed and accurate manner, visual, tactile, acoustic and above all kinesthetic information that is necessary to properly perform any motor act.

It is fundamental for athletes to become aware of their proprioceptive sensations and their differences (information coming from muscles, tendons and joints) in order to enhance the awareness of their body as a whole and "muscular sensibility", which plays a key role in helping the athlete master his body while practicing sport. In soccer, this capacity is therefore expressed in the "sense of one's body and motion" and in the "sense of the ball" as well, that is both while running smoothly and fluently or moving harmoniously, and while "mastering and handling the ball" – intended as the possibility to carry out effective, accurate and economical technical movements.

When a soccer player wants to make short, mid-range or long passes, he obviously needs to "weigh" his muscle power in relation to the distance of the teammate to whom the ball is delivered.

On the other hand, when the player has to meet and control passes made at different speeds, he needs to adjust his muscles' approach to the pass in order to deaden the impact with the ball and therefore help control the ball itself.

The ability to control and adjust the power of one's movements – that is the capacity to choose the suitable degree of muscle tension to carry out any technical movement, in relation to a specific goal – can be trained and enhanced by running, shooting, receiving and kicking balls of various weights, shapes and size; from different distances (long or short, near or far-off distances); at greater intensity (slow or fast); gradually increasing the level of accuracy of the movement.

This ability is strictly connected to space and time differentiation capacity, which refers to the individual's capacity to coordinate his motor performance in a very accurate and economical manner, in the close relation between the body, the ball, space and time in any situation of play where he is able to successfully master the technical movement in space, in relation to the time necessary to properly perform such a movement at a suitable rhythm. For example, when a player wants to make a pass to his running teammate, he first needs to carefully assess the distance and the speed of his running in order to exert the right power on the ball and therefore make the pass to his teammate at a suitable speed.

The activities aimed at enhancing this particular ability include games, exercises and special situations of play carried out on different playing areas (small and large), in different periods of time (before and after) and at varying speeds (slow and fast).

2.2.5 SPACE AND TIME ORIENTATION

Definition: The capacity to decide, adjust and modify the position and the movements of the body in space and time, in relation to definite points of reference.

Description: Every soccer player plays a match moving with or without the ball, in relation to given points of reference (like the boundaries of the field, the two goals, the corner-flags, the benches and so on) which clearly delimit the field of action (the playing field) or part of it (the penalty box, the center circle and so forth) and in relation to mobile points of orientation (the ball, his teammates, the opposition). The dynamic nature of every play situation inevitably forces the athlete to constantly re-decide, adjust and modify his position and perceive his movements in relation to all those variable elements in space and time that characterize the various contexts of play (path of the ball, the speed at which teammates and the opposition are moving, size of the playing area where the action is developing, rhythm of the performance).

Those who work in the field of soccer identify space and time orientation capacity with "the sense of position" that allows the player to "play a lot of balls" while building the offensive maneuver, which means that the athlete can touch the ball several times thanks to his ability to be in the right place at the right time.

This ability is one of the main criteria that help spot potential talented players. It allows attacking players to see free spaces where they can move unchallenged to receive the ball, understand when they can shoot at goal in relation to the position of the opposing goalkeeper, make timely movements and take the suitable position to shoot. Moreover, in the defensive phase, this important ability also allows players to move and act opportunely to cut off and "close free spaces", "intercept passes", challenge the player in possession of the ball and draw up or withdraw the defensive line. There are some players who "hide themselves" or fail to "come into play" and "get into the match" and, apart from general problems at a physical and athletic or psychological level, this is due to their inability to "find the suitable position" on the playing field, which simply means they are unable to orient in space and time.
In order to enhance this ability it is fundamental to practice:
- in playing areas and with goals of various size and shape (large and small, wide and narrow, high and low) and with mobile goals;
- adjusting, changing and making rules more complex: play with two balls, with more goals placed in different positions on the playing field, marking central and side lanes or special areas behind the goals;
- playing in situations of numerical advantage or disadvantage;
- playing with eyes closed or stimulating the use of peripheral vision
- playing at different rhythms and above all including changes of pace.

2.2.6 ANTICIPATION

Definition: A process that, on the basis of past experiences and on the prompt activation of the cognitive functions, allows players to anticipate and foresee the development of an action and plan how to act accordingly.

Description: In terms of probability, during the course of a match every player should be able to anticipate how a particular motor performance or action of play begins, gradually develops and ends. This is of critical importance since anticipating events and situations helps players to work out effective motor responses in advance.
For instance, this means that for a striker to successfully shoot at goal he should be able to anticipate the exact point where the ball is going to land, its bounce and rebound in order to forestall, beat the defender and take the suitable position to shoot. The midfield player should accurately perceive and follow the development of the offensive build up so that he can elude the marking and be spotted unguarded to receive the ball. The defender should understand the intentions of the opponent in possession of the ball in order to successfully intercept his pass, playing accordingly

in advance, or to drop back to cover and defend the area in front of his goal.

Anticipation capacity is based on acquired knowledge, past experiences and on perfect internalization of those experiences and can be further enhanced by refining personal perceptions and constantly processing them. Youth players should be educated in how to use their field of vision in order to understand and interpret different situations of play, selecting the information relevant to the case and excluding useless information; in particular, they should be trained to learn how to recognize "predicting signals", which means all those elements that allow for anticipation of the development of an action of play. The goalkeeper is standing in front of the striker who is about to take a penalty shot; he could anticipate the path of the ball by reading some important "predicting signals", like the path of the opponent's run-up, the direction in which the striker is looking, the position and orientation of his body, the posture of both his body as a whole and his lower limbs as well.

Perceiving those important signals is strictly connected to memory, since there is constant confrontation between the information that one is perceiving at that moment and the data that one has previously internalized in his mind. Thanks to the quality and the quantity of the experiences previously acquired and internalized in memory it will be possible to select and/or anticipate the best motor responses to carry out in relation to the specific objective. The quality of the motor reply is a clear indicator of the player's tactical ability.

2.2.7 REACTION

Definition: The individual's capacity to carry out quick motor actions in response to a particular stimulus.

Description: The varied and unpredictable nature of all the dynamic elements that characterize the various situations of play (space, time, the ball, the teammates, the opposition, the paths) require soccer players to solve the motor problems arising during the course of the match with "quick reflexes".

While playing a match the player should be ready to react to several stimuli including visual (the movements of the ball, of his teammates and of his opponents as well), acoustic (the referee blowing his whistle and any other form of verbal communication), kinesthetic and tactile (physical contact with his opponent, the ball or the ground) and vestibular stimuli (adjusting his balance). The motor responses that the player carries out must be prompt, quick, perfectly timed and suitable for the final objective: only in this way can his motor performance be successful and effective. The player's response to any known and expected signal – such as the referee blowing his whistle at restart plays, for example – is generally defined as simple reaction capacity, while the response to any unknown and unexpected signal – for instance, the ball suddenly deflecting from its path or an opponent who changes his running direction unexpectedly – is typically defined as complex reaction capacity.

Simple reaction strictly depends on age, the individual characteristics concerning the speed at which nerve impulses are transmitted and the composition of muscle fibers. It cannot be trained.

By contrast, complex reaction involves the player choosing among many different elements and information, often false and misleading or concealed, coming from the environment and situation of play. This type of reaction can be trained.

Such cognitive functions as perception, concentration and memory, together with the player's emotional condition in that particular situation, allow him to choose from a wide range of elements the most suitable and helpful information he needs both to anticipate and read what is going to happen and carry out prompt and effective motor responses.

In order to enhance this important coordination capacity it is advisable to suggest activities specifically designed to encourage the player to react to different stimuli in increasingly complex situations of play; these activities include:

❏ start running when the coach gives a known signal or immediately after an unexpected signal to make very short sprints or to shoot at goal from different positions;

❏ reduce the possibility of anticipating the signal and identify it in advance, for instance controlling a ball thrown by a teammate hidden behind a wall, or standing at the back of the player receiving the ball;

❏ increase the number of signals and the corresponding motor responses where, for example, if the coach whistles, claps his hands or sits down, the player must shoot at goal, stop and sprint dribbling the ball respectively;

❏ increase not only the speed of the performance but also the accuracy of motor reactions-performances;

❏ introduce special upsetting elements to prevent the player from clearly perceiving external signals: for example, close eyes, roll forward or backward, make a complete twisting movement and then shoot or control the ball.

2.2.8 RHYTHM

Definition: The capacity to perform motor actions rhythmically, which involves the ability to contract and relax all the various muscle groups, respecting particular sensorial stimuli.

Description: Play a match with regular rhythm flow, changing the rhythm of play or adjusting the rhythm of running periodically to simulate typical expressions that appear in soccer jargon. Every individual technical movement as well as every collective tactical action generally develop following a particular chronological sequence that determines the rhythm of the performance.

Experts commonly distinguish objective rhythm – which is set by the external environment through acoustic and visual signals – from subjective rhythm, based on the analysis and internalization of tactile and kinesthetic information.

The capacity to perceive and reproduce the rhythm of a movement allows players to carry out such a movement in a harmonious, economical and accurate manner. "Make the player feel", or better internalize, the rhythm at which a particular motor gesture should be performed – the rhythm of the performance may result from the sequence of steps in the player's run up to shoot the ball, or from the chronological sequence of touches between the foot and the ball when the player is juggling the ball, or from the succession of impacts between the foot, the ball and the ground while the athlete is dribbling the ball. This can help him learn basic technical movements.

Moreover, if the player is able to move rhythmically, this considerably helps him internalize all the various movements so that they soon become automatic. Besides, while playing sports games it is fundamental for every single athlete to carefully perceive and therefore adapt to the collective rhythm of the team, so as to integrate his individual rhythm.

It is important to underline that this capacity is largely conditioned by anthropological, environmental and cultural characteristics which are particularly evident in South American players who are known for the rhythm, the harmony and the esthetic sense of their movements.

2.2.9 TRANSFORMATION

Definition: The capacity to adjust, change or completely replace the motor action that was previously planned in the course of its development according to how the situation is changing in time.

Description: All the possible variations occurring in situations of play – either expected or absolutely unexpected – should not take the player by surprise. If the motor performance need not change radically - if the player only needs to modify or adjust some particular parameters of the movement such as time, space, speed, rhythm or range – we generally speak of adjusting capacity. This is the case of a player who is dribbling the ball and has to suddenly change the direction, the speed, the rhythm of his dribbling movement and consequently needs to adjust the range of his strides and the power he is applying in the impact with the ball when an opponent is running to challenge him.

By contrast, people generally speak of movement transformation capacity when the athlete absolutely needs to replace the motor action he is performing with another one. This is the case of an attacking player who is dribbling the ball to beat his opponent: the attacker typically makes feints and counterfeints so as to stimulate the opposing defender to act and react making suitable movements and countermovements.

In order to take each other by surprise, both the attacker and the defender try to conceal and disguise their own intentions, making faking movements so as to cause the opponent to react instinctively and effectively. Sometimes, the attacker "pretends" to take a powerful shot, thus causing the defender to take a defending position, "turning his back" to his opponent: meanwhile, the striker interrupts his shooting movement and changes it into a dribble, thus beating the defender. On the other hand, if the defender personally takes the initiative by challenging and pressing the attacker very closely, he could force him to give up dribbling the ball, causing him either to make a pass or to shield the ball.

Performing special technical movements and taking suitable decisions during the course of a soccer match should be adjusted and changed not only in relation to the opposition's behaviors and play – which are upsetting elements – but also according to those interfering elements resulting from the external environment such as the characteristics of the pitch and weather conditions.

The ability to transform movements depends on how accurately and promptly the player reads the changes in the situation of play, as well as on his past experiences.

The wider his background of acquired motor performances, the more he is likely to anticipate, adjust and change his movements with the opportunity to make the most suitable choices to fit any particular situation of play.

All the various multilateral activities a coach can suggest in training sessions should specifically aim at gradually building and enriching the player's motor background so that he can internalize a number of automatic movements.

The coach should accurately plan all the various activities and exercises so as to gradually introduce different variations – they can involve simple and predictable variations at the beginning, which become increasingly complex as time goes by, including significant factors of disturbance that cause the athlete to make suitable adjustments to those elements varying in space and time, or change the situations of play. I would suggest, for example, playing with an oval ball, either very light or heavy, on playing fields of different dimensions and shapes, under constant time pressure.

2.2.10 MOTOR IMAGINATION

Definition: The capacity to use one's own gestural, cognitive and expressive resources in an original and creative manner in order to solve motor, technical and tactical problems, and that allows the player to exploit his individual potential, spaces and objects out of any stereotype and rigid imitative scheme. It is possible to say that it is the result of all the various coordination skills combined together that the athlete can express thanks to his diverging intellectual activity.

Description: When a player is dealing with difficult motor situations, he is more likely to find the best solutions to those problems if he has ample motor imagination, since he is able to work out individual strategies resulting from his capacity to activate several cognitive functions including:

❏ **fluency:** ability to work out many different ideas in a very short period of time and put them into practice in different motor actions
❏ **flexibility:** ability to change the categories to which ideas or movements belong
❏ **associative originality:** capacity to work out original ideas and carry out unusual movements.

Among all the various roles and positions of the athletes in soccer, that of the tricky and skillful player – i.e. the highly creative player, who is able to make important and decisive moves that can break the monotony and predictability of codified playing – is undoubtedly one of the most discussed, loved and hated.

Motor imagination is not an inborn skill which is hard to enhance. It does not belong to skillful and talented players exclusively, but can be developed through varied experiences of different sports disciplines that offer several activities involving many different stimulus situations so as to stimulate and enhance all the other coordination skills.

Moreover, in order to develop this important capacity successfully and effectively the coach should use inductive coaching methods in training – like the method of research, for example – so that players can get accustomed to finding different personal solutions to the same problem.

By contrast, purely imitative training methods do not encourage or help the development of divergent or creative motor behaviors. The creative attacker can express his creative impulse by "inventing" new solutions to shoot and score under particular circumstances of play. For instance, he may shoot at goal after making acrobatic movements; using unusual parts of the body like his heel, chest or thigh to hit the ball; properly combining together a sequence of different motor patterns like running, jumping over the defender who is putting pressure on him with a sliding tackle and finally shooting with the toe.

2.3 GENERAL DIDACTIC AND METHODOLOGICAL CRITERIA TO DEVELOP COORDINATION SKILLS

In order to refine coordination and accelerate the learning process it is fundamental to use some particular didactic devices concerning the coaching method while suggesting training exercises; for example, they may include:

❑ encouraging the player to get accustomed to comparing – also verbally – the motor pattern that was previously planned with the final performance;
❑ suggesting multilateral motor activities involving a wide range of different motor experiences that help enrich the individual's motion skills;
❑ varying the way in which the athlete can receive external information (visual, auditory, acoustic, tactile, kinesthetic);
❑ respecting the level of difficulty of the motor activities suggested, that is starting from simple exercises and gradually shifting to increasingly complex experiences;
❑ asking the players to perform the exercises suggested symmetrically;
❑ adding new motor tasks;
❑ introducing variations in the performance of basic movements (unusual positions, changes in the rhythm and manner)
❑ changing environmental conditions;
❑ suggesting exercises to be performed in increasingly short periods of time;
❑ suggesting activities to be performed in a condition of physical fatigue;
❑ creating particular situations where the player needs to find personal solutions to solve problems.

Important studies carried out by professor Kurt Meinel confirm that motor coordination in sport is developed by the analysis and conscious learning of all the various sensations of motion, through the definition and verbal repetition (constantly stimulated by the teacher-coach) of those sensations.

BASIC TECHNIQUE 3

3.1 MASTERING/HANDLING THE BALL

Definition: The ability to handle the ball – with no opposition – within one's own area of action, which means a circle having a radius of about one yard and whose center is the non-kicking foot (i.e. the supporting limb).

Description: This is not a basic element of playing soccer, a real technical movement, but a prerequisite ability for the athlete to learn soccer technique and which immediately helps determine the player's skill in the relation between the body and the ball (it could be defined as a first important step to identify the player's real skills).
Handling the ball is the first important quality of any skillful player; this attribute is clearly expressed in the ability to master, control and "subject" the ball to one's will and not "be subjected to the ball" as inexperienced players often are. For this to be possible, the player must first be able to master his body and, in particular, all the various parts of it that may somehow come in contact with the ball; moreover, he also needs to have good balance capacities and developed muscular and kinesthetic sensibility.

Becoming familiar with the ball means discovering:
❏ its distinctive features: its weight, shape and dimensions.
❏ its qualities: hard or soft, smooth or rough, its elasticity and so on.
❏ its possibilities to move: (rolling, bouncing, flying) through special exercises and games involving contact between the ball and the body which the athlete should use as an instrument to "know and become familiar with the ball".

Rolling drills
The player begins to progressively grow familiar with the ball, putting pressure on it with the sole of the foot, making it roll forward and backward, to the right and to the left, clockwise and counterclockwise and finally standing in perfect balance on the ball for a few seconds.

Contact drills
The coaching progression continues with the player grazing and touching the ball very softly, enfolding it with all the other parts of the foot while skipping on the spot, always keeping it within his field of action.
What happens when the player touches the ball on its upper part, on its lower part or on its side?
The coach should always let the players discover what happens and understand the effects of their movements through personal experience.

Exercises to lift the ball
Combining the use of the various parts of the same foot or even of both feet together allows the player to lift the ball from the ground in many different manners in order to start juggling the ball. The most commonly used technique is to roll the ball

backward using the sole of the foot onto the instep of the same foot which will finally loft it in the air with a slight touch.

Prolonged contact drills
The player places and maintains the ball in perfect balance on any part of his body such as the forehead, the nape of the neck, the thigh, the shoulder, the instep and so forth while always moving freely in the space around him.

Juggling drills
From the main techniques used to lift the ball from the ground the coaching progression now shifts to enhancing juggling skills. Juggling technique helps the player develop considerable muscular sensibility which allows him to control the ball with a suitably relaxed contact area and to make economical movements and slight touches ("feel the contact with the ball").

In the following pages you will be offered a didactic coaching progression focusing on learning how to juggle the ball with the instep, using the methodological sequence suggested by Konzag (in 1991) for the development of technical skills. This is just one of all the various didactic methods one can follow to coach and enhance the main sports skills **(see table 1)**.

Order of the various stages in the development of the main sports skills
All the various methods and programs to coach and learn any sport specifically aim at enhancing the so-called **play capacity**, or the possibility to use and combine – in their mutual action and influence – motor skills, psychological attributes and the technical and tactical abilities one needs both in attacking and defensive situations in order to deal with and finally solve all the various motor problems and difficulties that may arise during the course of a match. In short, the essence of the so-called play capacity means the ability to properly combine all the factors bringing about the soccer performance and make them interact together perfectly. For a coach to suitably plan his coaching activity in youth soccer he should specifically "exploit" the most fertile periods for the development of these factors; in particular, as far as the players between the age of 8 to 12 are concerned, it is fundamental to plan the coaching activity so as to focus the attention on coordination technique. Soccer technical abilities are prerequisite elements in the player's sports performance capacity. In any sports discipline, athletes who are rather poor at the technical level are hardly likely to achieve great success; for this reason, it is necessary to enhance and optimize the means, the instruments and the methods one should use to coach soccer technical skills. Learning soccer technique concerns any age group as well as any level of performance. Improving and refining soccer technique is a never-ending process.

Skillful players also need to constantly train and enhance their technical skills; however, this aspect should obviously be given the greatest attention in youth soccer while coaching young players. The very first stage in coaching a particular technical movement is to provide the young player with a practical *performance of such a movement* in order to help him develop a precise mental image of it. The more information the player gets from the coach's performance, the more accurate the image he creates in his mind; in particular, his sight is affected by the coach's practical performance, his sense of hearing is stimulated by the coach's verbal explanation of the movement, while his kinesthetic sense is influenced by personal experience, which means by repeating the movement several times and "feeling" all the various parts. Inexperienced athletes want to see how the movement should be made and want to try to make it personally. While learning and training particular sports technical skills, athletes very often train the form exclusively, that is **the external image** of a movement. By this we mean the visible part of such a move, the positions and the movements of the limbs, the trunk, the head and their mutual relations characterized by such parameters as: extension, width, speed, frequency, rhythm. By contrast, the content, the essence, **the internal image** of the movement – which means the non visible parameters – are generally neglected; these non visible parameters of a movement include: the manifestation of one's will, muscle contraction and relaxation, muscle elasticity, one's muscular sense and kinesthetic sensibility. For an athlete to learn and enhance any particular technical skill in a successful and effective manner he needs to train both the external and internal components of that particular motor performance. This is specifically important in coaching children who typically imitate the technical movement shown by their coach and therefore acquire and master the external image of such a movement above all. The more skillful the child is, the more accurate his imitating the coach's performance will be; nevertheless, if the external and internal image are not properly combined at the right moment, the young athlete may fail to further improve his skills. The second stage in *coaching and developing* soccer technique is to select suitable preparatory training exercises - in order to make the learning process easier – and combine them with special activities carried out in favorable conditions. For example: using lighter balls, or allowing the players to use their hands to better handle and master the ball. The following step involves the coach teaching basic technical skills, with the players reproducing the basic structure of the technical move. Inexperienced athletes first try to reproduce the same pattern of the movement they are shown but often very approximately, neglecting many details, in order to acquire the basic standard technique – remaining in a stationary position first and then while moving – that is generally shown in drawings and pictures in special handbooks or described through verbal explanations or practical performances. While coaching his players the technical skills, should a coach accurately and literally follow the ideal technical models typically described in books or displayed by great champion athletes, or should he introduce individual changes to standard patterns?

If we agree with the definition of sports technique intended as the movement one needs to make to carry out a specific motor task – that goes beyond the psychological and physical characteristics of every single player - where we refer to a typical, ideal model to imitate and reproduce, which becomes the final purpose of training. By contrast, if we take into proper account the individual features of every single player – like his height, weight, motor skills and so forth – while suggesting this coaching model, in this case we should speak of individual technical abilities and personal style, referring to a personal and subjective interpretation of the ideal, standard pattern. From this point of view, all the possible changes introduced to modify the model technical move should not be considered a priory as mistakes to correct and adjust, specifically when they prove to be successful and effective and therefore allow the player to achieve the final goal. When the athlete has acquired the standard pattern

of any particular technical move, the movement needs to be *reinforced and enhanced*, always without opposition and suggesting possible variations to its basic structure; this means that the same technical move should be trained:
❏ at different speeds and rhythms
❏ along various distances
❏ in different directions and in a bilateral manner (using both feet)

Another significant stage in the development of technical skills is to properly combine the standard pattern of every single move with other elements to combine before or after it. The *process of reinforcement* of such a technical skill is further enriched by suggesting exercises and activities carried out in harder conditions, like:
❏ after or involving strenuous physical effort
❏ involving psychological pressure
❏ involving considerable coordination abilities
❏ involving pressure, effort and tasks that go far beyond what the athlete is
   generally subjected to during the course of a match.

Moreover, I would also like to underline the importance of the parallel and **BIUNIQUE/BIUNIVOCAL** development of coordination capacities and technical skills in a constant relation of interdependence. The period between ages 7 to 12 is generally considered as the best period for learning, the age characterized by considerable skill and motor intelligence, the most sensible phase for the development of basic coordination capacities and the first sensible phase for an individual to acquire sports motor abilities. Children of this age are still short, light and agile; height and body weight increase gradually and in a balanced manner; their limbs are not very long and this results in a positive and favorable relation between strength and levers; this means that all the premises exist for a child to quickly develop special technical skills in a condition of good coordination. Coordination is a genetic property of the nervous system and helps the learning of technical skills; however, highly coordinated athletes do not necessarily develop excellent technical skills, since learning sports technique properly is possible only through suitable coaching strategies. Coordination can be acquired and enhanced by learning new abilities and practicing new athletic and sports movements.

The higher the level of coordination of an athlete, the more he is likely to perform increasingly difficult motor tasks. In short, improving one's coordination capacities is strictly connected to improving one's technical skills peculiar to that sports discipline and viceversa. The coaching progression of the exercises suggested to *reinforce and enhance* technical skills in situations involving no opposition help the athlete learn basic technical moves, giving him the possibility to focus his attention on how the various movements develop exclusively. Moreover, it is also important to point out that technical movements should be trained both in standard conditions – repeating the same movements several times to better internalize them – and in conditions of constant change and variability (left and right, near and far, high and low, fast and slow, accurate and quick, and so on…) in order to make those moves become automatic so that they can be easily adjusted to the mutable conditions and to the unpredictable nature of any situation. Furthermore, it is also fundamental to consider that the time dedicated to practicing without opposition is being reduced considerably in favor of real actions and situations of play requiring the athletes to make decisions and focus their attention on the tactical aspect; in fact, the last stage in the process of ***enhancement and reinforcement of soccer technique*** involves training with active opposition. This phase specifically aims at enhancing the player's decision-making capacity, which means his capacity to make suitable technical and tactical choices in relation to the opposition's actions, in simpler conditions compared to those that he will have to deal with during the course of a match. The training methods a coach can use to coach basic technical skills include simple-game situations – from 1 v 1 to 3 v 3 – and activities approaching the competition, like conditioned games requiring the player to handle complex tasks, in contexts of play that constantly change: in this way, the athlete learns to distinguish the various situations of play and to use the technical moves he has acquired while training as a means to solve problems. Tactical actions and solutions involving a group of players or the whole team, for instance, can be learned through special conditioned games implying situations of numerical superiority and inferiority or competitions between groups consisting of the same number of players. The activities involving small numbers of players generally help enhance and refine technical skills, since the player needs to focus his attention on a smaller number of teammates and opponents, and can also move and play in a wider range of action. These forms of play generally have a high didactic value and considerable training effect: in fact, with the situations of play changing frequently, the player needs to adjust to constantly new conditions very quickly. The last stage in the process of learning technical skills – that is ***using*** such technical moves – aims at helping the player "**STABILIZE**", fix and refine complex play abilities, which is possible only in the real context of a competition and, therefore, through conditioning matches, matches played in favorable conditions, in adverse conditions and official competitions. While coaching and training coordination capacities, physical and psychological abilities and technical and tactical skills, great attention should also be focused on developing the so-called complex capacity of play through the competition. In fact, the above mentioned factors influencing the player's performance are simple prerequisites, while the real play capacity results from the combination of those factors and from the player's ability to properly use them in the match.

Learning basic soccer technique – Developing coordination	
Performance of the movement	
Preparatory conditioning exercises	Favorable conditions
Standard pattern	
From a stationary position	While moving

Learning basic soccer technique – Developing coordination	
Variation of the standard pattern	
In the speed while moving In the direction of the movement	In the distance In the ambivalence
Combining the standard performance with other elements: complex exercises Elements of connection prior to the standard pattern Elements of connection after the standard performance	
Enhancing and reinforcing the standard pattern in conditions More difficult after including heavy physical load Implying refined coordination Involving psychological effort Demanding more than one is usually required in competition	

Reinforcing basic technical skills with opposition (tactical aspect)
Simple and complex situations of play involving increasingly high pressure by the opposition Active opposition, but only in part Active opposition Several opponents
Real-game line-up in view of the competition

Using soccer technical abilities
In matches played in favorable conditions In conditioning matches In matches played in adverse conditions In sports competitions

Table 1 (by Konzag, 1991)

COACHING PROGRESSION (EXERCISES AND SITUATIONS)
TO COACH AND LEARN TECHNICAL SKILLS

Specific goal: Mastering the ball
Operative goal: Juggling the ball with the instep

Developing basic technical skills

Preparatory exercises
The balloon game
Every player has a balloon and tries to make it fly in the air without letting it fall to the ground using any part of the body.
Purpose: stimulate the knowledge and the perception of the body (all the various parts of the body that may come in contact with the balloon).

Posture games and imitation games
Lying face down: roll on the ball **(figure 1)**.
Lying on your back: bend and stretch your lower limbs, bend and stretch the soles of your feet **(figure 2)**.
On your knees: roll from the instep to the knee, with both legs together and on one leg exclusively **(figure 3)**.
From a sitting position: hold the ball with your feet, roll on your back and make movements forward and backward, to the right and to the left **(figure 4)**.
Standing upright: roll the ball against a wall, trying to keep the ball in close contact with both the instep and the wall **(figure 5)**.
Standing upright: keep the ball in perfect balance, holding it between the instep and the tibia; standing in a stationary position first, and then while moving **(figure 6)**.

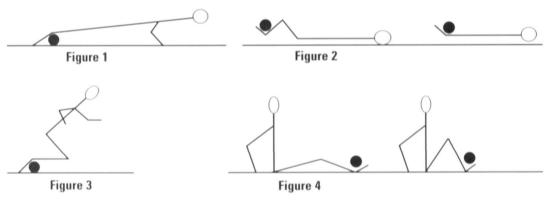

Figure 1   Figure 2

Figure 3   Figure 4

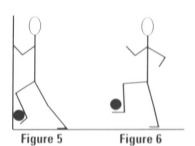

Figure 5   Figure 6

Purpose: Favor the knowledge and the mastering of your body, stimulate the perception of the contact between the instep and the ball; the instep, the ball and the ground; the instep, the ball and the wall.

Conditioned balloon game

Every player has a balloon and tries to make it fly in the air as long as possible without letting it fall to the ground using exclusively the insteps of both feet.

Purpose: Stimulate the knowledge and the mastering of the body (of the insteps, in particular).

Exercises performed in favorable conditions from a stationary position and while moving

Juggle balls of various sizes and weights, also using your hands
Hold the ball in your hands and juggle it

❑ hit the ball with the instep and then catch it again with your hands after it bounces on the ground once
❑ hit the ball with the instep and then catch it immediately with your hands with out letting it fall to the ground

Juggle the ball, letting it bounce on the ground

❑ juggle the ball alternating one juggle with the instep and one bounce of the ball on the ground in rapid sequence

Bounce the ball against the wall and catch it with your hands

❑ kick the ball against a wall and catch it with your hands after it bounces on the ground once or several times
❑ kick the ball against the wall and catch it with your hands immediately after it bounces on the ground once
❑ kick the ball against the wall and catch it with your hands before letting it fall to the ground

Standard performance from a stationary position

Unconditioned consecutive juggling
Conditioned consecutive juggling

❑ combine different parts of the body for the impact with the ball (only with the right foot, only with the left, alternating the right and the left foot)
❑ number of touches (for example: juggle the ball twice with the right foot and once with the left foot)
❑ in a free space
❑ in a circumscribed area (for instance: a 3 x 3 yards square area)

Standard performance while moving

Juggle the ball while moving

❑ walk or run: forward and backward, to the right and to the left, clockwise and counterclockwise

Juggle the ball while moving in a circuit track
❏ move along set paths previously marked out using small objects: flat cones, boundary lines, hoops, cones, posts and so forth

Juggle the ball while moving
❏ jump and skip: juggle the ball while skipping; juggle while jumping high, down, forward; juggle while jumping over small pieces of gym apparatus like hurdles, ropes, strips and so on

Reinforcing basic technical skills with no opposition

Variations to standard performance

Variations in the speed, the movement, and the distance. Adjust the height of the juggle to which the speed of the performance is directly connected
❏ juggle the ball over your head
❏ juggle the ball up to your head
❏ juggle the ball up to your pelvis
❏ juggle the ball up to your knees

Juggle the ball while making quick movements
❏ juggle at top speed (for instance: the player who first manages to juggle the ball twenty times is the winner of the game)

Enhancing coordination by juggling

Juggle the ball in a condition of static and dynamic balance
❏ Juggle the ball while standing in balance on one foot in a stationary position first, then while skipping on the supporting foot
❏ Juggle the ball keeping perfect balance on a step standing in a stationary position and then jumping down (down the step) and up (on the step)

Juggle the ball in a condition of differentiation
❏ juggle balls of different shapes, weights and dimensions. For example: use volley balls, tennis balls or rugby balls

Juggle the ball rhythmically
❏ juggle the ball following one's own rhythm
❏ juggle the ball following the rhythm set by somebody or something
❏ juggle the ball following a cyclic, an alternated, a varied and an acyclic rhythm

Juggle the ball in particular situations of space perception
❏ juggle the ball high and low, forward and backward, with the right and the left foot, clockwise and counterclockwise, near and far, long and short

Juggle the ball in particular situations of space and time perception
❏ juggle the ball high in the air and then pass below the flying ball once or several times

❏ juggle the ball and then pass over the ball bouncing on the ground
❏ juggle the ball and pass below the ball first and over it immediately afterwards

Juggle the ball adjusting and changing your movements
❏ juggle the ball while moving in traffic: 10 players are juggling the ball simultaneously in a small playing area (10 x 10 yards, for example), trying not to let the ball fall to the ground. The players of the two teams – each one juggling one ball – try to move from one side to the other of the marked area juggling the ball without running into each other and avoiding letting the ball bounce on the ground.

Combining the standard performance with other elements

Juggle the ball while also combining different movements

Elements of connection prior to the standard performance
❏ lift the ball + juggle
❏ control the ball + juggle
❏ play soccer tennis

Elements of connection following the standard performance
❏ juggle + stop + dribble the ball
❏ juggle + stop + screen the ball
❏ juggle + shoot at goal
❏ juggle + cross the ball
❏ juggle + leap over an obstacle
❏ juggle + pass the ball
❏ juggle + head the ball

Combining the standard performance with other elements in conditions

More difficult after or involving heavy physical load
❏ juggle the ball while moving uphill and downhill
❏ juggle the ball after strenuous physical exercise, for example: after sprinting over a distance of 50 yards, after making 1 v 1 exercises, or after jumping rope

Involving great coordination (juggle the ball and make pre-acrobatic movements)
❏ juggle + roll forward or backward + juggle
❏ juggle + roll to the right or to the left + juggle
❏ juggle + postures + juggle
❏ juggle + go up some steps + juggle
❏ juggle while sitting + get up + juggle while standing
❏ juggle the ball consecutively against a wall

Involving psychological load
❏ Exercise involving psychosensorial stress – concentrate on colors: three teams of three players each, each one wearing shirts of a different color, juggle the ball and pass it to each other: to the players of the same team (wearing shirts of the same color) or to the players of the other teams, following a fixed sequence of colors.

Involving emotional load
❏ Juggling competition in pairs along a circuit track like a parallel slalom
❏ Juggling competition against a wall replacing your teammate
❏ Juggling competition like a 4 x 100 speed relay race: in this case, the baton is the ball

Involving particular situations or conditions that go far beyond what the player is requested in competition
❏ Individual exercises with two balls: the player juggles one ball while, with the other ball, he is:
  • taking a throw-in or is throwing it
  • dribbling like a basketball
  • making it roll around his waist
  • juggling
N.B.: Abandon ball number 1, which is beginning to bounce on the ground, and start to juggle ball number 2, and promptly go back to ball number 1 before it ends its bounce on the ground.

Exercises in pairs with two balls (figure 7)
The players X and Y are standing one in front of the other 10 yards apart: each one has a ball and they are both juggling at the same time. When the coach gives the signal:
❏ they kick their balls in the air and change their positions
❏ they both kick their balls at the same time and pass them to each other, one high and one low

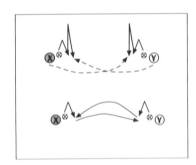

Figure 7

Reinforcing basic technical skills with opposition

Simple and complex situations of play involving marking by the opposition

Partly active opposition (figure 8)
The player juggling the ball tries to stand keeping his body between the ball and his opposing defender. The defender cannot touch the ball but, moving around his juggling opponent, forces him to constantly change his position to better shield the ball.

Figure 8

Active opposition
❏ Variation A: the defender attacks the ball actively, trying to take it away from the player in possession
❏ Variation B: the starting positions are the same, but in this case the exercise develops with a 1 v 1 situation for the final shot on goal

Several opponents (figure 9)
This exercise is carried out in a playing area whose dimensions depend on the skills of the players involved. 12 players: 9 of them are in possession of a ball each, while the 3 players without the ball can disturb – without touching the balls – their juggling opponents in order to cause them to make bad juggles or let the ball fall to the ground. In this case, they try to win possession of the ball and begin to juggle in their turn.

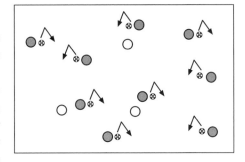

Figure 9

3.2 KICKING THE BALL

Definition: This is a basic technical skill in soccer that defines the part of the body that makes contact with the ball.

Description: Kicking the ball is the most common, frequent and important technical movement in soccer, since it is the real basic element of the sport.

In the attacking phase, players kick the ball to maintain possession by passing it to their teammates or to conclude the offensive build up by shooting at goal; in the defensive phase kicking the ball away (clearing shots) helps avoid possible dangerous situations or risks in one's penalty area, or disturbs and interrupts the opposition's offensive build up if the ball is intercepted. Four main phases can be identified in the act of kicking the ball.

1. **The player approaches the path of the ball** taking a suitable run-up, during which he follows and reads the path of the coming ball (its length, height, speed, spin) and and tries to anticipate the space and time coordinates for the impact with the ball; these points of reference in space and time correspond to the point in space where the path of the ball and the run of the player intersect. The last step of the player's run-up must be longer than the previous ones so as to help the kicking leg swing backward to shoot.

2. **The player prepares for the impact with the ball** which means he stores energy by taking the best position to come across the ball: this implies different muscle groups (the abdominal muscles, the quadriceps, the adductors of the thigh and the flexor muscles of the foot) to pre-stretch due to the swinging backward movement of the kicking leg. The whole body is actively involved in this process of preparation and in the mechanics of the kicking movement: the athlete arches his back slightly, while his arms try to counterbalance his posture, the upper limb corresponding to the non-kicking leg is thrown forward while the other arm is swinging backward and outwards. While the kicking leg is preparing to make contact with the ball, the non-kicking foot is also taking the best position to help the movement; in general, the non-kicking foot is turned in the direction one wants to aim the ball and is characterized by two different distances compared to the ball: the distance on the front plane (to the right or to the left) – that depends on the surface of the foot used to kick the ball - and the distance on the sagittal plane (in front of or behind) – that depends on the kind of path one wants to impart to the ball. For ground passes, the non-kicking foot should be alongside the ball, while it should be placed a little behind the ball for high or lobbed paths.

3. **The kicking foot makes contact with the ball.** The impact of the kicking foot with the ball immediately follows the movement of the kicking leg swinging forward as a consequence of the contraction of the muscle groups involved and previously stretched in the "preparation" phase. Stretching and immediately contracting those muscles conveys the power impulse to the ball through the foot, keeping the ankle joint in perfect tension. The ability of a soccer player can also be clearly understood by observing how he kicks the ball; his kicking skills depend on how

many and which parts of the foot he can use to kick the ball (the inside of the foot, the inner instep, the outer instep, the outside of the foot, the instep, the toe and the heel) and, in particular, on how he can use those parts, that is how his foot makes contact with the ball (power, speed, nimbleness of joints and coordination), including the rotation movement and the axis (rotating effect). The player should realize that the act of kicking the ball can cause the ball to rotate clockwise or counterclockwise around either its horizontal axis or the vertical one, thus imparting what in soccer jargon is typically referred to as "bend" to the ball. This directly depends on the part of the foot that makes contact with the ball and on the area of the ball absorbing the impact **(diagram A and table 2)**.

KICKING THE BALL				
PART OF THE FOOT	**FOOT**	**ROTATION AXIS**	**AREA OF IMPACT**	**DIRECTION OF ROTATION**
INSIDE OF THE FOOT ❑ The area of the foot between the inner malleolus, the calcaneum and the base of the big toe	RIGHT	HORIZONTAL	A	CLOCKWISE (seen from the right)
	LEFT	HORIZONTAL	A	CLOCKWISE (seen from the right)
INNER INSTEP ❑ The area of the foot between the inner malleolus and the base of the big toe	RIGHT	VERTICAL	E	COUNTERCLOCKWISE (seen from the top)
	LEFT	VERTICAL	D	CLOCKWISE (seen from the top)
INSTEP ❑ Area of the foot between the ankle joint and the metatarsal joint	RIGHT/LEFT	NONE	A	NONE
	RIGHT/LEFT	HORIZONTAL	C	COUNTERCLOCKWISE (seen from the right)
OUTER INSTEP ❑ The area of the foot between the outer malleoulus and the base of the fifth toe	RIGHT	VERTICAL	D	CLOCKWISE
	LEFT	VERTICAL	E	COUNTERCLOCKWISE
SOLE OF THE FOOT	RIGHT/LEFT	HORIZONTAL	B	CLOCKWISE (seen from the right)

Table 2 – by Bonfanti Mario, 1992: FIGC (Italian Soccer Association) course to coach youths

If a coach carefully reads the paths of the balls kicked by his players, he can see which part of the foot they have used to kick the ball and where the ball has been hit; moreover, he should also concentrate on their running to meet the ball and on their manner of positioning the non-kicking foot in order to give his players useful suggestions and help them suitably adjust their kicking moves.

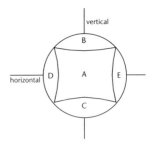

Figure A

4. **Compensation phase** occurring immediately after the kicking foot makes contact with the ball. In this phase the player should avoid interrupting the movement of his kicking leg abruptly, letting his leg complete its swinging movement forward so as to recover a position of balance and quickly place the foot on the ground to be ready for any tactical action occurring immediately afterwards – in this way, the player is ready to sprint to meet a cleared ball or to control a back pass.

For a player to kick the ball successfully and properly measure the power of his shot, not only does he need to develop some particular physical and athletic prerequisites - including **SPEED FORCE**, quickness of performance and nimbleness of joints – but also needs to enhance basic coordination skills to very high levels; in fact, coordination is crucial since it helps:

❏ assess the path of the coming ball (space and time perception)
❏ anticipate the path of the coming ball and, consequently, the final purpose of his technical movement (anticipation skill)
❏ take a suitable run-up (rhythm)
❏ get ready to make contact with the ball synergically combining the movements of all the various parts of the body involved in the action (connect and combine movements)
❏ position the non-kicking foot (orientation and balance)
❏ measure and control the force of the impact against the ball (differentiation)
❏ time the move and choose the right speed for the kicking leg to make contact with the ball (timing)
❏ handle unexpected situations that may occur while getting ready to kick the ball (adjust and change movements).

As to the various areas of the foot that a player can use to kick the ball:
1. **The inside of the foot** (push pass) allows the player to kick the ball with good accuracy but little power. In fact, the push pass is the most reliable technique for short and accurate passes because of the large surface of the foot presented to the ball. The player's run-up forms a straight line with the direction from where the ball is played; the non-kicking foot should be placed at a distance of 15 to 20 inches from the ball on the front plane (right and left); the kicking leg should rotate outwards (which is an unnatural position for the body) to make contact with the ball in area A so as to make it rotate clockwise around its horizontal axis – the movement of the ball is seen from the right side of the player.

2. **The instep of the foot** (instep pass) allows the player to add power and pace to

the pass, though accuracy is somewhat compromised. This kicking technique is valuable for long passing; the player takes a straight run-up to approach the ball; the non-kicking foot is placed alongside the ball about 10 inches away from it while the kicking leg takes a natural position (a running position). If the kicking foot makes contact with the ball in area A (Figure A) no spin is conveyed to the ball; by contrast, if the contact is made in area C, the foot imparts a counterclockwise rotating movement to the ball around its horizontal axis – the movement is always seen from the right.

3. **The inner instep** allows the player to make rather powerful and also accurate passes. This technique is generally used for long- and middle-distance passing. The approach to the ball is made from a slightly angled position: the run-up is taken from the left if the player kicks the ball with the right foot and from the right if the ball is kicked with the left foot; the non-kicking foot is placed at a distance of about 25 to 30 inches slightly to the side of the ball, while the kicking foot – the right one, for example – makes contact with the ball in side area E so as to make it rotate counterclockwise around its vertical axis (the movement is seen from the top). Obviously, the path and the direction of the kicked ball depend on where the foot makes contact with the ball; this means that if the inner instep hits the ball in area A, the ball could follow a straight direction and a flat path without any rotating effect.

4. **The outer instep** allows the player to make powerful and moderately accurate passes. This kicking technique is specifically used to hit the ball so as to make it follow "unexpected" paths characterized by considerable spin; the run-up to approach the ball is taken from a slightly angled position and the non-kicking foot is placed at a distance of about 25 to 30 inches from the ball; the kicking leg slightly rotates inwards before making contact with the ball. For example, if the right foot strikes the ball in its side area D, it makes the ball swerve counterclockwise around its vertical axis – the movement of the ball is seen from the top. The approach to the ball can also be made from in front: the player takes a straight run-up towards the ball and places the non-kicking foot much farther to the side of the ball. If the player takes a straight run-up towards the ball starting from an in front position and strikes the ball in area A, he can make it follow a straight path with no spinning effect even though this technique is rather difficult to perform.

5. **The outside of the foot** ensures moderate power and little accuracy of the pass; this technique can only be used over short distances and and for sideways passes to flick the ball through wide angles with heavy disguise. As a matter of fact, since this kicking technique does not interrupt the natural movement of running, it helps the player conceal his real intents.

6. **The tip of the foot** is used in very particular cases – when playing on muddy grounds, for example – and can help the player "anticipate" his direct opponent, catching him unawares by means of a rapid movement that involves short preparation and a quick approach.

7. **The heel of the foot** involves a biomechanical movement that is opposite to the

biomechanics of the moves we have analyzed up to now; this kicking technique is generally used to surprise the opponent and is a clear sign of a highly creative technical background.

8. **The sole of the foot** is not normally used to kick the ball, but is included in our list for a purely didactic purpose in order to complete our analysis on the directions and the axes of rotation.

Even though there are many different techniques for a player to kick the ball, it is possible to identify some typical *causes of errors* that I would summarize as follows:
❏ the player wrongly assesses the path of the ball and its speed
❏ the movement of the kicking leg to approach the ball is not duly completed
❏ the non-kicking foot is not placed in the correct position
❏ little balance on the standing leg
❏ the ankle joint is not perfectly rigid.

A player can kick the ball in three different ways: he can make ground passes, half-volley or volley the ball, either imparting spin to it or not, always trying to make accurate, powerful and quick moves; accuracy, power and quickness of performance are three crucial characteristics that help assess the real "technical background" of the player and should be constantly trained and refined in training, even though they are hardly compatible – in fact, players generally concentrate on one of them while kicking the ball to the prejudice of the others. At a didactic coaching level, it is usually recommended to ask inexperienced players to concentrate on the accuracy of passing technique first, then on rapidity and finally on the power of the performance, although some experts of motion do believe that it is fundamental to practice situations of play involving both accuracy and rapidity at the same time from the very beginning, even though they are in didactic conflict. From the physical formula **power = force x velocity** it emerges that the two factors are inversely proportional, which means that in order to generate the same amount of **power**, an increase in **force** should necessarily correspond to a decrease in **velocity**. When coaching young players, it is generally recommended not to work on enhancing **maximum force** in order to prevent pathologies resulting from physical overload – osteochondrosis – that affect articular capsules and joints which are particularly vulnerable in the developmental age.

Consequently, it is highly recommended to **avoid**:
❏ isometric exercise
❏ exercises involving physical overload higher than 6% of one's body weight; for example: lifting excessively heavy bars and dumbbells or carrying teammates on shoulders
❏ strengthening activities involving dangerous postures such as: bending one's lower limbs with the angle of the knee lower than 90°, jumping up and down high steps, jumping over high hurdles skipping once or several times, and so forth.
   Moreover, the coach should introduce in training sessions some specific activities aimed at coaching and practicing suitable correct postures. The coach could act as

follows:
1. help the player become aware of the correct postures and those positions he should avoid
2. **LOOSEN** joints and muscles to increase flexibility (specifically those of the back)
3. strengthen and develop the muscles supporting the back bone as well as the abdominals and the dorsals
4. tell the players which are the best relaxing and warming-down exercises to decontract the various segments of their bodies after strenuous exercise Furthermore, I also recommend that coaches suggest special conditioning activities to enhance **SPEED FORCE** (coaching and training how to jump) and the following aspects of **speed**:

❏ **Speed of reaction** defined as response to one single stimulus; this is an important characteristic which mainly concerns coordination and depends on the central nervous system. Shooting at goal to reply to a well-known input – the blowing of a whistle (sound stimulus), the gesture of a teammate (visual input), the touch of another player (tactile input), for example – is a clear expression of the player's simple reaction capacity; by contrast, reacting to a stimulus that is well-known but unexpected and disturbed by other signals (situation input) is an indicator of the player's complex reaction capacity.

❏ **Speed of performance** defined as the ability to make as many motor actions as possible in the unit of time, which is a characteristic concerning both the physical condition of the athlete and coordination as well. This important aspect of speed is clearly expressed while skipping, for example, which is the typical movement and pace of sprinters in track and field, and which involves the player bending his knees at right angles (90°) and stepping on the ground very quickly so that each step brings about an equal and opposite reaction resulting from the impact of the foot against the ground (speed **OF STEPPING**). This is why it is absolutely important to coach and train the running technique through several different running paces: from skipping, running by bending the legs backwards and raising the heels towards the glutei, bouncing along, stepping and taking off with sudden bounces, running sideways, hopping along by running on both feet together, to circular running where, in the two phases of the running movement – step (landing and take-off) and flight – the knees should describe a circular path, which is the expression of maximum harmony and coordination of the move. Great attention should also be focused on the stepping technique (landing phase with the foot making contact with the ground, and taking-off with the foot exerting pressure on the ground) and on those activities involving jumping over hurdles – about 10 inches high – which are very useful in educating and training the rhythm of stepping and paces. The speed of performance could also be trained by shooting 5 or 6 balls on goal very rapidly, in the shortest time possible, without stopping (frequence of the movement).

❏ **Speed of TRANSLOCATION** defined as the ability to cover a given distance as quickly as possible, which is a synthesis component of the two previously mentioned. One of the possible ways to express this skill is to run at top speed, with or without the ball, along straight or curved tracks of various lengths, starting from a stationary position or while moving.

In short, it emerges that power in soccer is not simply a function of the dimensions of the muscle (transverse section of the muscle to which the power it can convey is proportional), but is also connected to the speed of reaction and, consequently, to the capacity to involve the necessary muscle fibers, working to make a powerful technical move. This fundamental skill in soccer should be coached and trained in an alternated bilateral manner, which means the player should learn to kick the ball both with his dominant foot and his less skillful foot, since being able to kick with both feet is undoubtedly more beneficial. The dominant foot is that which can perform refined technical moves (the kicking leg, in this case), while the sensorial foot (the non-kicking or standing leg) is that which conveys stability and balance to the whole body and which offers the dominant foot the possibility to express its maximum skill, supporting the refined move.

When the coach plans the training activities he intends to suggest on the field to coach his players how to kick with their "less skillful" foot, he should not simply concentrate on the moment of the impact of the various areas of the foot against the ball – that is on the kicking foot – but should also focus the attention on the standing leg; in particular, he should help his athletes improve their balance capacity on which the stability of the body, the harmony and the accuracy of the movement directly depend. Although training activities generally aim at encouraging the player to use both feet to make technical moves, in competition he is more likely to use his dominant motor leg, even in unfavorable biomechanical conditions, since it is the quickest and shortest choice which also offers greater security. This fact should not discourage coaches; in fact, if they want to act in a truly competent manner and adopt a qualified approach to the subject, they should take care of both motor and sensorial education. In general, if they want to enhance their players' technical skills, not only do they need to work on strength, power, **SPEED FORCE**, speed and joint mobility, but also need to enhance their coordination capacity.

At a didactic level, one should also consider practicing kicking technique training barefoot – whenever the opportunity occurs – since this helps the player improve his perception of the contact between the foot and the ground and between the foot and the ball and also helps develop his muscles and enhances the reaction of the foot. An important methodological principle that should be used in training is that of "practice by opposites" and/or of contrast, which states that in order to enhance learning, it could be helpful to experience and perform contrary activities such as:

- kicking a heavy – light, hard – soft, rough – smooth ball
- kicking a fast – slow ball
- kicking a ball coming from in front – backwards
- kicking a ball so as to impart inswinging or outswinging spin to it.

Table 3 offers a recapitulatory picture of the subject and is therefore a useful reference for a coach to plan the coaching and learning of kicking technique.

KICKING THE BALL				
WHAT?	**WHERE?**	**HOW?**	**WHEN?**	**WHY?**
Areas of the foot	Space	Manner	Time	Purpose
• Inside of the foot • Inner instep • Outer instep • Outside of the foot • Instep • Toe • Heel	• Forward • Backward • Diagonally • To the right • To the left	• Referring to the movement of the ball • Ground pass • Half-volley • Volley kick	• After gathering information (visual contact) • Reading the situation	• **Defensive phase** • Deflect the ball • Intercept the ball • Clear the ball away • **Attacking phase** • Passing the ball • Shooting at goal
Player		**Ball**		
➢ Standing motionless ➢ While moving (run up)		➢ Stationary ➢ Moving • Direction from where the ball is coming (ball played from…) • Direction the ball is going (ball played to…)		
THE BALL IS PLAYED FROM		**THE BALL IS PLAYED TO**		
The ball comes	Path	The ball comes	Path	
➢ From in front Straight in front In front from the right In front from the left ➢ From the side	❏ Ground path ❏ Bouncing path ❏ Flat in the air ❏ Lob in the air	➢ Forward Straight forward Forward to the right Forward to the left ➢ Sideways	❏ Ground path ❏ Bouncing path ❏ Flat in the air ❏ Lob in the air	

Table 3

MONTHLY PLANNING FOR COACHING KICKING TECHNIQUE (PASSING AND SHOOTING AT GOAL)

The planning of the eight training sessions generally scheduled in a month of soccer activity should focus on setting the most significant motor, technical and tactical goals and selecting all the various activities to suggest to achieve those goals. Our coaching suggestion is based on the training method involving different phases and includes a series of didactic coaching progressions and contents that have proved to be useful to reach set goals (**table 4**).

MONTHLY PLANNING (8 TRAINING SESSIONS) MAIN GOALS TO ACHIEVE				
Basic motor patterns	Coordination Skills	Basic Technique	Individual tactical skills	Team tactical skills
• Jump • Strike • Throw	• Balance • Space perception • Time perception • Space and time perception	• Kick the ball	• Pass the ball (long pass – cross) • Shoot at goal	• Ball possession • Ball possession aimed at winning space on attack • Ball possession aimed at shooting at goal

Table 4

The training session should always begin with a warm up phase (lasting about 15 minutes), which first concentrates on practicing different paces (jogging, running) and then on training jumping technique, which means educating how to best use the ankle and the knee joints (walking or running by shifting the weight of the body on the toe and the heel, skipping and hopping at a moderate rhythm trying to maintain perfect balance).

The first warming up period is followed by the progression of starting games aimed at coaching and learning the kicking technique in a general form and, from the point of view of coordination, aimed at enhancing space and time perception, since the stationary and mobile targets the players are aiming for force them to carefully assess the distance, the height , the speed of displacement, movement and of the ball as well. If the same games are first played using only the hands, it not only helps the players understand the situation and the development of the exercise, but also improves and reinforces the basic motor patterns needed to learn how to throw in (which should be considered as a sub-goal of learning).

The training session further develops with the coaching progression of **analytical exercises** specifically designed to coach the technical move of kicking the ball in conditions of balance and space and time perception. These exercises focus on the four phases of shooting in a specific and analytical manner:
❏ approach to the ball (run up)
❏ preparing the kicking foot to make contact with the ball and placing the non-kicking foot in the best position (balance, the principle of sight)
❏ the contact of the kicking foot with the ball
❏ compensation phase: the condition of balance is restored and the next tactical action develops (try to restore the condition of balance by promptly putting the kicking foot down on the ground after shooting so as to be ready to sprint to meet the ball in case it bounces off the post or the goalkeeper clears it away).

These exercises can become real **situations of play** if they involve the goalkeeper and/or a defending player disturbing the attacker, who runs after him starting from a withdrawn position, for instance.

The coaching progression on the situations of play (**table 5**) allows the coach to make a synthesis of and revive the activities carried out on 1 v 1 and 1 v 2 and also to introduce new coaching suggestions on 3 v 2 and 2 v 2. One different situation of play is developed in each training session for a period of about 30 to 40 minutes according to the criteria of the example shown for 3 v 1 situation; in particular, greater attention should be given to:

❏ practicing ball possession if the coach realizes his players are poor at a technical level

❏ practicing ball possession aimed at clearing and winning space on attack if the players are poor not only at the technical level but also in playing in depth

❏ improving ball possession for the final shot on goal if they are poor in shooting and scoring technique.

In **table 5**, concerning the various situations of play, I have clearly pointed out the technical and tactical goals of both the attacking and the defending phase; moreover, it also shows the approximate dimensions of the playing areas where the situations should develop, which should be adjusted to the needs and the technical and tactical level of the players involved.

SITUATIONS OF PLAY				
Situation of play	Playing area in yards	Goals for individual tactical skills	Goals for team tactical skills
1. 1 v 1	8 to 10 x 8 to 10	Defending the ball Feinting and dribbling Shooting at goal Marking	Ball possession Clearing and winning space
2. 3 v 1	10 to 15 x 10 to 15	Eluding the marking Passing Shooting at goal Intercepting	Ball possession Clearing and winning space
3. 2 v 1	10 x 10 to 15	Eluding the marking Passing Shooting at goal Intercepting Marking	Ball possession Clearing and winning space Overlapping Playing one-two
4. 1 v 2	10 x 10 to 15	Defending the ball Feinting and dribbling Marking Tackling	Providing cover Double teaming
5 – 6. 3 v 2	20 to 25 x 25 to 30	Eluding the marking Passing Shooting at goal Marking Tackling	Ball possession Winning space Clearing space Diagonal running Overlapping Playing one-two Marking – covering
7 – 8. 2 v 2	15 to 20 x 20 to 25	Eluding the marking Passing Shooting at goal Marking Tackling Intercepting	Ball possession Clearing space Winning space Diagonal running Overlapping Playing one-two Marking – covering

The coaching progression on **conditioned games** points out the need for every player to express his own technical skills in order to achieve the tactical goals of the whole team; scoring a goal is obviously the ultimate purpose of the group, and for this to be possible, they need to maintain ball possession, moving forward and attacking the space towards the opposite goal by playing in depth (making long passes, through passes, playing one-twos) and in width (overlapping movements, diagonal outward passes, playing on the flanks of the field, crossing the ball).

At the end of each training session the coach should plan a **final game**, that is a conditioning match. This is the most attracting and stimulating event since it allows the players to freely express their motor, technical and tactical skills; in addition, it also helps the coach monitor and assess the work that has been done and the goals that have been achieved.

Planning the monthly activities suggested for coaching progressions whose difficulty level increases gradually offers to the coach the possibility to be rather flexible in selecting those exercises he intends to carry out:
❏ specifically concentrating on those that are more difficult for players to learn
❏ going back to those that he wrongly thought his players had perfected
❏ reinforcing variations to standard themes
❏ in particular, deciding to suggest exercises of greater complexity only at the right time and in the most suitable manner.

Starting games

1. Mark out a 40 by 40 yard playing area and place some cones and hoops at random inside it; each player has a ball and can touch it twice or three times to kick it into a hoop first and then strike a cone. Competition in pairs (**diagram 1**).
   Purposes: Make accurate ground shots to hit a stationary target. Space perception: assess distances.

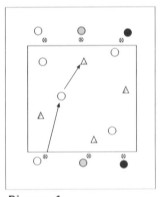

Diagram 1

2. Mark some targets of various size and at different heights on a wall or a wire-net fencing (you can use a piece of chalk or some tape). Each target corresponds to a particular level of difficulty and, consequently, to a different score.
   Variation: Shoot while moving.
   Purposes: Take accurate shots at different heights to hit a stationary target. Carefully assess distances and heights.
3. Every player runs through a fixed circuit previously marked by means of small goals and set paths consisting of various small pieces of gym apparatus (hurdles, cones, poles, hoops and so forth) where he has to kick the ball in sequence. The player who manages to run through the circuit kicking the ball with the smallest number of touches wins the competition.
   Purposes: Take accurate shots, alternating ground shots with high shots in rapid sequence. Assess distances and heights, measure the power of your shooting, anticipating the direction of the shot for the next target.
4. Two players grasp a pole at the two ends and hold it at the height of their pelves or shoulders; they run (at various speeds) along a marked lane at the sides of which

are other pairs of players, each with a ball. They have to kick the ball over and under the pole their teammates are holding, following the directions given by the coach to score one point.

Purposes: Take accurate shots at a mobile target, carefully assessing the speed at which it is moving.

5. Mark out a square playing area and divide the players in two groups: the hunters and the prey. The team of hunters are standing outside the square, they pass the ball to each other and try to choose the best moment to take ground shots and hit the members of the opposing team (the prey) who are free to move and run away within the boundaries of the marked area. The hunters try to hit as many prey players as possible in a given period of time (**diagram 2**).

   Purposes: take accurate shots at a mobile target, trying to cooperate with your teammates.

6. The team in possession of the ball are standing around the center circle; they try to strike a target, the triangle made up of three cones or poles inside the circle and defended by one or two keepers (**diagram 3**).

   Variation: The players defending the target can use their hands to touch the ball and therefore act as goalkeepers.

   Purposes: Take accurate shots at a stationary target, trying to cooperate with your teammates to elude the action of the defending keepers.

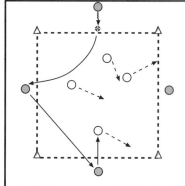

Diagram 2

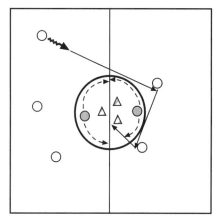

Diagram 3

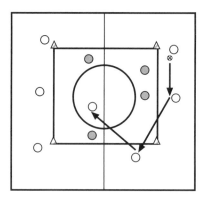

Diagram 4

7. The team in possession of the ball – outnumbering their opponents – position around the center circle; they pass the ball to each other and try to finally pass it to their captain standing inside the circle, eluding the marking of the defending team who can freely move in the playing area between the circumference of the kick-off circle and the square marked out around it by means of cones (**diagram 4**).

   Purposes: Take accurate shots at a mobile target, cooperating with teammates to elude the marking by the defending opposition.

8. For this exercise you can use the size of the penalty box at the edge of which you will place another goal, opposite to the regular one. Two or three players position on the flanks of the field along each of the two short lines of the penalty area: they make crosses towards the middle of the box from various positions and with different paths to the attacking players inside the penalty area who can take first-time shots at either of the two goals defended by the two goalkeepers **(diagram 5)**.

Purposes: Cross the ball and take volley shots at goal while making acrobatic movements. Carefully read the path of the ball and assess its speed.

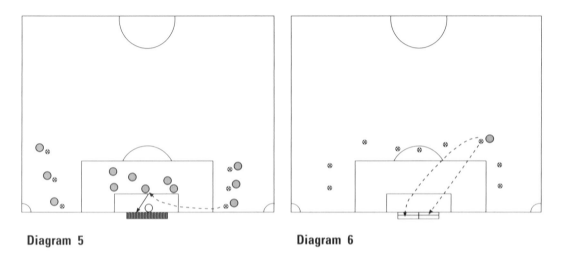

Diagram 5   Diagram 6

Analytical exercises

Training sessions 1 and 2

Exercises for the kicking leg without the ball

The pendulum exercise
Stand in perfect balance on one foot, on the ground or on an object (a block, a foot-stool, a brick or a step, for instance), and swing the free leg forward and backward, to the right and to the left.
Variations:
❑ In order to best concentrate on the movement of the swinging leg and avoid losing balance, you can use a support, leaning your hands against a wall, for example.
❑ The swinging leg can be relaxed and bent (the knee joint is free and loose) or perfectly stretched (the knee joint is rigid)
❑ Repeat the same exercise while sitting or lying on your back on special benches or high tables.

Exercises for the kicking leg with the ball

Kick a stationary ball from a stationary position

Every player takes a shot from a stationary position at one of the four sectors in which the goal has been divided, using the various parts of the foot. Kicking the ball from a stationary position forces the player to swing the kicking leg hard to generate power while also maintaining perfect balance on the non-kicking leg. In the first training session, the players shoot at goal from center-right positions, and in the second from center-left positions (**diagram 6**).

Variations: Change the positions from where the ball is kicked (nearer to or further from the goal, to the right or to the left).

Purposes:

❑ Enhance particular posture patterns concerning the positions of the lower limbs, that is all the various possible movements of the kicking leg (bend and stretch, rotate inwards and outwards, swing, fling and so on)

❑ Perception of and control over the kicking leg through a whip-like movement, maximum swinging and the pendular movement of the kicking leg itself (bending and stretching, abducting and abducting)

❑ Impact of the kicking foot against the ball (kinesthetic sensibility, differentiation capacity, balance).

Training sessions 3 and 4

Exercises for the standing leg (non-kicking foot) without the ball

Static and dynamic balance games

1. While trying to maintain a position of balance standing on the ground or on a block or footstool, take different positions (postures) moving the body forward and backward and to the right and to the left.

   Variation: Repeat the same postures slightly jumping down (jump down off the block or footstool) and up (jump up on the block).

2. Exercise in pairs: Player A is standing in perfect balance on the ground or on a block, while his teammate B tries to push him using various parts of the body (his hands, shoulders or chest, for example) in order to cause him to lose balance.

3. Exercise in pairs: Both players are standing in balance on their own block or foot stool and try to push each other – always with maximum caution and attention – in order to cause the opponent to lose balance.

   Variation: The two players standing in balance on the block start the exercise hand in hand or arm in arm and try to cause the opponent to lose balance by either pulling or pushing each other.

Exercises for the standing leg and the non-kicking foot with the ball

Shoot a stationary ball taking a suitable run up

Each player kicks the ball using the five different running paths to approach the ball in order to shoot at one of the four targets in which the goal has been divided. This exercise allows the player to focus his attention on the importance of placing the standing leg (non-kicking foot) in the correct position, that is the best distance on the front plane (right or left plane) of the ball in relation to the area of the foot the player wants to kick the ball with (the inside of the foot, the instep, the inner instep and so forth…) as well as the correct distance on the sagittal plane (front and rear plane) according to the kind of path the player wants the ball to follow (ground or flight path). In this situation the athlete also experiences the need to point the non-kicking foot towards the target (following the concept of the sight) (**diagram 7**).

In the third training session the players shoot at goal kicking the ball from center-left positions, while in the fourth sessions they kick from center-right positions.

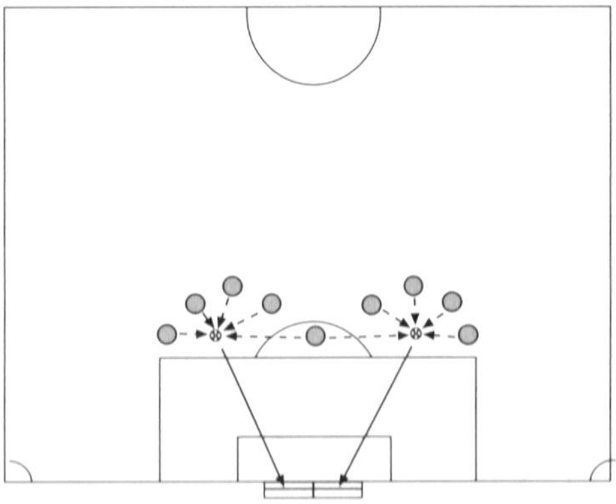

Variations:
❏ change the position from where the ball is kicked, that is nearer to or further from the goal, to the right or to the left
❏ focus the attention on the approach to the ball, adjusting the length, the running speed or the rhythm of your footsteps.

Purposes:
❏ Have a clear perception of the movements of the body (run up)
❏ Place the non-kicking foot in the best position (distance from the ball on the front and sagittal plane and concept of the "sights", aiming at the target)
❏ Perception of and control over the kicking leg
❏ Impact of the various parts of the foot against the ball
❏ Peripheral vision (instruct the players to shift their focus from the ball to the target at the moment of contact or even before. This trains the player to have a tactile and kinesthetic control over the ball, which means that he does not necessarily need to look at the ball to master it).
❏ Compensation phase (restore a position of balance).

Diagram 7

Training sessions 5 and 6

Exercises for the standing and the kicking leg without the ball

Swing and take off
Stand in perfect balance on the standing foot on a block or a brick, and swing the free leg (that is the kicking leg) alternately forward and backward, to the right and to the left while also combining and coordinating the movement with a slight jump on the standing foot, always trying to maintain balance on the block (or brick).

Variations:
❏ the swinging movement of the kicking leg is combined with the movement of the standing leg jumping down from and up onto the block or footstool
❏ swing the kicking leg while skipping rope or jumping back and forth over a tape lying on the ground or a boundary line marked on the playing field

Exercises for the standing and the kicking leg with the ball

Kick a moving ball after taking a suitable run up
The path of the ball and the path of the running movement to approach the ball run parallel with each other

Every player can touch the ball twice, kicking the ball into the square area marked out at the edge of the penalty box first and then shooting at goal. After kicking the ball the first time, the player sprints and adjusts his running movement to the speed of the ball in order to anticipate the position of the standing foot and therefore prepare for a suitable impact of the kicking foot against the ball to shoot at goal. For this to be possible, the player needs to develop good perception of the relation between space and time. In the fifth training session the players shoot from center-left positions, while in the sixth session they start from center-right positions (**diagram 8**).

Variations:
❏ Change the position of the square where the players first kick the ball (nearer or farther off, to the right or to the left of the goal) and its size (small or large)
❏ Vary the speed of the ball rolling towards the square area
❏ Vary the path of the ball kicked into the square

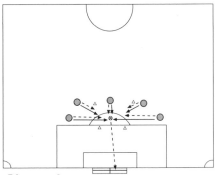

Diagram 8

Purposes:
❏ Stimulate the perception of the movement of the body (run up)
❏ Read the path of the ball
❏ Place the non-kicking foot in the correct position compared to the moving ball (anticipate the movement of the ball)
❏ Enhance the perception and the control of the kicking leg
❏ Impact of the kicking foot against the ball
❏ Enhance peripheral vision
❏ Compensation phase (restore a position of balance)

Training sessions 7 and 8

Exercises for the standing and the kicking leg with the ball

Kick a moving ball after approaching it with a suitable run up
The path of the ball and the path of the running movement converge

The players standing outside the penalty box, in the six different positions at center-right and center-left, play the ball with different paths into the reference square area marked out at the edge of the box. The exercise is carried out in pairs. The player waiting for the ball to be passed by his teammates kicks the ball while running forward, aiming it at the goal mouth. This means that the shooting player is able to properly read the path of the pass, carefully assessing the height of the ball, the length of the path and its spin. Great attention should also be focused on the speed of the ball as well as on timing the positioning of the standing foot and the swinging movement of the kicking leg to properly make contact with the ball. In the seventh training session the players cross the ball from the center-left, while in the eighth session the ball is crossed from center-right positions (**diagram 9**).

Variations:

1. Change the position of the square area where the shooting player runs to meet the cross (nearer or farther off, to the right or to the left of the goal) and its size (small or large)

2. Combine the eight different directions from where the ball can be crossed with different paths (ground, bouncing or flight paths) and different speeds (to play the ball into the square playing area)

3. Combine the four different directions where the ball can be played to towards the four different targets (shot on goal)

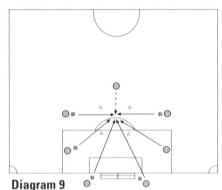
Diagram 9

4. Practice the eight different paths of the shooting player's run up to approach the ball

5. Practice the three different ways of kicking the ball (ground shot, half-volley and volley) Play with a goalkeeper defending the goal.

Purposes:

Approach to the path of the ball
❏ anticipate the path of the crossed ball
❏ perceive the movement of the body while running to meet the ball
❏ time the run to meet the crossed ball

Preparation for the impact against the ball
❏ swinging movement of the kicking leg
❏ distance between the center of gravity of the body and the ball
❏ position of the non-kicking foot in static and dynamic balance.

Impact of the kicking foot against the ball
❏ the kicking foot makes contact with the ball (whip-like movement)
❏ point of impact.

Compensation phase
❏ restore a condition of perfect balance in order to start and develop the tactical action following the shot on goal, for example: run to meet the ball in case the goalkeeper manages to clear it back

Peripheral vision
❏ read the situation
❏ elude the marking and the pressure by the opposition.

Situations of play

In the following page you will be offered an example for the development of the second situation of play concerning 3 v 1 (**table 5**).

3 v 1 for ball possession. Three attacking players play to maintain possession of the ball: they are allowed free or limited touches of the ball (unconditioned or conditioned play) moving within a playing area previously marked out. The game can develop following the rules of the 'monkey in the middle' exercise or in a set period of time. The coach counts the number of passes:
- made by the attacking players
- made playing the ball first time
- the defender manages to intercept.

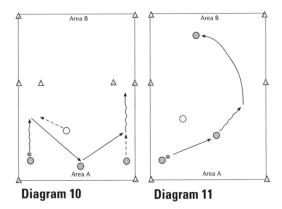

Diagram 10   **Diagram 11**

3 v 1 for ball possession in order to clear and win space
Three attacking players play to maintain possession of the ball and try to get into area B which is marked out with cones, dribbling the ball through one of the two small goals on each side of the playing field. The purpose of this exercise is to dribble the ball through either of the two goals as many times as possible (moving from one half of the playing field to the other and back) in a set period of time (**diagram 10**).
Purpose: Clear and win space so as to make play develop in width.

The game continues with the two attacking players in area A who try to maintain possession of the ball in order to make an end-to-end pass to their third teammate standing in square B, so as to shift the situation of play to that zone. The purpose of this exercise is the same as in the previous game (**diagram 11**).
Purpose: Clear and attack space forward so as to make play develop in depth.

3 v 1 to maintain ball possession in order to finally shoot at goal
Mark out a playing area (as large as the goal area) with cones. Three attacking players in possession of the ball try to gain space by dribbling the ball forward (they are challenged by a defender) in order to shoot at the goal defended by the opposing goalkeeper in the shortest time possible.

Conditioned games

1. Place five cones in one half of the regular playing field as in **diagram 12**. Two teams compete playing 4 v 4 to strike the cones. One point is awarded if the ball only touches the cone, and two points are awarded if the player manages to knock it down.
   Purposes: Maintain ball possession in order to take accurate shots and to favor a uniform and harmonious distribution of the players on the playing area.

2. Two teams play 4 v 4 in a 20 x 30 yard playing area; they have to strike a special target consisting of three cones forming a triangle at a distance of about 10 yards from the goal line (**diagram 13**).
   Variation: Increase or decrease the size of the target-triangle
   Two points are awarded if the ball stops inside the triangle.
   Purpose: maintain ball possession in order to take accurate shots.

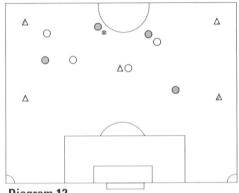

Diagram 12

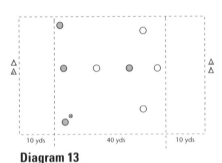

Diagram 13

3. Two teams play 7 v 7 or 8 v 8 in a 30 x 50 yard playing field with two target areas defended by the two goalkeepers. Each team, after making at least five consecutive passes, can lob the ball to their goalkeeper who must catch it before it bounces on the ground.
   Purpose: Maintain ball possession in order to shoot at a mobile target.

4. In the middle of a 30 x 40 yard playing area mark out a hexagonal zone at the center of which there is a two-mouth goal defended by a goalkeeper.
   Two teams play 5 v 5 or 6 v 6: they are allowed to play one touch inside the hexagonal area and unconditioned touches outside it. The two teams compete to try to shoot at goal and score (**diagram 14**).
   Purposes: Play so as to favor shooting at goal, long play and cross-field passes.

5. Two teams play 7 v 7 or 8 v 8 in one half of the regular playing field (with two goals, one at each end) in the middle of which there is a free area – 10 yards – where both the ball and the players of the two sides can move, but where the players cannot touch the ball.
   Purpose: Encourage the players to play in depth, making long passes.

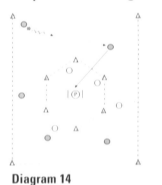

Diagram 14

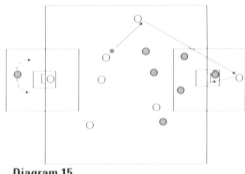

Diagram 15

6. Two teams play 7 v 7 or 8 v 8 in one half of the regular field, with two two-sided goals (one at each end) and two penalty boxes at each goal – one in front and the other behind the goal.
Two support players are standing in the zones behind the two goalkeepers: these players can take first-time shots on goal or make crosses from the goal lines to their teammates, who can try to score from the opposite side (**diagram 15**).
Purposes: Stimulate the players to play in depth, give crosses from the goal line and shoot at goal.

7. Two teams play 7 v 7 or 8 v 8 in one half of the field with two goals placed on the two side lines: play develops from one side line to the other (in width) with two external areas (marked by the goal line and the mid line, respectively). Any player who manages to receive the ball after making an overlapping movement in the opposing half of the field is allowed to enter one of the two external zones. When a player moves unchallenged in one of these areas, he can easily cross the ball for his teammates, thus avoiding the marking by the opposition.
Purposes: Stimulate the players to play on the flanks of the field and give crosses to their teammates.

8. Two teams play 7 v 7 or 8 v 8 in one half of the regular field (with two goals) divided in three different areas.
When the team starting from the goal line are attacking, the two sides are allowed to play unconditioned touches of the ball in the zone including the goal area; three touches in the central area; and two touches in the zone including the center circle – and viceversa when the opposing team are on attack.
Purposes: Stimulate the players to play very rapidly and shoot at goal, while also clearing and gaining space forward.

3.3 DRIBBLING THE BALL

Definition: A basic technical skill in soccer which refers to the player's ability to make a sequence of passes directly to himself while moving on the playing area.

Description: During the course of a soccer match, when a player wins or gets possession of the ball, he can decide to dribble it (make it roll on the ground) from one point on the playing field to another, running at different speeds, striking it with a variable number of touches, changing his running direction, while always maintaining control and possession of the ball. The ball should always be very "close" to his feet. For this to be possible, the player needs to run with very short and quick steps, enhancing the kinesthetic sensibility in the impact of the kicking foot against the ball that allows him to make the ball roll by means of slight and accurate touches. If the player sees open spaces on the field, he could increase his running speed, **LENGTHENING HIS STRIDE**, touching the ball with greater power so as to make it roll away from his foot in relation to the speed and to the presence of the opponents in the direction he is dribbling the ball. At the very moment when the foot makes contact with the ball, the body is standing directly above the ball with the eyes looking down, while in the period between one touch of the ball and the following one, the player needs to raise his head and look around in order to get helpful information on the position of both his teammates and opponents so as to "read" the situation of play while he is moving with the ball. If the player who is dribbling the ball is disturbed by one of his opponents, he should use his body as a screen between the ball and the marking opponent, in order to shield the ball and prevent the opponent from tackling or intercepting it.

The most common areas of the foot that players use to dribble the ball are:
❏ the inside of the foot to change direction
❏ the outside of the foot to change direction
❏ the outer instep to change direction and dribble the ball straight ahead
❏ the sole of the foot to adjust or completely change direction.

In the context of a soccer match, the act of dribbling the ball is never an end in itself and the technical ability to successfully orientate the dribbling of the ball towards various specific directions also has some important tactical implications and purposes when this becomes a means to:
❏ gain and attack space upward
❏ take a new position on the playing field that allows for further development of the tactical situation
❏ dribble past an opponent
❏ avoid a challenge or a tackle successfully
❏ shoot at goal.

When a coach plans his coaching and training activity, it is therefore fundamental to concentrate not only on practicing basic technical skills concerning the ability to dribble the ball as an end in itself (which involves the relationship between the player and the ball, exclusively), but also on applied technique which refers to the combination of two or several movements aiming at one particular purpose, that is combining such moves as (**table 1**):

❏ dribbling and passing
❏ dribbling and shooting
❏ dribbling past an opponent and beating him
❏ controlling the ball and dribbling.

SITUATIONS OF PLAY				
Before the move	**Technical move**	**Technical move**	**After the move**	
1. Tackle 2. Intercept 3. Receive 4. Shield and cover 5. Dribble past the opponent	Dribble Dribble Dribble Dribble Dribble	Dribble Dribble Dribble Dribble Dribble	Tackle Shoot at goal Pass Shield and cover Dribble past the opponent Stop	A B C D E F
Before the move		**Before the move**	**Before the move**	
Tackle Tackle Tackle Tackle Tackle Tackle		Dribble Dribble Dribble Dribble Dribble Dribble	Tackle Shoot at goal Pass Shield and cover Dribble past the opponent Stop	1A 1B 1C 1D 1E 1F
COMPLETE COMBINATIONS				
1A 2A 3A 4A 5A	1B 2B 3B 4B 5B	1C 2C 3C 4C 5C	1D 2D 3D 4D 5D	1E 1F 2E 2F 3E 3F 4E 4F 5E 5F

Table 1

The most common mistakes players make while dribbling the ball include:
1. running with excessively long strides (this is a common mistake in the running technique)
2. using the least suitable area of the foot to make contact with the ball in relation to the situation of play (bad choice)
3. eyes constantly looking down (bad use of the visual analyzer)
4. the ball is touched with excessive power (bad use of the kinesthetic analyzer).

The following **table** shows a recapitulatory picture of what has been explained up to now, while the second table is a synthesis of the coaching unit focusing on dribbling the ball in situations of set rhythm, which should be developed in at least three or four training sessions.

DRIBBLING THE BALL				
WHAT?	**WHERE?**	**HOW?**	**WHEN?**	**WHY?**
Areas of the foot	Manner	Space	Time	Purpose
• Inside of the foot • Outside of the foot • Outer instep • Sole of the foot	• Compared to the path of the ball • Straight dribbling path • Curved dribbling path • Compared to the direction and the dribbling technique • Change the direction completely • Adjust the direction • Adjust the speed	• Forward and backward (in depth) • To the right and to the left (in width) • Diagonally	• After getting visual information • After reading the situation of play	• Clear and gain space upward • Take a favorable position to develop the action of play • Shoot at goal

COACHING UNIT

Age: 11 to 13 year olds
Primary specific goal: dribbling the ball
Secondary specific goal: setting a particular rhythm
Instruments: stopwatch
Equipment: cones, flat cones, 16 soccer balls, colored shirts
Contents: group games, individual exercises, 1 v 1, 2 v 1 and 1 v 2 situations, 4 v 4 and 8 v 8 team games
Methods: deductive – inductive
Test: observation of the conditioned game
Suggestion for the following session: depends on the outcome of the test
Starting games: dribbling the ball in traffic, the four corners, the statues
Analytical exercises: individual exercises to dribble the ball in situations of set rhythm
Situations of play:
1. The cat and the mouse (1 v 1)
2. Run to the finishing line gaining positions (1 v 1, 1 v 2, 2 v 1)
Conditioned game: 1 v 1 chase, rugby soccer 4 v 4 and 8 v 8
Final game: unconditioned game with two goalkeepers in one half of the field

Starting games

1. Dribbling the ball in traffic: Mark out a playing area whose dimensions vary according to the number of players involved and to their skills. Every player has a ball and dribbles it in the playing area, trying to avoid running into the other players without dribbling out of the playing area.

2. The four corners: Four players, each in possession of a ball, position at the four corners of a square playing area in the middle of which there is another player with a ball. The players standing at the four corners frequently change their positions, dribbling the ball from one corner to another, while the player standing in the middle tries to take the position left free by one of his teammates. If he manages to reach one of the four corners, he remains there, while the player who failed to position at one of the four available corners plays at the center of the square.

3. The statues: Mark out a 20 x 20 yard square area. Twelve players with a ball each move freely dribbling the ball inside the playing area, while four magicians (without the ball) run after them in order to touch them. If the magician manages to catch one of the players, that player becomes a statue, which means he stops on the spot with his legs wide apart holding the ball in his hands over his head. The statues can be rescued and set free by means of sorcery, if one of the free prey players succeeds in dribbling the ball through their legs.

Purposes of the starting games
❏ Adjust your dribbling to the behaviors of your teammates and the opponents, completely changing direction, adjusting the direction and the speed
❏ Direct the dribbling of the ball towards free areas
❏ Use your peripheral vision

Analytical exercises

Dribbling the ball in situations of cyclic, alternated, varied and acyclic rhythm

1. Every player dribbles the ball along set paths
   - moving straight ahead or making a slalom through the posts – marked out with hurdles or cones placed at equal distances so that the rhythm of the dribbling movement remains constant (**diagram 1**).

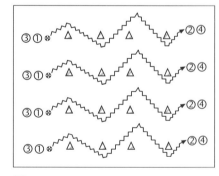

Diagram 1

2. Placing the same hurdles or cones at various distances, the player needs to vary the rhythm of his movements, alternating faster with slower movements (alternated phase).
   In this way, it is possible to plan special coaching progressions modifying the length, the form of the track (straight path, slalom or geometric figures) and change the areas of the foot making contact with the ball, in the form of relay races (rapidity) or penalty competitions (accuracy).

3. Each player dribbles the ball along special tracks marked out using different pieces of gym apparatus (hurdles, cones, poles and so forth). While dribbling the ball from

one end to the other, the player also makes different technical moves (like shifting from dribbling the ball with the left foot to dribbling with the inside of both feet and so on) so that the rhythm of the performance varies in relation to the type of gym equipment and to the dribbling technique (varied phase).

4. In the last sequence of exercises suggested in this context, the young player tries to express his ability to adjust his own rhythm of performance to the rhythm set by the coach, a teammate, an opponent or a situation of play. An example of this is the shadow game. This game is played in pairs: one player is standing behind the other and each has a ball. The player in front leads the game by dribbling the ball at will, often changing direction, speed and dribbling technique, while his shadow teammate follows him closely, adjusting his movements to the rhythm set by the leading player (acyclic phase)

Purposes:

❏ Practice dribbling technique using and combining different areas of the foot to make contact with the ball

❏ Perceive and internalize the rhythm set by your own movements resulting from the contact between the foot and the ball and the foot and the ground.

Using small pieces of gymnastic apparatus and planning activities properly

An inefficient planning of the coaching and training activities (due to several different reasons, such as unsuitable placement of the pieces of gym apparatus on the playing area, the inability to properly set tasks or decide the beginning and the end of the exercises, or the inability to time the rotation of roles, spaces and positions) may result in "dead periods", which means waiting lines, frequent stops, numerous interruptions and chaos. These situations do not only cause a considerable waste of time, but also negatively affect attention and concentration, thus impairing the learning process itself. It is therefore fundamental for a coach to increase the periods of time dedicated to motor performance to maximum levels, planning the activities he intends to suggest in the best way possible in order to cut dead periods but specifically to be able to observe, examine, intervene, give suggestions and correct at the same time. **Diagram 1** shows one of the possible solutions to organize analytical exercises focusing on dribbling, where sixteen players – divided in four different groups standing in lines – practice using four balls (one for each group), dribbling through slalom paths marked with cones. The exercise develops as follows: the coach is standing in a strategic position as in **diagram 1**; when he gives the starting signal, all the number one players (that is the first player in each line) in possession of the ball, dribble in a slalom through the cones until they reach their teammates (number twos), who receive the balls and dribble them backwards in the opposite direction, leave them to their next teammates (number threes) and so forth. The practical advantage of this situation lies in the regular sequence of movements as well as in the fact that the coach can observe and monitor the movements of four players at the same time with the possibility to intervene, stop and correct them – which would be difficult, or even impossible, if the players dribbled the balls simultaneously, moving freely on the playing area.

Situations of play

The cat and the mouse (Diagram 2)
Moving around the perimeter of a square playing area (2 to 3 x 2 to 3 yards) – whose dimensions depend on the skills of the players involved in the exercise – player M dribbles the ball away from his opponent C. Player C is also in possession of a ball and dribbles it around the boundaries of the square running after his opponent M, trying to catch or touch him within one minute.

Variations:
❏ both the cat and the mouse play without the ball
❏ the pursuer in possession of the ball dribbles running after the prey who runs away without the ball and/or viceversa.

Purposes: Dribble the ball using your peripheral vision to read and assess the moves of your opponent.

Diagram 2

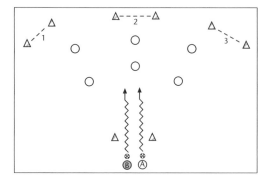

Diagram 3

Run to the finishing line, gaining positions (diagram 3)
Player A in possession of the ball is awarded two points if he manages to dribble the ball up to one of the three finishing lines – marked and placed as in **diagram 3** – gaining as many intermediate positions as he can, which consist of several hoops placed on the playing area (free zones) where the player can stop and restart as he likes, dribbling the ball in other directions (another point is awarded for every intermediate position the player manages to reach).

Defender B tries to hamper his opponent A, preventing him from reaching intermediate positions or dribbling up to the finishing line; the defender manages to neutralize his opponent's action if he manages to touch, intercept or win possession of the ball according to the rules and the defensive goals set by the coach.

Changing the starting positions of player B compared to his opponent A (he can start in front of him, behind, from the right or the left at various distances, for example) is key for the game to be successful and effective.

Variations:
❏ Several pairs of players play the game at the same time
❏ The attacking players play in numerical superiority or inferiority compared to the defenders.

Purposes:
❏ Dribble the ball to gain free space and favorable positions
❏ Dribble and screen the ball.

The chase (diagram 4)
The attacking player in possession of the ball tries to dribble it rapidly along a marked path 20 to 30 yards long and 10 yards wide before shooting at goal, trying to elude the marking of the defender, who starts from a position 2 to 3 yards behind him.

Diagram 4

The coach can suggest a team competition with the groups alternating in the attacking and defending phase.
Variation: Two defenders run after one attacking player to hinder his movements
Purposes:
❏ Dribble the ball to finally shoot at goal
❏ Dribble the ball to get in the defender's way
❏ Cover and screen the ball.

Conditioned games

Rugby-like soccer
Two teams compete playing soccer on a playing field suitably marked out so as to include two target areas along the two goal lines. One point is awarded every time a player of the attacking team manages to dribble the ball up to the target area.

At a didactic level it is convenient to introduce the following coaching progression so as to gradually increase the difficulty level of the game:
❏ dribble the ball up to the goal area
❏ dribble the ball up to the goal area touching it at least five times
❏ pass through the goal area (5 to 6 yards) dribbling the ball
❏ start to dribble from the offensive third of the field (10 to 15 yards)
❏ dribble up to the goal area following one of the basic rules of rugby: players are not allowed to make forward passes.
Purposes: Clear and gain space forward by dribbling the ball forward and making backward passes.

Enhancing Dribbling Skills Through Suitable Variations

Learning basic technical movements from the biomechanical point of view – that is the ideal, the most suitable, economical, effective and successful move to make in a particular situation of play – is not enough. It is fundamental to learn any technical movement in its variety of forms and expressions, which means all the various possibilities for a player to perform the same move in the dynamic mechanisms of the match in order to adjust and adapt to the unpredictable nature of playing soccer (which is a sport of situations).

All the soccer skills that can be internalized and therefore become automatic through constant repetition should be used and applied to any particular situation of play as plastic automatism, that is as situational moves involving several expressive variations and performances to be used in different contexts and varied manners, contrary to rigid and stereotyped automatism that can only be used in certain situations, with fixed and repetitive performances (consider individual sports disciplines such as high jumping, putting the shot, swimming and so forth).

These automatism can be activated and developed through suitable adjustments, changes and combinations while performing the movement, which can obviously be defined in relation to space, time, quantitative and tactical variations or, more generically, according to the particular situation of play.

Consequently, the same technical move can be carried out varying the manner of the performance in relation to several different parameters.

For a coach to properly plan and suggest these kinds of activities he needs to use suitable playing areas and small pieces of gymnastic apparatus and objects like hoops, hurdles, disc cones, tape, cones of various heights, poles and so forth.

Moving along the same path dribbling the ball through disc cones or making a slalom through the poles taking care not to touch them is a variation of the same exercise, since it forces the player to make more rapid and accentuated changes of direction, involving more evident and significant movements of the body in order to avoid touching the poles with his shoulders.

Enhancing dribbling technique with no opposition

Athletic variations

Combine dribbling and speed force
Dribble the ball through a well set path marked out using low hurdles placed at different distances and oriented in different directions. The ball passes below the hurdle while the player is jumping over it.

Plan the number of repetitions and sets for each exercise. (For example, three sets of 10 jumps each). Combine dribbling and rapidity (**diagram 5**)

Relay racing, running and dribbling
Two teams compete playing in a 10 x 15 yards rectangular area.

When the coach gives the starting signal, the first player in line (player 1) runs at top speed along the long side of the playing area from A to B, takes one of the two balls inside the hoop lying at corner B, dribbles the ball diagonally from B to D, stops it inside the hoop placed at corner D and sprints without the ball along the short side of the field from D to A to "pass the baton" to his teammate number 2 and joins the line behind the other players.

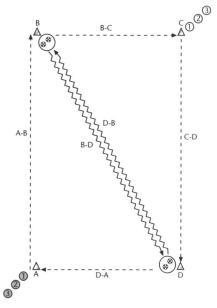

Diagram 5

Simultaneously, the opposing player moves following the same path, but in the opposite direction, that is along the long side of the field from C to D without the ball, dribbles the ball diagonally from D to B and runs without the ball along the opposite short side from B to C to relieve his teammate. At the beginning of the game there are two balls in each hoop. If the two players actively involved in the exercise run and dribble the ball at the same speed, there will always be a situation of balance since one ball is taken from the hoop at corner B, dribbled diagonally through the playing area and placed in the hoop at corner D, and viceversa. By contrast, if the players of one team run faster than their opponents on average and are able to benefit from the mistakes of the opposition, they can break the situation of balance by dribbling the third ball into one of the two hoops which would promptly cause the end of the game. On the other hand, if the players manage to maintain the situation of balance, the game ends when the coach stops it, at his own discretion, according to the goals he has set and his players may have achieved after 3, 4 or 5 repetitions. The coach should carefully measure the distance his players have covered (10 + 11 + 5 = 26 yards), the time they have taken to perform the exercise, the number of repetitions, and the recovery interval between a repetition and the following one.

Combine dribbling and endurance

Mark out a long training circuit – the perimeter of the playing field, for instance – using many different pieces of gymnastic apparatus, including the boundary lines. The coach can either set how many times the players have to cover the distance dribbling around the field and the running speed (that is moving at constant, moderate, or average speed, including changes of speed or fartlek running) and time their performances; or he can set the time of the exercise and consequently measure the distances or the segments of the circuit they have covered in that period of time.

Coordination variations

Dribble in condition of balance

Dribble the ball making a slalom through the cones, skipping on the standing foot without the dribbling foot touching the ground.

Dribble using different balls

Repeat the same activities explained in the previous pages but using balls of various weights and different sizes, like tennis balls, sponge balls, volleyballs or basketballs and so forth.

Combine dribbling and space perception

Space variations

In a playing area (small or large) mark out a dribbling track or circuit (open or closed) using all the various small pieces of gymnastic apparatus available. The players start (near or far) from the goal, dribble the ball (inside or around) some hoops, pass (over or under) some hurdles, through cones and posts (high or low), along special lanes (large or narrow) and mattresses (long or short). It is also possible to change the dribbling direction (forward and backward, to the right and to the left).

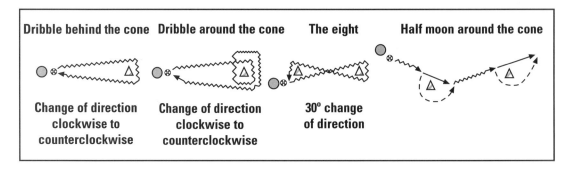

Dribble behind the cone **Dribble around the cone** **The eight** **Half moon around the cone**

Change of direction clockwise to counterclockwise **Change of direction clockwise to counterclockwise** **30° change of direction**

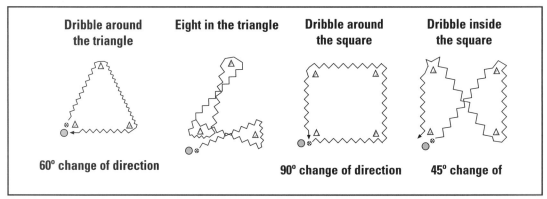

Dribble around the triangle **Eight in the triangle** **Dribble around the square** **Dribble inside the square**

60° change of direction **90° change of direction** **45° change of**

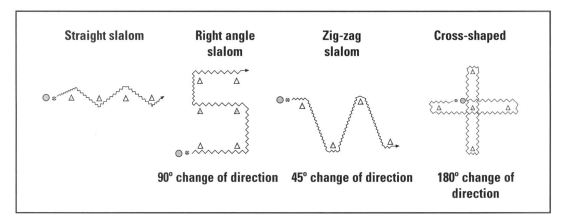

Straight slalom **Right angle slalom** **Zig-zag slalom** **Cross-shaped**

90° change of direction **45° change of direction** **180° change of direction**

While planning and arranging training tracks, slaloms and circuits it is highly recommended to suggest them as individual competitions, or team contests or games in pairs (competitive component) and score, time and penalty relay competitions (combining playing and enjoying) so as to enhance players' motivations.

Combine dribbling and time perception

Suggest the same exercises shown in the chapter "Dribbling the ball in situations of cyclic, alternated, varied and acyclic rhythm", specifically stressing and focusing the attention on time variations.

Time variations
In sequence (before and after) and simultaneously.

Dribble the ball adjusting and changing your movements
The crossing (diagram 7)

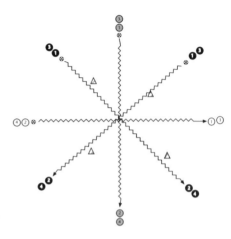

Diagram 7

Four groups of players are divided in teams standing in opposite lines, like the arrangement shown in the diagram. Each group starts with a ball. The first players in line with a ball (number 1's) dribble to the line opposite them and "hand off" to the next players (number 2's) and so on.

All players must pass through the square (5 x 5 yards) marked out inside the playing area. While dribbling in this square area every player has to adjust his dribbling pace, accelerating, slowing down or stopping and promptly restarting, in relation to the presence, the speed and the behaviors of the other players who are dribbling the ball at the same time.

Dribble the ball combining different movements
Combine different technical moves that can be made before and/or after the dribbling of the ball **(diagram 1)**.

Dribble the ball combining enhanced coordination capacities
Dribble the ball while also combining acrobatic movements (rolling forward or backward, to the right or to the left, diving, falling on the ground and so forth…)

Dribble the ball combining qualitative variations
Dribble a (heavy or light, rough or smooth) ball moving on a (soft or hard) playing surface, touching and kicking it (slightly or powerfully).

Dribble the ball in difficult conditions or situations involving heavy physical load
Dribble the ball on a slight slope or on a very uneven ground. Dribble the ball after strenuous physical exercise.

Dribble the ball in conditions that go far beyond what the player is required to do in standard matches
Arrange a relay competition dividing the players into several groups and asking each player to dribble two or three balls simultaneously from one place to another.

Tactical variations

Enhancing dribbling technique with opposition
Suggest all the various situations of play arranging them so as to follow a particular coaching progression.

3.4 CONTROLLING THE BALL

Definition: Controlling the ball is one of the basic techniques of playing soccer, which implies the ability to read the path of the ball so as to control and direct it in a particular direction, choosing the most suitable part of the body to make contact with the ball before receiving it.

Description: When a player is particularly skillful at receiving and controlling the ball, in general this means that his technical skills have achieved a considerably high standard. If a player never (or almost never) fails to make "the first control of ball", this ensures his team the opportunity to maintain possession of the ball and further develop the play. As a matter of fact, in this way the player can avoid – even in very restricted spaces – defensive actions such as pressure and double teaming.

Modern soccer is constantly trying to reduce time and space in order to favor quick actions, one-touch play and, in more general terms, to increase the speed of the performance of any technical move. Consequently, this has obviously contributed to shorten the time available for a player to "stop" the ball as close to his body as possible and control it in the best way possible, thus making the following technical move (passing, shooting, dribbling and so forth) much easier to perform.

It is possible to classify all the various ways to control the ball according to the different parts of the body which a player uses to make contact with the ball and according to the paths of the ball itself. It is also fundamental to remember that the player should carefully assess any particular situation of play and consequently decide if it is better to control the ball on the spot or stop it and run in relation to the movements and the positions of the opposition.

The main principles every player should remember while controlling the ball in any way include:

❏ decide early which part of the body will make contact with the ball
❏ retract the part of the body touching the ball as soon as it makes contact with it
❏ try to relax the part of the body in contact with the ball

If we analyze the technical movement of controlling the ball more carefully, we realize how important it is for a player to enhance his coordination capacities, since coordination is a prerequisite element to learn any technical move. For a player to successfully stop and control the ball, it is first of all necessary to properly read the path of the coming ball, which means assessing the height, the length, the speed and the exact point where the ball coming towards him will land (perception of the relation between space and time).

If he wants to control the ball successfully, he should also stand as close as possible to the place where the ball is falling. If he cannot move and take the right position at the right time, he cannot but stretch out with part of his body to reach the ball and is therefore likely to make a bad control of the ball because of his moving late and standing in poor balance while touching it (perception of one's body moving in space and time).

After moving and taking the right position to control the ball – that is the point in space where the path of the ball and the path of the player moving towards the ball meet – the player prepares to make contact with the ball by putting all the weight of his body on the standing leg and keeping his arms wide open so as to find and maintain a posture of maximum stability (balance).

Meanwhile, the leg the player uses to control the ball begins to move towards the ball itself until it slightly retracts just before making contact, so that the body surface touching the ball is kept as relaxed as possible, otherwise the ball would bounce away. The muscles involved in the movement should be relaxed in order to deaden the impact and consequently reduce the power of the ball. This is why the player should be asked to make a slight jump with the standing leg towards the ball, which would allow the controlling leg to decontract more to make the movement (which involves kinesthetic-muscular sensibility, differentiation capacity, perception of the time and the width of the movement of the leg receiving the ball).

Furthermore, the player should decide as soon as possible how he is going to control the ball; obviously, the more the player has enhanced his technical abilities, coordination and skill, the more he is likely to change his mind suddenly and stop the ball successfully. By contrast, the lower the technical level, the greater the need to make decisions early (ability to adjust and change one's movements).

From this short analysis of this technical move, it emerges that the most common mistakes that players make while controlling the ball are due to:
❏ inaccurate reading of the path of the ball
❏ waiting for the ball to approach without moving towards it
❏ focusing solely on the ball, thus reducing the field of vision
❏ not relaxing the part of the body making contact with the ball
❏ poor muscular sensibility.

Diagram 1 summarizes very synthetically what we have been pointing out up to now.

The following **coaching unit** mainly aims at coaching and enhancing controlling skills, both standing on the spot or while moving, to receive and control a ball describing a lobbed path with the most suitable part of the body. This work unit also helps focus the attention on perceiving the relation between time and space, that is on those space and time operations necessary to make contact with the ball successfully in the best way possible.

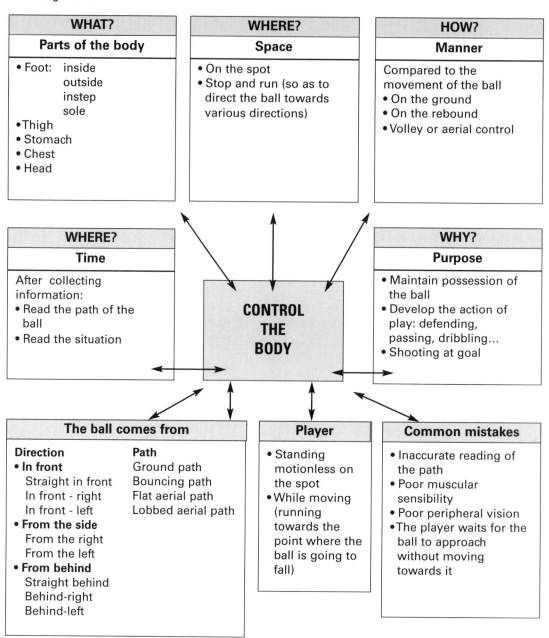

WHAT? **Parts of the body**	WHERE? **Space**	HOW? **Manner**
• Foot: inside outside instep sole • Thigh • Stomach • Chest • Head	• On the spot • Stop and run (so as to direct the ball towards various directions)	Compared to the movement of the ball • On the ground • On the rebound • Volley or aerial control

WHERE? **Time**		WHY? **Purpose**
After collecting information: • Read the path of the ball • Read the situation	**CONTROL THE BODY**	• Maintain possession of the ball • Develop the action of play: defending, passing, dribbling... • Shooting at goal

The ball comes from		**Player**	**Common mistakes**
Direction • **In front** Straight in front In front - right In front - left • **From the side** From the right From the left • **From behind** Straight behind Behind-right Behind-left	**Path** Ground path Bouncing path Flat aerial path Lobbed aerial path	• Standing motionless on the spot • While moving (running towards the point where the ball is going to fall)	• Inaccurate reading of the path • Poor muscular sensibility • Poor peripheral vision • The player waits for the ball to approach without moving towards it

The starting games are generally designed to help the player gradually become familiar with reading and assessing high and short paths (through such games as "**NAME THE BALL**"), or high and long lobs (like in "**THROW OR PASS THE BALL OVER THE OPPOSITION**"), while always practicing in a ludic and playful atmosphere. Obviously, the coaching progressions and the variations suggested in these pages cannot be condensed in one single training session, but should be considered as a point of reference for a long-term planning of one's coaching activity. The exercises carried out in pairs are intended to help players learn and improve ball control on the spot – both while standing motionless and while moving – which involves refined balance skills and the capacity to control one's muscles.

It is evident that, according to the level of skill the player has achieved and in relation to the progressive development of one's coaching controlling technique, it will

be necessary to adjust or modify:
❏ the size of the square playing areas
❏ the distances between the players
❏ the speed at which the ball is played
❏ the weight and the form of the ball
❏ the type of path
❏ the number of sets and repetitions for each exercise

COACHING UNIT

Age: 11 to 13 year olds
Primary specific goal: controlling technique
Secondary specific goal: enhancing space and time perception
Instruments: stopwatch
Equipment: cones, 8 colored training pinnies, 8 balls
Contents: practice in pairs, 1 v 1 and 2 v 1 situations, team games 4 v 4 and 8 v 8
Methods: directive and prescriptive coaching method, problem solving
Test: accurate observation of the conditioned game
Suggestion for the following session: defend and screen the ball
Starting game: "NAME THE BALL" AND "THROW OR PASS THE BALL OVER THE OPPOSITION"
Analytical exercises: exercises in pairs to practice and improve ball control on the spot
Situations of play:
• 1 v 1 control and screen the ball
• 1 v 1 control and dribble the ball
• 2 v 1 control and pass the ball
• 2 v 1 control the ball and support
Conditioned game: 6 v 6 with two players receiving and controlling the ball moving on the playing area
Final game: unconditioned practice match with two goalkeepers on one half of the field

---

In practice, the coach should change all the variations affecting the manners of the performance which will help the player – if properly combined together – internalize and reinforce flexible automatic mechanisms which can be easily adjusted to the unpredictable nature typical of situational sports. In fact, great attention is focused on enhancing "open skills" which the player will apply to in the development of the situations of play suggested, that require the player to control the ball in the way that best suits the situation and allows him to achieve the final goal. For example, if there is enough room to dribble the ball forward, the player should concentrate on receiving and controlling the ball in a way that favors dribbling. By contrast, if the opponent is standing at his back (very close to him) the player should control the ball in front, shielding it with his own body in order to prevent the opponent from tackling him.

In short, the player learns to choose the best way to control the ball by reading the opponent's behavior and movements while always trying to make the next technical move (screening the ball, shooting, dribbling, passing and so forth) as easy as possible to perform. This is why it is also fundamental for a player to enhance peripheral vision before, while and after making the technical move. The coach can use **table 1** (on page 124) "Combining technical moves before or after dribbling the ball" as a point of reference to plan his coaching suggestions on ball control, including all the possible movements that may either precede and therefore prepare or follow the controlling move and at which this technique is aimed.

The conditioned game is a test that allows the coach to monitor the level of skill the player has achieved; in particular, it helps evaluate the controlling technique from the point of view of the effectiveness of the move and of the quality of the technique as well. This is an exercise based on ball possession involving directional pressure, which can develop through short or long playing, according to the circumstances and situations occurring during the course of the match.

Playing the final game at the end of the training session is always an enjoyable and stimulating experience for the players and also allows the coach to check the information his players have absorbed and internalized in a context that is similar to real-game situations. In order to complete the progression on practical suggestions, diagram 10 shows the basic exercise to coach and learn controlling technique involving stopping the ball and running, that is the ability to direct ball control towards different directions in relation to the needs of the match. This ability involves the player anticipating the play and, in particular, the movements of the opponents standing closer to the action, in order to spot open spaces where the ball should be played. Starting from this analytical exercise the coach can plan and build the whole coaching unit to practice stop and run, using the training method structured in several different phases; the last step is the conditioned practice match (2 or 3 touches of the ball are allowed).

Starting games

Play the ball over the opposition

The kicker of the attacking squad standing in area A makes a lob pass into zone C – occupied by the opposition - passing over central zone B. One point is awarded every time the ball hits the ground in the case where the defenders are allowed to catch it with their hands or – when they are only allowed to control the ball with their feet – they make a poor touch, letting the ball roll out of the playing area, for example. We suggest organizing the game as follows, so as to plan a suitable coaching progression concerning the performance of both the kicking and the controlling technical movement (**diagram 1**).

Kick the ball	Control the ball
The goalkeeper holds the ball in his hands and kicks it into area ⇨	with the hands
The goalkeeper holds the ball in his hands and kicks it into area ⇨	with the feet
The player kicks the ball off a stationary cone (tee)	⇨ with the feet
The player kicks the ball after juggling	⇨ with the feet

Variation: Every time the attacking squad score one point, the players of the two teams switch their positions, rotating like in volleyball.
Purpose: Read the lobbed path of the ball and control the ball in a global form in various manners.

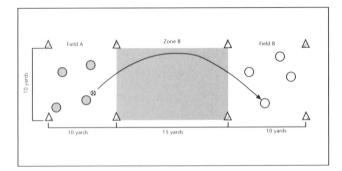

Diagram 1

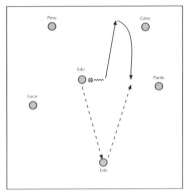

Diagram 2

Name the ball
A group of 5 or 6 players without the ball position on the playing area to form a circle at the center of which is the player in possession of the ball. The player in possession has to sky the ball, hitting it as high as he can, so that it lands inside the circle; while kicking the ball he also calls the name of one of his fellow players who has to leave his outside position and sprint into the circle to meet and control the ball, while the kicking player runs to take his position. There is a penalty if the player controlling the ball lets it fall to the ground (when he can catch it with his hands) or if he makes a bad control of the ball (when he is only allowed to use his feet). We suggest you develop a suitable coaching progression focusing on the performance of both the kicking and the controlling technical movement (**diagram 2**).

Kick or throw the ball	Control the ball
The player throws the ball high in the air with both hands	⇨ with the hands
The player throws the ball high in the air with both hands	⇨ with the feet
The goalkeeper holds the ball in his hands and skies it with his foot	⇨ with the hands
The goalkeeper holds the ball in his hands and skies it with his foot	⇨ with the feet
The player skies the ball high in the air after juggling	⇨ with the feet

Variation: Play using two balls.

Purpose: Read the lobbed path of the ball and control the ball in a global form, in various manners.

EXERCISES

In **diagram 3**, player A plays the ball to his teammate B with a lobbed pass. B is standing inside a 5 x 5 yard square area and has to control the ball while trying to keep it within his own playing area.

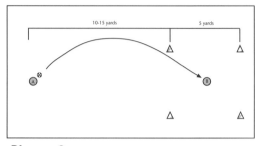

Diagram 3

How to play the ball: Throw it with the hands, kick it like a goalkeeper clearing the ball away, kick it after juggling.

How to control the ball: Control the ball using the most suitable parts of the body to meet lobbed passes (the instep, the inside of the foot, the thigh, the chest and the head, in particular) on the volley, that is taking the ball to the ground by retracting the controlling body surface as soon as it makes contact with the ball.

Purpose: Learn and improve controlling technique standing in a stationary position to receive balls describing lobbed paths.

Variations:

❏ Player B starts from outside the square, running forward to meet the ball inside the square.

❏ Player B starts from outside the square, running backward to meet the ball inside the square area.

Purpose: Learn and improve controlling technique moving in different directions to meet lobbed balls.

In **diagram 4**, player A, standing in a 5 x 5 yard playing area, plays the ball to his teammate B, who is standing at a distance of about 10 to 15 yards in a square area of the same size. Before giving the starting signal, the coach sets the conditions for the two players to play and control the ball; the game

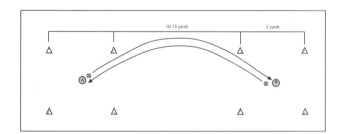

Diagram 4

can develop as a competition in pairs. Count the number of successful controls (inside the marked playing area) or bad traps out of 10 repetitions.

Variation: Play and control two balls at the same time.

Purpose: Test the players' ability to stop and control lobbed passes.

Situations of play

1 v 1 situation (**diagram 5**). Player A is standing in an 8 x 8 yard square area: he juggles the ball freely and then skies it high in the air. At the moment when the ball

reaches its peak and then begins to fall down, player B - who was standing outside the square – promptly sprints inside the area to try to win possession of the ball, challenging his opponent A who has to control the ball and screen it for about 10 seconds. Player B is awarded one point if he manages to kick the ball out of the square, and two points if he manages to win possession of the ball and maintain it for the set time (10 seconds).

Purpose: Control and screen the ball.

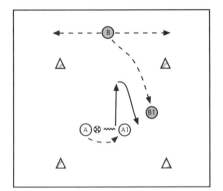

Diagram 5

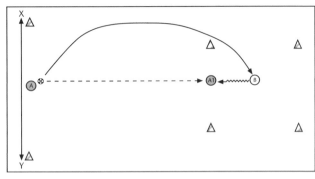

Diagram 6

1 v 1 situation (**diagram 6**). Player A is defending line X and Y between the two cones placed at a distance of about 30 yards from a 5 x 5 yard square playing area where player B is standing. Player A lobs the ball to B and promptly sprints to attack and put pressure on his opponent in order to prevent him from dribbling the ball past him and gaining space upward, crossing the X-Y line.

Purpose: Control the ball and dribble.

2 v 1 situation (**diagram 7**). In a 12 x 8 yard rectangular area marked out at the edge of the penalty box, player C makes a lobbed pass to his teammate A who is standing inside the rectangle to meet the ball and is immediately pressed by his opponent D, who sprints from the penalty spot as soon as the ball leaves the penalty box. Player A controls the ball and decides whether to move to shoot at goal playing 1 v 1, (dribble past his opponent) or play 2 v 1 with the help of player C who has approached to support the attack

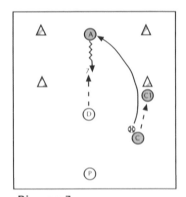

Diagram 7

and perform a wall-pass if necessary.

Purpose: Shoot at goal with the help of a supporting teammate.

2 v 1 situation (**diagram 8**). Mark out a 12 x 8 yard rectangular area at the edge of the penalty box; player C lobs the ball to A. Player A is standing in the rectangle to meet the ball; he is promptly pressed at his back by his opponent D, the defender, who starts from outside the marked zone when player A touches the ball. At this point, there are two different solutions for the player in possession of the ball; he can either:
❏ control the ball and turn around either to dribble or shoot at goal;

❏ or control the pass, screen the ball and make a back pass to his supporting team-mate to play 2 v 1 for the final shot on goal.

Purpose: Control the ball while being pressed from behind by the defender and play to shoot at goal with the help of a supporting teammate.

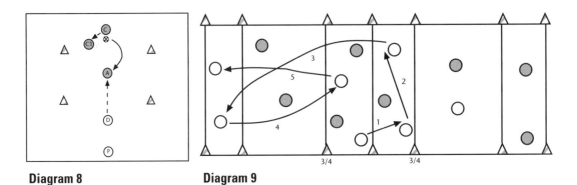

Diagram 8   **Diagram 9**

Conditioned game

Mark out a 40 x 25 yard playing field where two teams play 5 v 5 or 6 v 6 to maintain ball possession making lobbed passes. The lobbed passes can only be made from the central zone and must be directed towards one of the two target areas. Two players are standing in each of the two target areas and move to meet the passes and control the ball. When they receive the ball, they promptly kick it back into the playing field with lobbed shots or ground passes. Any one of the players standing in the playing area can move to meet the ball and give a return pass to one of the receiving teammates in the target area: in this case, the team is awarded one point (**diagram 9**).

Variations: The players receiving the ball in the targets areas can move freely and play with no conditions; they can move freely but play 2 or 3 touches; they are marked very closely (man-to-man marking).

Purpose: Alternate situations where the players control the ball while playing over long distances (making lobbed passes) and over short distances (giving ground passes).

Stop the ball and run (diagram 10)

Player A plays the ball to his teammate B with various paths (ground, bouncing or aerial passes). Player B is standing in a 5 x 5 yard square and is only allowed 2 or 3 touches of the ball to control the pass and dribble the ball out of the square area to pass it back to his teammate A and immediately restart the game. Player B can direct his control of the ball to the eight possible directions so as to form 45° - 90° - 135° - 180° angles between the path of the ball played into the square and the path of the ball played out of the square.

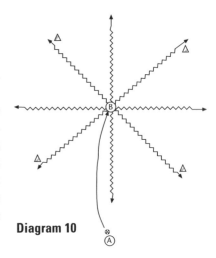

Diagram 10

3.5 HEADING THE BALL

Definition: Heading the ball is another basic technique of playing soccer, which refers to the ability to hit the ball with one's head in both attacking and defensive situations of play.

Description: In many cases, heading the ball is a particularly exciting and extraordinary movement attracting the attention of the public; think of the frequent aerial struggles between an attacker and the opposing goalkeeper, or a diving header at goal.

The technical movement of heading the ball can be divided into three different phases:

1. The starting phase or preparation phase when the body prepares to make contact with the ball, arching the back backward because of the contraction of the sacrospinal muscles.
2. The main phase or "closing" phase when the head makes contact with the ball; the impact results from a stimulating strength impulse starting from the lower limbs vigorously stretching out, thus projecting the body towards the ball by bending the trunk forward and ending with the head rapidly bowing to meet the ball.
3. The final phase or compensation phase when the player needs to restore a position of balance, allowing him to perform the next tactical action. For example, if the player ends his heading move standing with his legs wide apart on the sagittal plane (that is one leg in front of the body and the other at the back) as if he were taking a step, this position allows him to quickly start running to elude the opponent's marking or to sprint to meet the ball kicked back by the goalkeeper.

A player can head the ball with his forehead (the frontal bone), which ensures power and accuracy of the move; with the right or the left part of the head (the parietal and temporal bone) in order to swerve the ball; or with the area of the head between the hair line and the nape so as to aim the ball backward. When heading the ball backward, the preparation phase involves bending the trunk forward, while in the "closing" phase the trunk and the body stretch out backward.

This technical move can be used both in the defensive phase (aerial tackle, clearing pass, intercepting the ball) and in attack (shooting at goal or passing, for example).

For a player to head the ball effectively and successfully, not only are such attributes as elevation, speed force and muscular features of critical importance, but it is also fundamental to properly time the perception of the relation between time and space, which allows the player to carefully assess the path of the ball and consequently time his movements. In fact, practicing heading skills considerably helps activate the sense to anticipate the paths of the ball.

The player can head the ball:
❏ while standing in a stationary position
   1. with his feet in contact with the ground

❏ while moving
1. running to meet the ball
2. taking off
3. diving

Many players are inhibited from performing this technical move by fear of injury and consequently refuse to engage in aerial challenges or tackles. Brave players who can properly time their movements and have suitably enhanced their elevation capacities do not stand waiting for the ball to come and letting the ball touch them, but directly attack the ball moving towards it so as to meet its path with great determination and opportunism, always keeping the muscles of the neck perfectly stretched out while the head is making contact with the ball. At a purely didactic level, it is important for a coach to help his players become familiar with this technical movement in order to avoid creating in them inhibitory restraints. This is why children should first practice this technique using small and soft balls describing slow and lobbed paths. When the children have experienced the pleasure of heading the ball by playing and enjoying themselves, the coach can then start examining the technical movement in all its different phases, using larger and heavier balls, inflated at a measured pressure, and practicing heading balls with faster and flatter flight paths.

The mistakes players commonly make while heading the ball include:
❏ closing the eyes when the head makes contact with the ball
❏ waiting for the ball to approach
❏ using only the movement of the head without flinging the whole body forward
❏ mainly using the right or left part of the head to make contact with the ball
  instead of the frontal area

The following **tables** briefly summarize what has been explained up to now.

HEADING THE BALL				
WHAT?	**WHERE?**	**HOW?**	**WHEN?**	**WHY?**
Areas of the head	**Space**	**Manner**	**Time**	**Purpose**
• Frontal area (forehead) • Right or left area (parietal bone) (temporal bone) • Upper area (from the forehead to the nape)	• Forward • Backward • To the right or to the left	• In relation to the player's state of motion • From a stationary position • While moving 1. Run up 2. Take off from a stationary position 3. Run up and take off 4. Dive	After collecting the necessary information: • Read the path of the ball • Assess the situation of play That is after anticipating: • The coordinates for the impact with the ball • The goal to achieve	• **Defensive phase** 1. Clear the ball 2. Intercept the ball 3. Aerial tackle or challenge • **Offensive phase** 1. Shoot at goal 2. Pass the ball

THE BALL COMES FROM		THE BALL COMES FROM	
The ball comes from	**The path**	**The ball is headed**	**The path**
• **In front**	• Ground path	• **Forward**	• Ground path
Straight in front	• Bouncing path	Straight forward	• Bouncing path
In front – on the right	• Flat aerial path	Forward – to the right	• Flat aerial path
In front – on the left	• Lobbed aerial path	Forward – to the left	• Lobbed aerial
• **The side**		• **To the side**	path
The right		To the right	
The left		To the left	
• **Behind**		• **Backward**	
Straight behind		Straight backward	
Behind – on the right		Backward – to the right	
Behind – on the left		Backward – to the left	

COACHING UNIT

Age: 11 to 13 year olds
Primary operative goal: head the ball with the forehead, standing in a stationary position, head a ball coming from in front describing a lobbed path aiming it forward so as to make it follow a flat path
Secondary specific goal: static balance and dynamic balance
Instruments: stopwatch
Equipment: disc cones, training pinnies, 16 balls
Contents: exercises in pairs and in groups of three players each, team games, 5 v 5, unconditioned game
Coaching methods: deductive – inductive
Suggestion for the following session: depends on the outcome of the test
Warm up phase:
• Free standing exercises to stretch one's muscles
• Coach how to make step
• Heading juggles
Starting games: attack the castle
Analytical exercises: throw and head the ball in pairs
Situations of play:
• 1 v goalkeeper to score a goal
• 1 v 1 + goalkeeper to score a goal
Conditioned game: 5 v 5 + 2 heading players (the towers) from the goal line
Final game: unconditioned game with two goalkeepers in one half of the playing field

THE WARM UP PHASE

1. Free standing exercises
The very first minutes of each training session are dedicated to warming up which means loosening up one's muscles and suitably moving the backbone, the neck and the shoulders to make them more relaxed and mobile; the coach should suggest very easy exercises and light activities aimed at bending, stretching, twisting and rotating the various segments of the body.
Purpose: limber up the various segments of the body involved in the act of heading the ball.

2. Coaching how to make steps
The act of heading the ball standing in a stationary position starts from the feet, in the sense that it is fundamental to maintain a posture of perfect balance on the feet in order to convey greater power to the ball. For example, in order to head the ball while standing in a stationary position with the legs wide apart on the frontal plane, the starting phase of the movement (i.e. the preparation phase) involves the player transferring the weight of his body on his heels, while in the main phase of the move (when the head makes contact with the ball) the weight of the body is equally distributed on the soles of the feet, and in the last phase (the compensation phase) the weight of the body concentrates on the front parts of the feet. It is also true that the whole movement can be made while standing in a position of balance on the front parts of the feet , starting from total "suppleness"; however, it is very important for a player to learn how to control all the various pressures that the movements of his body combined together put on his feet. It is therefore advisable to ask the player to swing his body forward and backward, to the right and to the left - and suggest other combinations of movements – without losing balance or accentuating the postures to the maximum degree until he finally loses balance.
Purpose: perceive and internalize different postures of balance.

3. Heading juggles
The last few minutes of the warm up phase are dedicated to individual heading juggles suitably suggested to follow a special coaching progression: the players start the exercise holding the balls in their hands, then they make some repetitions of consecutive heading juggles and finally juggle the ball heading it against a wall.
Purpose: make the player more sensitive to the contact between the forehead and the ball.

Starting game

Attack the castle (diagram A)
The three players on the team standing in area A cooperate with the three players occupying zone C and pass the ball to each other by throwing it with their hands in order to head the ball while standing in a stationary position to hit one of the opponents, who are free to move within their zone B. Count the number of opponents they strike by heading the ball in two minutes' time.
Variations:
❏ for the attacking players:

- pass the ball while making heading juggles
- pass the ball while throwing in
❏ for the defenders:
- move on the knees, while sitting or while lying face down
- play using two balls

Purpose: Gradually become familiar with the heading movement in a global form.

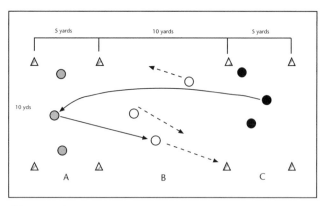

Diagram A

Analytical exercises

Throw and head the ball in pairs (diagram B)
Player A lobs the ball forward to his teammate B. Player B heads the ball using his forehead while standing in a stationary position so as to passing it forward with a flat path (at various heights, downward, upward). How should the ball be headed? Where should it be headed?
Variations:
Different postures

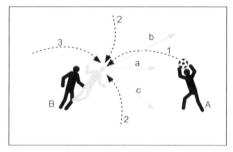

Diagram B

Player B learns to head the ball while remaining in a stationary position, while sitting first, then down on his knees sitting on his heels, down on his knees and finally standing on his feet.
For the lower limbs: Player B is standing without moving and tries to head the ball while balancing on one foot, on both feet close together, with his feet wide apart on the frontal plane, and wide apart on the sagittal plane (one foot in front of the other). What are the differences? What are the advantages and the disadvantages of these positions?
For the upper limbs: Player B first heads the ball without the support of his upper limbs which he keeps perfectly rigid at his sides as if he were a soldier, then while crossing his arms in front of himself and finally at his back. What are the differences? What are the advantages and the disadvantages of these positions?
Purposes:
❏ Feel the importance of keeping the arms wide while heading the ball in order to favor the movement of the trunk and maintain balance
❏ Perceive the importance of the supporting bases (position of the feet) helping to maintain steady postures
❏ Directly experience that the possibility to convey power to the ball depends on the postures of the body as a whole and on the harmony of the movements of all the various body segments
❏ Head the ball so as to change its aerial path: the lobbed path of the coming ball becomes a flat path after the header.

Situations of play

1 v goalkeeper (diagram 15)
The goalkeeper throws the ball towards the attacking player trying to make it follow a lobbed path. The attacker is standing near the penalty spot and tries to head the ball at goal without moving. He can try ten times; how many goals can he score?
Variations:
❏ After throwing the ball, the goalkeeper leaves the goal line and sprints towards the attacker. What should the attacking player do to score a goal? A lob? Where should he head the ball?
❏ After throwing the ball, the goalkeeper moves towards the post on his right or on his left. Where can the attacking player score a goal? What should he do to aim the ball at the top or at the bottom corner of the goal? Does he need to position so as to direct his body towards the target keeping his head steady or does he need to turn his head? In either of the two cases, where should he hit the ball?
Purpose: Use the most suitable heading technique to achieve the final goal: to score a goal.

1 v 1 + goalkeeper
The goalkeeper throws the ball towards two contending players. They start from different positions (sitting on the ground, lying face down, or on their knees, for example), stand up and struggle to win possession of the ball first and score a goal.
Variations:
❏ After deciding who is the attacker and who is the defender of the two contending players, the attacker starts before the defender, one yard ahead. How should the attacker move while always trying to keep the defender at his back? How can he look at the ball, the goalkeeper and the opponent at the same time?
❏ The defender starts before the attacker, one yard ahead. Imagine that the defender manages to win possession of the ball first, what should he do? Does he pass the ball back to the goalkeeper? Does he score an own goal? Does he aim the ball at the goal line for a corner kick? Does he aim the ball backward towards the playing field?
Purposes:
❏ Choose the right movement at the right time to achieve the goal
❏ Head the ball both in the defending and in the attacking phase

Conditioned game

Heading pass (tower) from the goal line (diagram C)
5 v 5 or 6 v 6 conditioned match played on a 40 x 30 yard field with two goals, two goalkeepers and two heading players (the towers) for each team, standing behind the two goal lines as in the diagram.

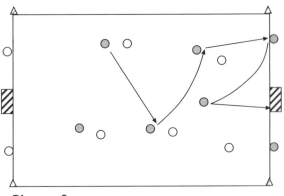

Diagram C

The two teams play trying to cross lobbed balls to their own towers, who promptly head them back, making passes into the playing field to their teammates who continue the game trying to shoot at goal.

Variations:

❏ Play handball to achieve the same goals

❏ Play trying to make ground passes to the two towers. They are allowed two touches of the ball to control the pass and make a cross towards the playing field for their teammates to head the ball at goal.

Purpose: Favor and use the heading technique also while playing matches – both in the defensive and in the attacking phase – to meet crosses coming from in front and following lobbed paths.

Diving Header

The heading technique can be considered as one of the most complex movements to coach and learn in soccer, both due to biomechanical and technical causes and because of psychological reasons as well. There are schools in which playing soccer – typically considered as something athletic and vigorous - is essentially based on physical challenges and aerial tackles; so, if the players are able to perform these movements effectively and successfully, the exciting and spectacular nature of soccer is revealed. This is why it is undoubtedly fundamental to develop players who are particularly skillful at heading the ball, both in the defensive phase and on attack. In particular, this type of tactical and strategic solution encourages the contestants to make acrobatic technical moves, such as scissor kicks, volleys, sliding tackles, falls to the ground after being tackled and diving headers. We now want to focus the attention on the diving heading technique, encouraging coaches to think that coaching and training pre-acrobatic skills should not be considered as an end in itself, since in the match pre-acrobatic abilities are directly combined with many different technical moves and consequently involved in various situations of play. Our coaching suggestion is based on the standard training method involving several phases and includes a set of progressions which should be considered as points of reference. The following coaching progressions should be distributed in different training sessions, always carefully considering the level of physical and athletic maturation and the coordination capacities of the players – specifically when planning the coaching activity in relation to the various age groups. Anyway, good heading skills both while standing in a stationary position and while jumping are prerequisite in the following coaching progressions.

The starting games favor a global approach to the heading movement in general, and to the heading technique while diving in particular, in a fun context which creates a positive atmosphere conducive to further learning.

The progression of free standing exercises is aimed at learning how to fall first and then dive; this means that it helps overcome the fear of getting hurt, which represents the emotional factor inhibiting many players from making acrobatic technical movements. Overcoming the fear of the impact of the body against the ground by learning and enhancing suitable landing techniques is the primary goal in this case. In fact, all the activities suggested put the young player in the condition to gradually become familiar with the ground and the various parts of his body – or better, the different body segments – through special exercises and games involving contact between the body and the ground. In particular, we want to insist on the coaching progression on palmar supports (i.e. the hands) which will prove fundamental to deaden the force of the impact of the body against the ground after heading the ball while diving.

Training and mastering all the various postures while standing in a stationary position and while moving also favors the development of the arm muscles – which are often ignored in the conditioning of soccer players – and tones up the muscles of the stomach and the back as well. Obviously, these exercises should be combined and alternated with special activities stimulating joint mobility and muscle stretching, as well as with relaxation exercises (**diagrams 12 and 13**). Actually, strenuous exercise should always be followed by or combined with light, moderate and relaxing activity. We also recommend – specifically at the very early stages of the learning process and while developing more complex skills – using suitable equipment including thin foam-rubber mattresses or other soft landing surfaces which can be found in gymnasiums, for example, maybe with the support and assistance of a trainer. Preventing injuries – specifically in training sessions - is a duty of the coach and a right of every young soccer player. In this way, the player grows and matures while acquiring self-confidence and assurance and progressively enhancing the capacity to control and master his body in dynamic situations and in conditions of aerial balance, from which result the spirit of daring needed to make acrobatic technical movements and the "rashness" of getting into the scrimmage to head the ball while diving.

The progression of analytical exercises offers the youth soccer player the possibility to test his capacity to control his body while dealing with the ball and making movements in the air. Also in this case, the fear of getting hurt when heading a hard and heavy ball may inhibit the player; this is why it is recommended to approach the standard conditions gradually, using soft and light balls to practice at the beginning – foam rubber balls, for example – specifically if we ask them to perform the various exercises several times. While practicing these activities the youth player will progressively become aware of the need to properly perceive the relation between time and space in order to:
❏ assess the path of the coming ball
❏ assess the speed of the ball
❏ time the heading movement so that the head makes contact with the ball at the right time
❏ anticipate the exact point in space where the head will make contact with the ball
❏ anticipate and direct the path of the headed pass.

The progression on the situations of play allows the player to perform acrobatic technical moves in relation to a specific goal. In simpler playing situations, the final purpose is to score a goal trying to elude the goalkeeper and using peripheral vision. As the situations of play become more complex, the players try to achieve the same final goal but have to deal with the active resistance of their opposition, which should be introduced gradually so that the fear of tackles, physical challenge and body contact does not become a negative factor inhibiting players from learning and refining the technical move in a context of competitive "duel".

Lastly, **the conditioned game** becomes a helpful and convincing test for the coach to monitor the quality of the coaching and learning process he is developing; consequently, the conditioned practice match allows the coach to assess the capacity of the young athlete to properly master his body and control his movements in any situation of play, performing moves of refined coordination and technique in real-game conditions.

Starting games

Strike a fixed target
Mark out a 25 x 10 yard playing area and divide it in 5 different zones: two A zones, two B zones and a central lane 5 yards wide where you will place some cones representing the fixed targets that the players will try to strike. This is a competition between two teams who position on the playing field as follows: the players in zone A have a ball each and head or throw the ball to their teammates in zone B; the players in zone B head the balls delivered by their teammates trying to strike or knock down the cones; they score two points if they manage to strike a cone with a diving header. The players in zone A, after delivering the ball, try to prevent the headed balls from hitting the cones using their bodies as shields (they are allowed to use their hands or not) (**diagram 1**). How many points can each squad score in a 3 to 5 minute game?
Variation: Play with two balls.

Strike a moving target
Mark out a 25 x 10 yard playing field with a central zone 5 yards wide dividing the

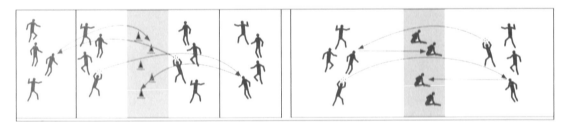

Diagram 1   **Diagram 2**

field in two halves. In this central lane are four target players who, starting from a sitting position, can move within their playing area on all fours, rolling or crawling, but without standing up. In the two halves of the playing field are two groups of players who throw the ball to each other; they try to hit the target players by heading the ball. The player who manages to strike the target by heading the ball while diving scores two points (**diagram 2**). How many points can they score in three minutes? What is the final individual score for each player and the global score of each team?
Variation: Play using two balls.

Progression of fitness exercises (pre-acrobatic skills)

Abdominal exercises
Do three sets of 6 to 7 repetitions of abdominal exercises, keeping your legs bent and without completely closing the angle between the trunk and the lower limbs in order to protect the lumbar region of the back bone (see **diagram 3**).
Purposes: Improve stomach muscles, use your arms as a sort of balance bar, exploiting their flinging movement to overcome the inertia of the trunk.

In front of a wall
Stand facing a wall and push your hands against the wall. Three sets of ten repetitions (**diagram 4**).
Variation: Start from a standing position in front of the wall and fall towards the wall pushing with your hands so as to reduce the force of the impact and promptly push your body back to recover the starting position.
Purposes: Tone the upper arm muscles, enhance the sensitivity of the palmar supports (keep your hands wide open so that the surface of contact between the palm of your hand and the wall is larger) orienting them in any direction (up and down, to the right and to the left).

Keep your body straight moving on all fours
Practice and master the posture shown in the diagram below lying in a stationary position and while moving to and fro (forward and backward, to the right and to the left); turning around your axis. In order to prevent injuries and pain, you should avoid arching your back (hyperlordosis of the lumbar region), keeping the pelvis straight in line with the legs and the trunk (**diagram 5**).

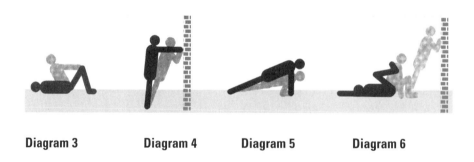

| Diagram 3 | Diagram 4 | Diagram 5 | Diagram 6 |

Variation: Do a quarter push-up.
Purpose: Improve the muscle groups of the arms and the back, enhance the sensitivity of the palmar supports while supporting the weight of the body.

Crawl and roll on the ground
Crawl and roll on the ground freely or using special techniques to move: for example, moving at a leopard's pace.
Purposes: Reinforce and enhance basic motor patterns; perceive and master the impact with the ground, in particular the contact between your chest and the ground.

Roll on your back and…stand up (fall down sitting on the ground and…roll on your back)
Roll on your back, leaning the palms of your hands on the ground while sitting and, in contrast, the backs of your hands while rolling on the ground in order to avoid compressing the cervical region of the back bone. We also recommend keeping your knees wide apart in order to avoid hurting your face (**diagram 6**).
Variation: Roll on your back, sit down and stand up by pushing your arms down on the ground (the hands offer a solid support to reach a standing position) with no pauses, that is without interrupting or breaking your movements, and viceversa.
Purposes: Perform and master the rolling backward and the standing up movements using your hands as helpful supports both to push down on the ground and to absorb the shock of the impact with the ground.

Sit down
You are sitting on the ground moving forward and backward, to the right and to the left, turning around yourself using your hands as supports and orienting them in any direction (**diagram 7**).
Purposes: Tone up the arm muscles, handle and combine the supports of your hands, feet and pelvis.

Move on all fours
Start from a position on all fours (four supports) with your hands and feet on the ground and let your body fall down and forward, absorbing your weight and the shock of the movement with your arms (**diagram 8**).
Purpose: Handle and overcome the first level of difficulty in falling forward (capacity to fall down properly).

Kneel down
Starting from a kneeling position, let your body fall down and forward on the ground, absorbing the shock of the impact with your arms (**diagram 9**).

Diagram 7   Diagram 8   Diagram 9   Diagram 10

Purpose: Handle and overcome the second level of difficulty in falling forward (don't be afraid of letting your body fall).
Squatting position
Start from a squatting position sitting on the ground with your knees drawn up close to your body and let your body fall down and forward, absorbing the shock of the impact against the ground with your hands (**diagram 10**).
Variation: Push off with your legs so as to turn the fall to the ground into a real diving movement, describing increasingly high arcs while diving.

Purpose: Handle and overcome the first level of difficulty in diving forward (capacity to dive properly).

Standing position
Start from a standing position and let your body fall forward, keeping it perfectly straight, trying to absorb the shock of the impact with the ground using both your arms and a thin foam rubber mattress or a soft surface (sandy or soft grassy ground, for example) (**diagram 11**).
Variation: Take a suitable run up and dive forward.
Purpose: Handle and overcome the second level of difficulty in diving forward (don't be afraid of diving).

Run, take off on the spring board and dive forward
Purpose: Handle and overcome the third level of difficulty in diving forward, which involves the need to prolong the time of the flight to cover increasingly long distances (express courage, spirit and motor skills to make acrobatic diving movements).

1) Relaxing postures
You are lying prone (face downwards) on a table with your legs slightly bent and the balls of your feet on the ground: relax and let the force of gravity cause traction of the lumbar region (**diagram 12**).

2) Relaxing postures
You are lying on your back with your feet up on a chair or another object so as to form a right angle: this position helps decrease the tension and contraction of the lumbar region of your back bone. If you lie in the same position but also use a cervical support (a tennis ball or a rolled towel, for instance) under your nape, in the socket of your neck, you can also relax the cervical region of your back bone (**diagram 13**).

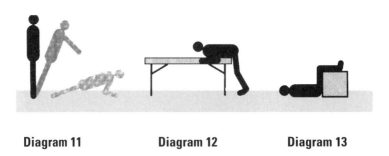

| Diagram 11 | Diagram 12 | Diagram 13 |

Coaching progression of analytical exercises

The first coaching progression includes all the exercises performed with the ball we have shown up to now where it is possible to push a ball using the head so as to make it roll in all the various directions – for example, crawling or moving on all fours in order to enhance the perception of the contact between the body and the ground and the head and the ball at the same time.

The second coaching progression involves the repetition of nearly all the fitness exercises shown in the previous paragraphs which are now performed in pairs with a player holding the ball in his hands and throwing it to his teammate who receives the pass and heads the ball back.

By way of an example, we suggest the activities on heading technique which involve the player falling forward to head the ball starting from a kneeling position and then repeat starting from different postures, following a special progression where the exercises suggested become increasingly difficult. Player A throws the ball forward (1), to the right or to the left (2) and backward (3) using both hands, while his teammate B heads the ball: a) straight, b) up, c) down (**diagram b, page 148**).

Coaching progression on situations of play

In the following situations of play the player scores two points if he manages to score with a diving header. Every player can try ten times: how many goals can each player score?

Situations of play in pairs
The goalkeeper throws the ball towards the attacker who heads the ball to try to score a goal (**diagram 15**).
Three player situation
Player A makes a cross, first throwing the ball and then kicking it to his teammate B who heads the ball to try to score (**diagram 16**).

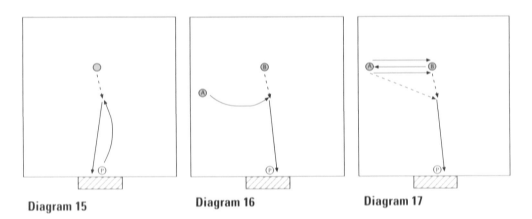

Diagram 15   Diagram 16   Diagram 17

Three player situation
Players A and B head the ball making passes to each other while moving in any direction to finally head at goal and score (**diagram 17**).

Three player situation

The goalkeeper throws or kicks the ball towards the two opposing players who start from different positions and struggle to win possession of the ball and score a goal (**diagram 18**).

Variation: Another player (four player situation) makes a cross from the flank of the field towards one of the two opponents to score.

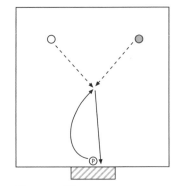

Diagram 18

Four player situation

Player C makes a cross to his teammate
A who tries to elude the marking by his defending opponent B to finally head at goal (**diagram 19**).

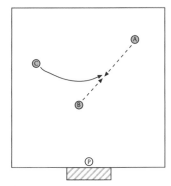

Conditioned game

Play a conditioned practice match using six goals: each team defends and attacks three goals (one in the middle and two at the sides). They are allowed to score heading the ball at goal or taking a volley shot on goal after receiving a headed pass. When a player manages to score with a diving header his team score two points.

Diagram 19

3.6 TAKING THROW-INS

Definition: Basic technique of soccer allowing a player to restart the game by throwing the ball from the point where the ball crossed the touch line.

Description: The laws of the game in soccer prescribe that when the whole of the ball passes over one of the two touch lines, either on the ground or in the air, it shall be thrown in from the point where it crossed the line in any direction, by a player of the team opposite to that of the player who last touched it. At the moment of delivering the ball to restart the game the thrower must face the field of play and use both hands to throw the ball from behind and over his head. As to the practical performance of this basic technical movement it is important to consider two main aspects: the technical and the tactical.

Technical aspect (how to throw in). The player can throw the ball standing in a stationary position or after taking a suitable run up and should hold the ball firmly with his thumbs and fingertips so as to form a sort of a heart turned upside down. He is standing with his legs wide apart on the frontal plane (right and left plane) to take middle-range throw-ins, and wide apart on the sagittal plane (that is one foot in front of the other) to take long-range throw-ins. In fact, keeping the feet wide apart offers a solid supporting base (providing equilibrium) favoring the movement of the legs; the trunk stretches backward, the arms bend to hold the ball behind the head first and then stretch forward over the head to convey power to the ball, transmitting the final drive through the movement of the wrist. It is possible to take longer throw-ins when the player throws the ball after taking a suitable run up. This movement requires refined coordination skills, since the player shall combine: the run up, the movement of the legs, the trunk and the arms in a rhythmical sequence and, in particular, without interrupting or breaking the movements.

Tactical aspect (where to throw the ball). After reading the situation of play (the position of his fellow players and of the opponents on the playing field) the player decides where he should throw the ball; he can take:
❏ a zone throw-in, towards an open area of the field, generally along the running path of one of his teammates; he could also decide to make the ball bounce on the ground before it reaches his teammate
❏ a man-to-man throw-in, which means directly to one of his fellow players, making the ball describe an aerial path aimed at the legs of his teammate; in particular, the ball should be thrown towards the part of the leg between the knee and the foot so that it is much easier for his teammate to control the ball, or directly towards his head so that he can make a heading control or pass.

In modern soccer, 50% of all goals are scored at set plays (direct or indirect free kicks in particular) or in actions directly resulting from these situations of play and the balance of a match – also in youth soccer – is often broken by the abilities of one of the two teams to exploit set play situations successfully due to the individual skills of one single player (the top class player particularly skillful at taking free kicks, for example) or due to the collective abilities of the whole team, able to make organized and effective tactical movements practiced in training sessions.

Throwing-in is a basic technical movement that deserves greater attention from youth coaches, since – at a didactic level – the opportunity to play also using the arms offers significant inputs for the development of coordination capacities and basic motor skills. Furthermore, coaches of higher level teams can undoubtedly benefit from playing athletes who are particularly skillful at taking long throw-ins, since their throw-ins can become real crosses towards the center of the box or strategic passes on the flanks of the field. How can you forget Roberto Baggio's exciting move at USA '94 World Cup when Italy were playing against Bulgaria and Baggio scored a goal after controlling a ball directly from a throw-in?

The coaching unit you will be shown in the following pages is specifically designed to offer hints and suggestions concerning the organization and the order of the various exercises and activities. Using the coaching method involving several progression phases it is possible to set the primary goal and also the secondary purpose of each activity; in this case in particular, among the various inputs of coordination offered by special training, the attention is focused on enhancing space perception and the relation between time and space.

The warm up phase includes the **starting game** which is an example of how it is possible to combine elements of various sports disciplines and apply them to soccer: the players practice different passing and controlling techniques peculiar to various sports and can freely express their skills and creativeness in order to learn how to handle balls of different shapes, sizes and weights with their hands.

In order not to let the ball fall to the ground, the players need to focus their attention on the accuracy of their throwing, after carefully assessing the distance separating them from the point where the ball is controlled. Moreover, they also need to be able to communicate by establishing eye contact, without which it is practically impossible to make the pass; the situation can become more difficult to handle if on the playing field there are several balls and the opposition at the same time, which can create confusion, obstruction, feints, obstacles and interferences that only suitable direct communication can counter.

The **analytical exercises** constitute the second phase of the training session and begin with a game in which the players practice all the various throwing techniques after they have acquired and enhanced basic skills including holding the ball properly in their hands and making the throw-in from their shoulders (the ball makes contact with the back of the neck). When making the throw-in standing with both feet close together the players can feel the need to stretch their body completely (dorsal arch) in order to convey greater power to the ball; avoid excessively intense activity and too many repetitions of the same exercise so as not to hurt or damage the back bone. By contrast, when throwing in with the feet wide apart, the player understands that this conveys greater power to the ball since he is standing on a larger supporting base and in a condition of greater balance (these factors are further improved when the player is standing with his legs wide apart on the sagittal plane, that is with one foot in front of the other). When throwing the ball standing in a stationary position, the players should understand that for the throw-in to be successful, effective and as long as possible, it should start directly from their feet, that is from a solid supporting base which favors the movement of the body (dorsal arch) and that of the upper limbs. The players should also gradually experience that they are more likely to make longer throw-ins if they take a suitable run up. This technical move requires refined coordination, since the player needs to properly combine: the run up, the dorsal arch and the stretching of the upper limbs to throw the ball in rhythmical sequence and progression all in one motion. Doing the exercises suggested in our coaching progression, the players gradually become more familiar with the technical move, learning to assess the coordinates in space (height, length and distance) necessary to throw the ball towards a fixed target (throw-in towards a player) and to evaluate the coordinates in time and space they need to throw the ball towards a moving target (zone throw-in).

In the **situations of play** suggested in the following pages the players can apply the techniques they have practiced in a playing context characterized by the typical elements of a match: the presence of their teammates, the opposition, the goalkeeper and the goal. In particular, the player taking the throw-in should be able to read the situation and communicate with his teammate in order to understand his movements to elude the marking and immediately choose the best solution between throwing the ball towards his teammate or into the open space.

The **conditioned game** is a real test for the coach to understand how the players can make such a technical move also in unconventional situations of play, for instance to take a corner kick, a goal kick or a kick off. In this way, the coach can evaluate the player's creativeness, his capacity to take the initiative and surprise or anticipate the opposition; these skills are particularly important specifically if they are combined with and support technical abilities and tactical intuitions.

The **final game** – the inevitable practice match – places the players in a game context that is closer to the reality both at the technical and tactical level; moreover, from the psychological point of view, it represents a situation of mental discharge (intended as release of tension), free expression and motivational charge for the players which, in short, completes and enriches the testing (already begun in the previous phase) of set goals, on which the coaching suggestions for the next training session strictly depend.

Starting game

Two teams made up of 8 players each move freely in a playing area previously marked out, each one using one of three different balls (1 rugby ball, 1 basketball and 1 volleyball) to make passes with the hands, trying not to let the ball fall to the ground; a penalty is assessed to the team whose player lets the ball land on the ground. The team with less penalties than the opposition win the game. In the first part of the game, the players are completely free to choose the passing technique they want to use, while in the second phase the coach will suggest special motor performances and patterns recalling particular techniques of throwing and receiving the ball peculiar to the three different team sports disciplines. For example: the passing technique typical of basketball, that is the two-hand pass thrown from the chest, the two-hand pass from the bottom upwards in rugby and the passing technique after throwing the ball high in the air typical of volleyball.

Purpose: Properly handle the ball holding it with both hands when throwing and receiving.

```
COACHING  UNIT
```

Age: 11 to 13 year olds
Primary specific goal: throwing-in
Secondary specific goal: enhancing space perception and the perception of the relation between time and space
Instruments: stopwatch
Equipment: cones, 8 soccer balls, 2 rugby balls, 2 volley balls, 2 basket balls, 8 colored training pinnies
Contents: exercises in pairs, exercises in groups of four players, team activities, 1 v 1, 2 v 1, 4 v 4, 8 v 8
Coaching methods: assigning tasks, problem solving
Testing: observation of the conditioned game
Suggestion for the following session: depends on the outcome of the testing
Starting game: passing game using passing techniques typical of various sports disciplines
Analytical exercises: exercises in pairs (to improve long throwing, throwing towards a fixed target and towards a moving one)
Situations of play: 1 v 1, 2 v 1 to make crosses or to finally shoot at goal
Conditioned game: 4 v 4, 8 v 8 always restarting the game with a throw-in in dead ball situations
Final game: unconditioned game with two goalkeepers playing in one half of the field

Analytical exercises

Who can throw the ball the farthest?
The exercise develops as a competition in pairs to see who can throw the ball the farthest taking a throw in from the following positions:
❑ with the feet close together
❑ with the legs wide apart on the frontal plane
❑ with the legs wide apart on the sagittal plane (first standing in a stationary position and then taking a suitable run up to throw the ball) **(diagram 1)**.
Purpose: Help the players understand which position generates the greatest power to the ball.

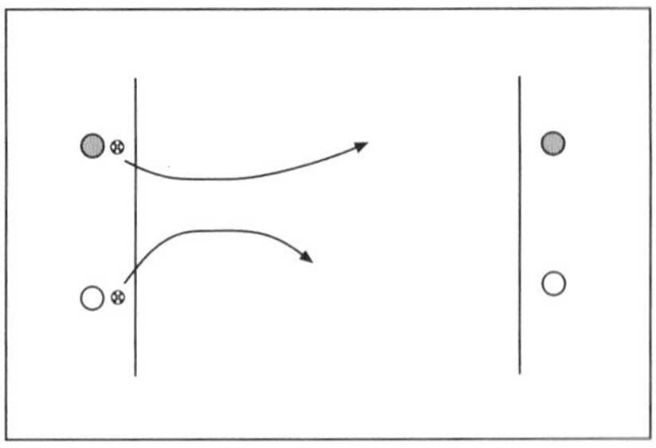

Diagram 1

Throw the ball to a fixed target
Competition in pairs; the players play in the penalty box trying to hit one of the sectors in which the goal has been divided. After three consecutive throw-ins the players change the position from where they throw the ball so as to vary the distance from the goal line and the angle compared to the goal and also decide the target at which they are going to aim the ball **(diagram 2)**.

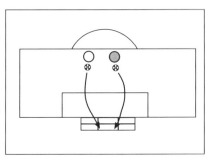

Diagram 2

Purpose: Assess the distance and the height of the target and consequently choose the most suitable throwing technique to hit the target.

Throw the ball to a moving target

The two players C and D throw the ball to each other or pass a hoop making it roll on the ground, while the two opponents A and B throw the ball in trying to hit the moving ball or send the ball through the hoop rolling on the ground (**diagram 3**).
Purpose: Enhance space and time perception, carefully assessing the speed of the ball or the hoop and properly timing the technical move: in short, throwing the ball in at the right time.

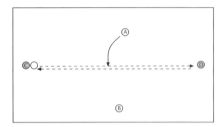
Diagram 3

Man-to-man or zone throw-in

Competition in pairs in a playing area where several hoops have been placed. The throwers are standing along the line where they take the throw-in, while their teammates can move from one hoop to another to receive the ball (**diagram 4**).
a) The player receiving the ball is standing in one of the hoops before his fellow player throws the ball in (man-to-man throw-in)
Purpose: Assess the distance the ball should be thrown.

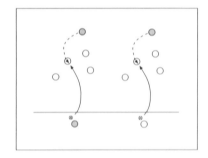
Diagram 4

b) The player receiving the ball moves into one of the hoops exactly while he is meeting the pass by his teammate (zone throw-in).
Purpose: Enhance space and time perception.

Situations of play

1 v 1 starting from the throw-in

Player A takes the throw-in aiming the ball towards his teammate B who is marked by an opponent. Player B needs to elude the opponent's marking and can move how and when he wants, with the intent to either receive the ball thrown in by his teammate in order to make a cross towards the goalkeeper who is leaving the line of the goal or to finally shoot at goal. In the first part of the exercise the players are free to experience personal solutions and move as they want, while in the second phase the coach will suggest some possible solutions (**diagram 5**).

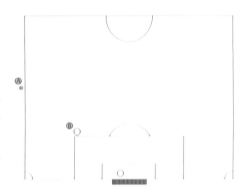
Diagram 5

Solution a) Player B makes a feint towards his teammate A and promptly sprints on the wing to meet the throw-in in order to cross the ball towards the box.

Solution b) Player B runs towards his teammate A to meet the throw-in, screens the ball and sprints towards the goal or on the wing towards the goal line dribbling the ball and beating the opposition.

Solution c) Player B makes a feint towards his teammate A and promptly sprints in the opposite direction directly towards the goal where he can receive and shoot at goal.

Variation: 2 v 1 starting from the throw-in. The same situation as above, but in this case player A can take part in achieving the offensive build up immediately after taking the throw-in. The offside rule is in force in this situation.

Conditioned game

Two short 4 v 4 practice games played in a 25 x 20 yard area followed by a conditioned 8 v 8 practice match played in a 40 x 30 yard field: the condition is that every time one of the players of the two teams breaks one of the laws of the game a throw-in is awarded to the opposite side. Kick-offs, corner kicks and goal kicks are also taken as throw ins. The final purpose of this game is to help the players become familiar with this technical movement, always trying to suggest new and different solutions.

INDIVIDUAL TACTICAL SKILLS WITH BALL POSSESSION **4**

1.1 ELUDING THE MARKING

Definition: Individual tactical skill of a player without the ball who manages to get free from the opponent's marking and wriggles out to search for open playing areas where he can freely meet a pass by one of his teammates or offer other opportunities for new tactical solutions to his teammate in possession of the ball.

Description: When a player gains possession of the ball, his teammates all need to elude the opposition's marking, which means they immediately position on the playing field so as to offer a passing option to their teammate in possession or to further develop the playing action. This action obviously implies the player's ability to orient in space in relation to some fixed points of reference (such as the goals, the boundary lines and so forth) and to other moving ones (i.e. his teammates, the opponents and the ball) in order to spot open playing areas and free passing lanes where neither opponents nor teammates are standing. The most elementary movement to elude the marking is "to make oneself visible", which means to occupy an open area in the ball handler's line of vision, offering him a possible solution of play. Should the player in possession be challenged, the movement to elude the marking should be made outside the "shadow cone" created by the marking opponent, in a light zone, that is in the "cleared area" where it is possible for the two teammates to develop visual contact and communication and consequently "open a passing lane". By contrast, should the player without the ball – which means the player who is more likely to meet the pass – be marked by an opponent, he could get free of the opponent thanks to his ability to fake which involves making one or more movements to deceive and fool the opponent (he could change direction, pace or completely turn in the opposite direction, for example) and elude his marking. The movements to elude the marking can be made in any direction:

➤ forward and backward gaining or losing depth;
➤ to the right and to the left in width across the field, in order to widen or narrow the attacking line;
➤ diagonally so as to anticipate the defender and use the body as a shield to screen the ball while facing the opposing goal.

It is possible to distinguish movements to elude the marking to support a teammate and receive his forward pass - with the player moving before the line of the ball (to provide support and depth and develop forward play) - which are generally made by the forwards, from movements to support a teammate and meet a backward pass – with the player moving behind the line of the ball (backward play) – which are usually made by the defenders supporting the maneuver of their midfield teammates or by the midfielders to support their attacking teammates. In particular, a player should move to get free from the marking approaching the ball when the ball is "closed" by the pressure of an opponent and cannot be played forward or, in any case, far from the position where he is standing, forcing him to meet the pass while turning his back to the opposing goal; by contrast, the challenged player can elude the marking moving off the ball when the ball is "free" from the pressure by the opposition and can therefore be played forward or, in any case, far from the place where the player is standing, allowing him to receive the pass while facing the opposing goal and gain space forward. In general, for each movement and action to elude the opponent's marking to be truly effective it must be properly timed (when the player has established eye contact with his teammate in possession of the ball and the ball handler is consequently able to play the ball to him). Eluding the marking usually involves feinting and faking in order to deceive the challenging opponent and temporarily get free from his marking; feints are movements of the body or runs (faking movements) in the direction opposite to that in which the situation of play is developing (intentional movement). In typical soccer jargon, some coaches summarize this concept using the expression "elastic movement" or "countermovement" referring to go-and-come movements (move far off the ball and get close to the ball) and come-and-go actions (get close to the ball and move away). "Come" refers to the player's movement to approach the ball so as to reduce the distance between the ball and the player who is likely to meet the pass (get close to the ball), while "go" defines the action of the player moving off the ball which obviously involves increasing the distance between the ball and the possible receiver (stretch out the maneuver). Some coaches also use the expressions "compact - expand" or "expand – compact" considering the width of the playing field; in particular, the verb "compact" defines a movement converging on the goal (cutting movement towards the inside) while the verb "expand" refers to the player's movement moving off the goal towards the touch lines (cutting movement towards the outside).

From these basic movements derive all the possible combinations (such as "go and compact", "expand and go") which are nothing but changes of directions combined with changes of pace. Individual movements off the ball to elude the marking are made by single players; however, in order to offer the ball handler more opportunities and solutions of play, any individual movement should be carefully coordinated at a collective level by several players, who will take the best positions on the playing field, synchronizing their movements in different directions in order to create, clear,

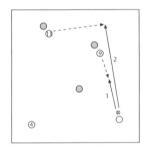

Diagram 1

open and occupy free spaces. Consider, for example, the typical movement of cooperation and team play made by the two attacking players (**diagram 1**) to support their midfield teammates: one of the two forwards moves backward to get close to the ball handler in order to clear a playing area at his back; the other forward promptly sprints to occupy that cleared space moving off the ball towards the opposing goal to make the action of play develop in depth and therefore offer his midfield teammate in possession of the ball two different solutions.

Table 1 is a brief recapitulatory picture of the basic skills to elude the marking. The **coaching unit** below shows an example of a standard coaching and training session focusing on the abilities to get free from the marking in particular conditions and situations involving accurate time perception (timing).

ELUDING THE MARKING			
WHERE?	**HOW?**	**WHEN?**	**WHY?**
Position	Manner	Time	Purpose
❏ Compared to the player in possession of the ball: • Forward – backward • To the right – the left • Compared to the ball: • Moving off the ball (facing the goal) • Approaching the ball (with one's back to the goal)	❏ In relation to: • Change of direction • Movement in the opposite direction • Change of pace • Diagonal running	❏ Immediately when eye contact is made	❏ Get free from the opponent's marking ❏ Offer tactical solutions to the player in possession ❏ Clear space ❏ Move to meet the ball

Table 1

COACHING UNIT

Age: 13 to 15 year olds
Primary specific goal: elude the marking
Secondary specific goal: Perceive and time the movement to elude the marking
Instruments: stopwatch
Equipment: disc cones, training pinnies, balls
Contents: exercises in pairs, situations of play involving three, four and five players, team game 8 v 8, 4 v 4 and 6 v 6, unconditioned game
Coaching methods: deductive – inductive
Testing: careful analysis of the conditioned game
Suggestion for the following session: depends on the outcome of the testing
Starting game: ten passes throwing the ball with the hands
Analytical exercises: pass the ball moving in pairs in traffic
Situations of play:
1. 2 v 1 for ball possession
2. 3 v 1 and 3 v 2 monkey in the middle along the boundary lines of the playing area
3. Elude the marking and shoot
Conditioned game: play with the captain
Final game: unconditioned game with two goalkeepers played in one half of the field.

Starting game

Ten passes throwing the ball with the hands

Mark out a playing area where two teams play 8 v 8 or 4 v 4 competing for ball possession with the aim of making ten consecutive passes throwing the ball with their hands. The members of the two groups are divided in pairs of opposing players marking each other. When the ball handler gains possession of the ball after receiving a pass by one of his teammates, he can neither move nor be challenged or obstructed by his own direct opponent, since he needs to be able to read the situation of play and his fellow players' movements to elude the marking and sprint to meet the pass without being disturbed.

Variation: Playing to maintain ball possession can be aimed at reaching a target area marked out along the goal lines.

Purposes:
1. Read the situation of play (eye contact) to support the player in possession of the ball.
2. Improve and become familiar with the basic movements to elude the marking (combine different techniques to elude the marking typical of various sports disciplines).

Analytical exercises

Pass the ball moving in pairs in traffic

In a 15 x 15 yard playing area previously marked out, four pairs of players – each with a ball – play the ball to each other combining passing and dribbling, adjusting their movements and techniques to the presence of several players and various balls at the same time.

Variation: Another player takes part in the play of each pair of players: he can disturb and obstruct their action but is not allowed to touch or play the ball.

Purposes:
1. Elude the marking in a cleared space.
2. Get free from the marking within the field of vision of the player in possession of the ball.
3. Clear space to move freely and pass the ball.

Situations of play

2 v 1 for ball possession (diagram 1b)

Play 2 v 1 to maintain ball possession in a 15 x 15 yard playing area. When committing the opposing player A, the defender D is forced to tackle, challenge and press the opponent in possession of the ball, completely disregarding the ballhandler's supporting teammate.

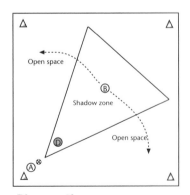

Diagram 1b

Purposes for the supporting teammate:
1. Elude the marking and move into open space
2. Elude the marking moving out of the shadow cone
3. Elude the marking moving freely towards the ball.

3 v 1 monkey in the middle along the boundary lines of the playing area (diagram 2)
Play 3 v 1 along the boundary lines of the square playing area (10 x 10 yards); the player in possession of the ball always has two possible solutions to pass the ball towards the two corners of the square nearest to his position.
Variation: The player in possession of the ball can dribble the ball from one corner of the square to another. Unconditioned ball possession inside the square.
Purposes:
  1. Elude the marking to move into open space
  2. Cooperate and support the movement to elude the marking by offering the ball handler two different solutions to pass the ball (to the right and to the left).

3 v 2 monkey in the middle along the boundary lines of the playing area
Play 3 v 2 in the same manner and using the same rules and variations suggested in the above 3 v 1 situation; the player in possession of the ball is allowed to both pass and dribble the ball diagonally from one corner of the square playing area to the opposite one.

Elude the marking and shoot (diagram 3)
Players A (facing the goal) and B (with his back to the goal) make one touch passes along the ground. When B receives the ball and turns to face the goal, his teammate C sprints to elude the opponent's marking in order to meet the pass and shoot at goal while being challenged by the opposing defender.
Variation: The movement to elude the marking cannot be made towards the passer.
Purposes:
  1. Get free from the marking.
  2. Elude the marking in depth, moving off the ball.
  3. Time the movement to elude the marking.

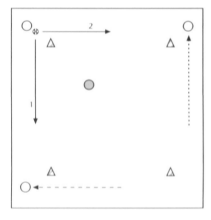

Diagram 2

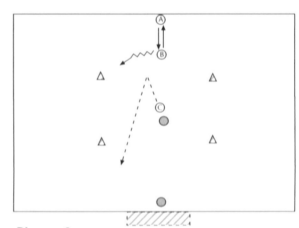

Diagram 3

Conditioned game

Play with the captain (diagram 4)

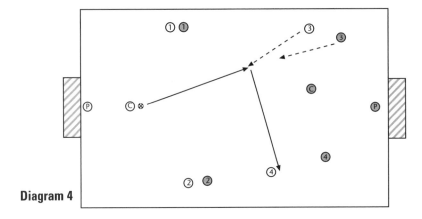

Diagram 4

Play a 6 v 6 practice match on a 40 x 30 yard playing field; each team is made up of: a goalkeeper, a captain and four players. The players on the two teams compete playing man-to-man marking (individual guarding), which means they form fixed pairs of opposing players who can be supported and helped by the captain of their own squad. The two captains can play freely in their own defensive halves of the field and cannot be obstructed, challenged or tackled by other players. The practice match includes two halves of 15 minutes each and also involves the players switching their roles and positions on the playing field.

Variation: The two captains are allowed to play in the opposing offensive halves of the field but when they do, they can be challenged, obstructed and tackled by the opposing captain.

Purpose:
1) Elude the marking in situations of play
2) Apply the basic principles to elude the marking.

Basketball and Skills to Elude the Marking

The age period between 6 and 12 is generally considered as a particularly fertile period for learning since any stimulus brings about highly fruitful and effective responses. Practicing different individual or team sports disciplines helps enrich and improve basic motor skills (abilities to run, jump, bend, see, roll, perceive, keep one's balance and so forth...), that is all those functional and structural prerequisites that a young athlete needs to learn any sports technique.

The more the player can improve and enrich basic motor skills, the higher the technical and tactical level he is likely to achieve. This approach to various sports disciplines and varied techniques typical of each sport favors the application of the principle of **MULTILATERALITY**, which refers to the didactic aspects of coaching and, in particular, to the need to vary training methods and contents as much as possible in order to arouse interest and stimulate active participation (for example: work using small pieces of gym apparatus, balls of different shapes and sizes, using marked tracks, practice circuits and multiple tests or competitions). All this should always be suggested using different methods and various coaching styles, which means the coach should follow the principle of polyvalence. In this way, sports specialization would be delayed – in fact, it should only begin from the age of 12 or 13 on – and it would also be advisable that the player chooses what sport he prefers to practice freely and independently on the basis of a varied and significant sports background. In this way, it would also be possible to promote the sports culture of individual athletes, encouraging in them the mentality of sport intended as a unique discipline embracing various disciplines, which – among other things - would allow him to choose the sport that best suits his needs and skills or to shift from one sport to another. The culture of **INTERCHANGEABILITY OF ROLES** would consequently spread out, which could enrich the technical and tactical background of the player in the developmental age, thus avoiding deleterious early specialization in sport while also encouraging serious motivation to sport. This means that transferring motor skills from one sports discipline to another would become practically automatic, increasing and improving the learning of basic sports abilities, that is those basic movements that can be adjusted to constantly mutable contexts of play, as sports always require (sports of situation).

On these theoretical premises is based the following coaching suggestion including exercises and situations taken from basketball to enhance the learning of basic individual movements without the ball. It has been statistically proven that every player is in possession of the ball for about three to four minutes in a typical soccer match, while he is forced to play and move without the ball for the remaining eighty-six or eighty-seven minutes. This means that, the factors determining the performance in sports being equal, the team who is more likely to win the competition is the one who can outplay the opposition without the ball both in the defensive phase (taking the suitable position, marking, covering and sealing off spaces, supporting one's teammates) and in the offensive build up (clearing spaces, eluding the marking, supporting one's teammates and so forth…) always acting according to special strategies of cooperation, collaboration and communication typical of any team game.

Basketball accurately analyzes and focuses an important part of training on coaching and practicing basic individual movements and techniques without the ball, which can be used in competitions to favor the movements to elude the marking, in particular to temporarily get free from the opponent's guarding in order to better receive the ball. The didactics of coaching and learning those basic individual techniques starts from the analysis of the player's **fundamental position** without the ball, that is the position which allows him to keep his balance and react faster to challenge his direct opponent in any situation of play. The player can stand in the fundamental position:

1. keeping his feet parallel, shoulder width apart, keeping his weight on the balls of his feet: this means he should slightly raise his heels from the ground so as to enhance the sensibility of the supporting bases, the taking-off movement and the balance on the front part of his feet;
2. slightly bending his knees;
3. keeping his trunk upright and slightly bent forward;
4. holding his head high;
5. looking forward in order to favor peripheral vision.

In order to get free from the opponent's control and marking or anticipate him in a given area, the player without the ball can use a **change of pace** either from slow to fast, pushing from the balls of his feet, slightly bending the trunk forward helped by a wide movement of the arms on the front-back plane; or from fast to slow, slowing down the speed using the front parts of the feet and slightly raising the trunk so as to help decrease the speed of motion.

Changing direction (diagram 5) is another technique to get free from the opponent's guarding; it involves the player suddenly and unexpectedly moving in another direction.

❑ the player pushes against the ground to change direction (the left foot to move to the right and vice-versa) turning the inside of the front part of the foot to the new running direction, in line with the trunk (**diagram 5**);

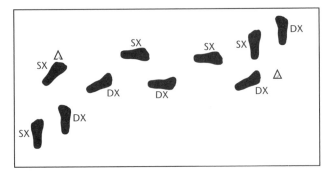

Diagram 5

❑ the other foot – the non-standing one – takes a long step in line with the new running direction;

❑ the weight of the body is transferred forward;

❑ the player now changes his running pace.

Turning about and running in the opposite direction involves a movement similar to a common change of direction with the sole difference that this situation implies a 180° change in the direction of the player's motion. This is a basic technique in the transition phase, in recovering one's position on counterattack and, in some cases, it is also used to elude the marking in very restricted playing areas. This movement is generally made as follows: after an abrupt stop, he turns towards the side of the back foot, pushing it against the ground and taking a long step in the new direction. The real effectiveness of these movements also depends on the player's ability to simultaneously combine them with successful changes of pace and synchronize them with the movements of his center of gravity, while also combining them with the action of the lower limbs pushing against the ground.

These aspects of motion represent the key elements of any basic individual technique without the ball and will consequently become significant factors which the coach should carefully observe, analyze, assess and correct, if necessary.

Our coaching suggestions also include some **games** in which the players can personally experience how these basic individual techniques without the ball are applied in ludic situations, at speed and, in particular, in relation to a given final goal; in each one of the games suggested in the following pages - from the "shadow teammate" to the game to elude the marking – this goal is to act and play according to the presence of an opponent with the aim of receiving or passing the ball.

At a later stage you will be shown some **simple play situations** in which the players' movements to elude the marking are carried out to control a pass and dribble, cross the ball or shoot at goal, always in relation to the presence and movements of the opponent.

The **complex play situations** (2 v 4 and 2 v 5) that we have included as example situations could appear more exhaustive and significant if they were carried out and developed in special exercises between opposing lines such as 6 v 4 or 7 v 5 situations in which the midfield and the attacking lines play against the defending and the midfield lines, for example. In these exercises, the application of basic individual techniques and movements, both with and without the ball (how to perform such movements), is important only if they are made in relation to the general understanding of the situation of play (what the player should do, when and why he should play in such a way).

In fact, understanding the situation of play means being able to read what is happening on the playing field in that particular moment and what problems may cause a particular situation of play, anticipate in your mind the solution to those problems and the action to choose and perform the most effective basic techniques and successful movements in order to carry out the task assigned by the "problem-situation".

Practice drills

Exercise to improve change of pace
Four players – standing in line with player A who leads the game – run along a 40 yard track marked with cones and divided in several sections by perpendicular lines marking the points where the players have to change pace, accelerating or slowing down (**diagram 6**).

Exercise to improve turning in the opposite direction
Four players standing perfectly lined up run from the starting line up to the 1st line, promptly turn around and sprint in the opposite direction back to the starting line, and so forth (they run up to the 2nd line and sprint back to the 1st one; up to the 3rd line and back to the 2nd one) up to the finishing line (**diagram 7**).
Variation: Combine changing your running pace and turning around to sprinting in the opposite direction.
Exercise to improve change of direction
Every player runs from the starting line to

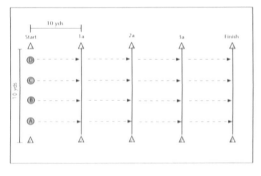

Diagram 6

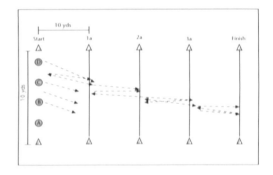

Diagram 7

the finishing line making various changes of direction, always placing the pivot foot (the foot pushing against the ground to change direction) inside of the reference cones (**diagram 8**).

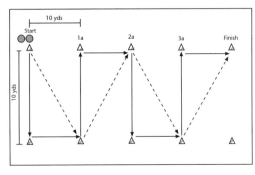

Variation: The player can follow different paths, running along the sketched or the straight line, or combine them; combine changes of direction with changes of pace.

Diagram 8

Exercise to improve turning in the opposite direction, change of direction and change of pace

Eight to twelve players run freely at various speeds according to their own level of skill in a 10 x 10 yard square area. Each time two players run into each other, they change direction – sprinting to the right or to the left – or turn about and run in the opposite direction, according to the coach's instruction, while always combining those movements with a change of pace.

Purpose: The players try to avoid touching or running into each other.

Touch the prey

In a 10 x 10 yard playing area, one or two hunters run after six to eight prey players with the intent to touch them at a given part of their bodies using their hands (for example, the coach can decide they have to touch the preys at their backs or legs). If a hunter touches a prey player the two players switch roles.

Purposes: Turn about or change direction in a condition of motor rapidity and in relation to a final goal: that is catching or touching for the hunters and running away or avoiding being touched for the prey players.

The shadow teammate

In a 10 x 10 yard playing area, four pairs of players all play the "shadow teammate game" at the same time. While the player leading the game (the guide) moves at various speeds within the playing area combining changes of directions and turning-about movements stopping and restarting, his shadow teammate – standing at his side or behind him – follows him very closely, reacting to his movements.

Purposes: The player leading the game (the guide) tries to get free from his shadow teammate's contact, while the shadow teammate constantly seeks contact with his leading player or tries to stand close to him.

Elude-the-marking game

In a 15 x 15 yard square marked out inside the playing area, the attacking player A, challenged by defender D, tries to elude the opponent's marking to control the ball freely and play it to one of the four supporting teammates standing outside the square; each one of the four supporting players is in possession of a ball (**diagram 9**).

Purpose: Elude the marking in order to control the ball freely.

Variation: Play using just one ball which the supporting players outside the square can pass to each other; they are only allowed two touches of the ball, while the attacking player inside the square can play unconditioned touches.

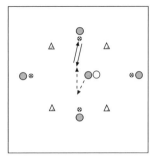

Simple play situations

2 v 1 for the final shot on goal

Solution a) Player A, marked by D, runs towards his teammate C who is in possession of the ball. The opposing defender D does not follow him so A can control a ground pass with his feet, turn and dribble the ball diagonally forward playing 1 v 1 against D while facing the goal (**diagram 10**).

Diagram 9

Variation: C plays as a supporting teammate ready to control a back- or forward pass.

Solution b) Player A, marked by the opposing defender D, runs towards his teammate C in possession of the ball at midfield. Defender D reacts and follows the attacker to mark him closely; consequently, A can decide to move to meet a zone pass:

a) making a change of direction (1) sprinting diagonally to the position A1 to play 1 v 1 on the flank of the field;

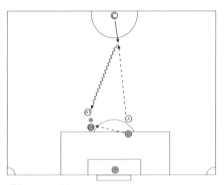

Diagram 10

b) turning (2) and sprinting in depth to the position A2 to play at the back of the defender and shoot at goal (**diagram 11**).

Variation: After giving a through pass, the midfield player C moves to support his teammate A, ready to control his back- or forward pass.

Complex play situations

2 v 4: avoid being caught offside against an in-line defense (static)

The attacking player A moves to give his teammate C the opportunity to make a through pass

Diagram 11

against a static defense standing in line. In order to avoid being caught offside, the attacker does not sprint towards the goal immediately, but first runs horizontally parallel to the halfway line in front of the defensive line and then sprints in depth into the A1 position, making a prompt change of direction suitably combined with a change of pace in order to meet the pass by his teammate and shoot at goal (**diagram 12**).

2 v 5: avoid being caught offside against an in-line defense (dynamic)

The attacking player A starts the game in possession of the ball, screens it and then makes a backward pass (1) to his midfield teammate C who is immediately pressed by the opponent C, supported by the whole defensive line who move upward to force the opposing attacker offside. In order not to be caught offside when his midfield teammate C passes the ball in depth (2), the attacking player A tries to elude the marking by turning and making a change of pace so as to control the ball in position A2 and shoot at goal (**diagram 13**).

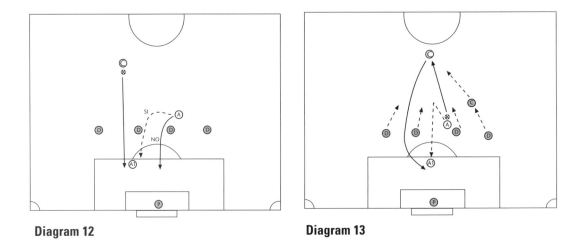

Diagram 12   **Diagram 13**

1.2 DEFENDING AND SCREENING THE BALL

Definition: Individual tactical skill characterized by the ability to handle and master the ball, maintaining possession when challenged by one or more opponents.

Description: "Hold the ball", "Don't lose it" are just some of the exclamations typically heard from the sidelines in soccer matches. Nevertheless, in training sessions many coaches fail to suggest special activities to develop this basic individual tactical skill defined as "ball defense and screen" or, in other words, "ball control".

This particular ability – helpful for all players in any area of the playing field – becomes specifically important for attacking players, who are generally marked very closely by the opposition and are often forced to play with their backs to the opposing goal. Attackers who are able to maintain ball possession – even for a short period of time – allow the whole team to organize and develop the offensive build up; moreover, in difficult situations (for example, when the team are suffering the opposition's play and pressure), they also allow the defender to "take a breath", temporarily releasing psychological tension and pressure.

From the very first period when a child begins to practice soccer activity – it is important to accustom young soccer players to use their bodies as a means to defend the ball. This important goal can be gradually pursued by practicing ludic activities expressly designed for this purpose and which also act as an instrument to help build the body structure, a factor of critical importance between the ages of 6 to 12. While regularly practicing polyvalent and multilateral activities the players should be put in suitable conditions to understand the basic principles underlying the particular action of play. In order to screen and shield the ball successfully it is fundamental for a player to stand with his body between the ball and the opponent, using the foot furthest from the opponent to control the ball, trying to keep the ball as far as possible from the marking opponent. Moreover, he needs to use his arms, slightly raising them in order to keep his balance and also to create another obstacle to his opponent; he should always take care not to open his arms in an aggressive manner so as to avoid committing a foul. Finally, the player should never show the ball by holding it between his legs or too close to his body, which would give the opponent an opportunity to steal or kick the ball away.

For a player to learn and improve this basic individual tactical skill, we think that he should first improve some prerequisite elements and abilities including: pulling and pushing as basic motor patterns; receiving and controlling the ball at a technical level; and, from the psychological point of view, the capacity to handle body contact with courage and determination. When a player fears body contact, this often inhibits the development of his technical and tactical skills: in fact, the players who cannot fully trust their own abilities avoid any tackle and body contact while also jeopardizing the ability to defend the ball successfully and maintain possession of it. Consequently, the coach's job is of crucial importance: through a suitably planned sequence of exciting and non-traumatic exercises and games he could actually encourage the player to gain confidence in his own skills, which is absolutely fundamental to fully exploit his potential in the struggle and body contact with the opposition.

Sport in general involves socialized forms of competition. As the young player grows, his self-confidence is more and more stimulated and reinforced in increasingly competitive situations. When a player can test his real skills in a situation of competition against other players, it certainly helps him to enhance self-control and confidence and also increase the awareness of his own sense of identity. Our coaching suggestion on this theme involves a progression of activities from exercises in pairs without the ball to simple play situations. The exercises focusing on pulling and pushing – suggested in the form of a competitive game – involve great motivational and emotional charge, which is able to create a positive atmosphere and a favorable coaching and educational environment helping basic learning.

Duel games and team games offer a significant preliminary support to the understanding of the basic principles of defending the ball (cover, shield and screen the ball). On the other hand, the situations of play shown in the following pages allow the player to apply this particular ability in the context of actions occurring commonly and repeatedly during the course of a match.

In the table below we have tried to make a synthesis of the key concepts of defending the ball.

The **coaching unit** shown below focuses on defending and screening the ball in conditions of motor differentiation. For a suitable and complete planning of coaching and learning how to defend the ball as a basic individual technique – including the technical movements involved in preparing such an action (prior to it) and those immediately following it and at which it is aimed (made after screening the ball) – you can refer back to the coaching unit dealing with "**the combination of technical moves in dribbling the ball**".

DEFENDING AND SCREENING THE BALL

WHERE?	HOW?	WHEN?	WHY?
Position	Manner	Time	Purpose
❏ In the attacking area near or inside the opposing penalty box ❏ At midfield ❏ In the defending area near or inside one's own penalty box or near the goal lines	❏ Using the body: • as a shield • as an obstacle	❏ While receiving the ball and immediately after	❏ Maintain possession of the ball in order to: • Turn with the ball to... shoot, dribble or pass (attacker) • Pass or cross the ball (midfield player) • Defend the goalkeeper leaving the line of the goal • Defend the ball crossing the goal line (defender)

COACHING UNIT

Age: 11 to 13 year olds
Primary specific goal: defend and screen the ball
Secondary goal: motor differentiation
Instruments: stopwatch
Equipment: disc cones, training vests, balls
Contents: exercises in pairs, situations of play in pairs and groups of three, individual games, team games 4 v 4, practice match
Coaching methods: deductive – inductive
Testing: careful analysis of the conditioned game
Suggestion for the following session: depends on the outcome of the testing
Starting game: preys and hunters among goalkeepers; kick the ball out; preys and hunters
Analytical exercises: exercises in pairs to improve catching (contact) and pushing
Situations of play:
1. 1 v 1 "hold the ball and don't lose it"
2. 2 v 1 "run, control and screen"
Conditioned game: 4 v 4 playing towards one goal
Final game: unconditioned game with two goalkeepers in one half of the field

Starting games

Prey and hunters among the goalkeepers
In a 20 x 20 yard playing area, 8 players (the prey) move freely dribbling the ball, followed by 8 other players (the hunters) without the ball. The hunters try to win possession of the balls from the prey players in order to be allowed to switch roles. If the prey players are in situations of danger, they can curl up on the ball to protect and cover it as if they were goalkeepers; in this case, the hunter must turn to seek other prey.

Kick the ball out
The players are all in possession of a ball and can move and dribble freely in a 20 x 20 yard playing area. Everybody plays against everybody and they all try to kick the balls of their opponents out of the playing area while also defending their own balls. Every time a player manages to kick the ball of an opponent out of the square field, the ball handler is given a penalty. The game develops in a set time and those who are awarded the smallest number of penalties when time is over win the competition.

Prey and hunters
In a 20 x 20 yard playing area, 13 players (the prey) can move freely dribbling the ball, followed by three players without the ball (the hunters) who try to touch the prey players' balls, kicking them away in order to be allowed to switch roles.
Variations:
1. The hunter tries to kick the ball out of the square playing area
2. The hunter tries to win possession of the ball
3. Vary the ratio between the number of prey players and hunters.
Purposes of the starting games: Acquire and improve the ability to defend the ball in a ludic context.

Analytical exercises
Pull and push

Diagram 1

Diagram 1 shows some example exercises in which the two players get accustomed to body contact with their direct opponents, trying to use their strength when pushing the opposing player and keep their balance.

Purpose of duel exercises: Defend and occupy the space marked out by an imaginary line separating the two contestants or by the line drawn due to the presence of the ball.

Struggle for ball possession

The player lying on all fours curled up on the ball tries to defend the ball, preventing the opponent from touching it and winning possession. The player standing at his side tries to upset his opponent in order to take the ball away using his hands.

Purpose: Cover and shield the ball using your body; body contact; screen the ball.

Situations of play

1 v 1 "hold the ball, don't lose it"

A player juggles the ball freely within a 10 x 10 **Diagram 2**
yard playing area in the presence of a passive opponent. When the coach gives the starting signal, the juggling player immediately stops the ball and screens it so as to prevent the opponent from winning possession. The duel lasts ten seconds. The attacker scores one point if he manages not to lose possession of the ball, while the defender is awarded two points if he succeeds in winning possession of the ball and keeps it inside the square playing area. The players score no points if the ball moves out of the marked area.

Purpose: Handle (ball possession), stop and screen the ball.

2 v 1 "run, control and screen the ball"

In a well-marked playing area, player A – marked by the opposing defender D - starts from the goal line and runs towards his teammate C to meet the pass from the opposite side of the field. Attacker A controls the ball and screens it from his direct opponent for the time it takes his fellow player C to run around a cone placed at a distance of 10 yards and sprint back to control his teammate's back pass. Each successful back pass scores one point.

Purposes: Control, screen and pass the ball.

Variation: As an alternative to the back pass, the attacker can decide to turn with the ball and dribble up to the goal line.

Purposes: Control, screen and either pass or dribble the ball.

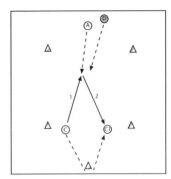

Diagram 3

Conditioned game

Play towards one goal

Play 4 v 4 using one goal defended by a goalkeeper, near the penalty box. A goal is valid only if it scored after dribbling the ball into the penalty area and suitably screening it from the opponent's attempt to win possession. The defending team who manage to gain possession of the ball first need to dribble it out of the penalty box before starting the offensive build up.

Purpose: Defend the ball in the context of a match for the final shot on goal.

1.3 PASSING THE BALL

Definition: Individual tactical skill whereby a player intentionally plays the ball to one of his teammates.

Description: When the player in possession of the ball "intentionally delivers" the ball to one of his teammates, this means that the two players (the one playing the ball and the one receiving it) have previously established eye contact and developed non-verbal communication (i.e. gestural communication) which is the action of passing the ball from one to another. Verbal communication develops through words and sentences, while soccer communication is carried out passing the ball from one player to another.

The teams who are able to build the maneuver at a collective level (team play) and are particularly skillful at maintaining ball possession are those who manage to enhance mutual understanding and act accordingly, which means that intentions and non-verbal messages are all interpreted and understood in the same manner by all the players involved. Players can develop mutual understanding while practicing and gradually refine it while playing matches using signals and codes which allow all the members of the team to understand each other, but which the opposition find hard to "decode". Making a feint which involves a movement to elude the marking or to pass the ball to a teammate is aimed at deceiving the opponent and not a teammate, who will obviously need to keep alert so as to anticipate and properly interpret the movements of his passing teammate, also using verbal and non-verbal conventional signs – which have been previously agreed upon by the two players – in order to make communication truly successful and effective. Now, who is the protagonist in soccer communication? The ball handler who "reads the situation of play", "sets the rhythm of play" and "lights up the maneuver" or the supporting player who is able to suggest to his teammate where he should pass the ball, making suitable movements to elude the marking? The diatribe is still open between those who are in favor or against one or the other theory; in any case, they all agree that team games are all based on the principle of cooperation which, in our case, involves two players – the player in possession of the ball and his supporting teammate – to act in perfect harmony in order to achieve a common final goal: passing the ball successfully. Consequently, the successful performance of this technical move depends on the combination of various factors:

1. **Ability** to elude the marking by the teammates without the ball
2. **Position of the body** and posture of the player in possession of the ball
3. **Capacity to read the situation** of play of the ball handler.

In particular, the third factor refers to the ability of the player in possession of the ball to get visual information (read the situation of play) concerning the position of the ball, his teammates and his opponents. Maintaining possession of the ball and properly handling it while also reading the position of both teammates and opponents in order to choose the best solution in that particular situation of play are absolutely prerequisite to develop soccer communication and team play. With regard to this important aspect, the action of the soccer player in this particular context of play should develop following an ideal sequence of operations which include:

1. **Read the situation and understand**
2. **Choose**
3. **Receive**
4. **Pass**

This sequence implies the capacity to read the situation of play and make decisions before receiving the ball, a skill that is fully expressed when playing one-touch, since controlling and passing the ball combine in one single touch of the ball.

Consequently, the didactics of coaching and practicing should not focus on the pure performance, on the biomechanical aspects of the movement and how to make such a move exclusively, but should also and specifically concentrate on both perception and the decision-making process, which play a role of critical importance when reading the situation of play and choosing what, when and why one should perform a particular move. In synthesis, the player first of all needs to analyze the situation in order to make the best choice (optimum decision) and finally carry out the most suitable movement. The quality of the performance of the passing move can be synthesized in the following characteristics: space, time and power.

Space: where is the pass aimed?
❑ The pass also defines the movement of the ball on the ground and, according to the directions in which the ball is played, could be classified as follows:

Forward pass

The main goal of any sports game, which also foreshadows the possibility of scoring, is gaining space forward. Passing the ball in depth or making through passes are part of the technical skills of top players and represent priority solutions of play since they allow the player to approach the opposing goal while also putting the supporting teammate receiving the ball in a favorable condition to play facing the opposing goal itself. For example, examine the through pass made by the midfield player to his wing teammate cutting diagonally to meet the ball (**diagram 1**).

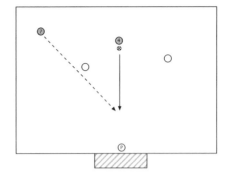

Diagram 1

Diagonal pass

When it is to difficult or too hazardous to play in depth, making a diagonal pass could be a helpful alternative solution.

Imagine, for example, the central midfield player giving a diagonal pass (OPEN UP) on the vertical upward running movement of his outside midfield teammate on the flank of the field (**diagram 2**).

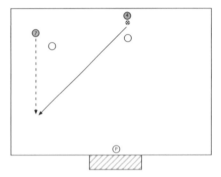

Diagram 2

Horizontal pass

When the build up cannot develop forward in depth, playing the ball horizontally – or "playing in width" - may be a helpful solution for the development of the maneuver and to maintain ball possession in some situations. However, horizontal passes can become dangerous and risky if they are made from the flanks of the playing field towards the center of the field; in fact, if the opposition manage to intercept and win possession of the ball, the two imprudent players are "**CUT OUT OF PLAY**", even though only temporarily. This is why it is important to make horizontal passes only in conditions of maximum safety.

Backward pass

In situations of danger, when players try to avoid the opposition's pressure (double-teaming and pressing in general), it could sometimes be advisable to make a backward pass, in order to spot open spaces to set up the offensive build up in another direction.

Obviously, this solution should not be used to excess, specifically to avoid maintaining ball possession as an end in itself. In order to encourage attack-minded mentality, passing the ball backward should be used as a device to favor the subsequent build up to developing in

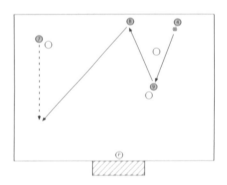

Diagram 3

depth towards the opposing goal. Consider, for example, the attacking player passing the ball backward to his midfield teammate who promptly plays it diagonally (open up the maneuver) upward to the wing player sprinting on the flank to meet the pass (**diagram 3**).

Man-to-man pass

When play develops in very restricted spaces - for example, at the edge of the opposing penalty box – it is recommended to pass the ball directly to the feet of the receiving teammate, so as to avoid losing control and possession of the ball. Backward passes are usually man-to-man passes since they are undoubtedly much safer. Man-to-man passes are very common and frequently made to play the ball to slow players.

Zone pass

Specifically when play develops in large open spaces and on counterattack it is important to pass the ball in a given area of the field, on the running movement of the teammate receiving the pass. This type of pass – the zone pass – is often combined with the forward pass to play the ball to fast players.

Playing **one-two** is a very important team tactical solution which includes the principles of both man-to-man and zone passing at the same time; this tactical strategy is used as an alternative to dribbling in order to beat one or more opponents and consequently gain space upward. The first pass (**one**) given to the supporting teammate is a man-to-man pass, while the second one (**two**) is made delivering the ball into a particular playing area, on the run of the player who is moving to meet the pass (zone pass). Moreover, it is also possible to distinguish some types of passes characterizing both the players passing the ball and also the possible build up development of the teams to whom they belong.

For example, the "**FINISHER**" is the player who is particularly skillful at making the last pass, the crucial pass whereby the attackers are put in the condition to shoot at goal or, in any case, to play facing the opposing goal. The players on the wings of the field generally "finish" their actions making **crosses** towards the penalty box, a distinct basic technical move which should be given greater importance and trained accordingly. Crossing the ball into the penalty area inaccurately is actually completely different from reading the situation of play and consequently choosing the best solution to cross the ball; in fact, a cross can be made from a stationary position or while moving, immediately after making a feint or not, it can be aimed at a particular player or at a given area of the field, it can follow a flat, lobbed or ground path, it can be an inswinging or an outswinging cross and can be made at short, long or middle distance in relation to what the particular situations of play requires.

The player who is specifically skillful at taking powerful and accurate shots can help his team play on counterattack making long passes, for example, or base the offensive build up on ball possession (short play) playing in a certain direction and suddenly switching the maneuver in the opposite direction by means of a "**cross-field pass**"; this solution is possible and successful only when the player giving the pass is able to accurately play the ball over long distances. At this point, we should also remember the player's ability to disguise his own intentions by making a **FEINT PASS** so as to upset and bewilder the opposition and gain more opportunities to beat them. The English generally speak of "**golden pass**" to refer to a pass made to the right when the player's body is oriented to the left, which defines a pass given in the opposite direction compared to the position of the passer's body.

Time: when should the pass be made?

"Time the pass" or "Set the rhythm of play" are two typical expressions used in soccer jargon which refer to the player's capacity to choose the right moment to carry out a particular move (timing). This capacity to successfully time the performance depends upon some fundamental coordination skills underlying the following operations:

❏ Ability to change or adjust the position and the movement of the body in space and time, in relation to a particular field of action (the playing field) delineated by objects and persons including the ball, the teammates and the opposition (space and time orientation).

❏ Evaluate the direction and assess the distance at which the ball should be played (space perception).

❏ Assess the time it takes for a player to prepare and carry out the movement of the kicking leg to approach the ball and the duration of the forward movement of the foot that will make contact with the ball (time perception).

❏ Examine the concepts of succession/progression (before and after) and simultaneity (occurring at the same time) necessary for a player to choose the right time and rhythm of the move.

❏ Assess the speed at which the teammates without the ball are moving (space and time perception).

Power: how powerful should the pass be?

The ability to make perfectly accurate passes exactly aimed at the teammate receiving the ball strictly depends on the ability to control and adjust one's muscle strength to exploit the correct joints' range of motion (differentiation capacity). A popular expert on youth soccer likes to constantly repeat to his young players that "what is really difficult in soccer is to do simple things" and that " a good player is he whose margin of error is close to zero while making basic moves"; this means that "simplicity" should be the common feature characterizing the performance of any technical movement. For this reason quality passes are generally simple passes that are easy to make and control, which ensure the development of the action and favor continuity of play without such useless wastes of time as over-refined technical moves which satisfy aesthetic taste but not the real effectiveness of playing. **Table 1** is a recapitulatory picture of what has been explained up to now. For a comprehensive planning of coaching and learning passing techniques – including the technical movements involved in preparing the action (prior to the pass) and those at which passing is aimed (immediately after the pass) – you can refer back to the table 1 "**combination of technical moves in dribbling the ball**".

Most coaches operating in the youth sectors of amateur clubs often have to work in extremely difficult conditions both due to functional logistic reasons (several teams practicing at the same time, poor lighting, impossibility to use the main training grounds and so forth…) and because of problems of time (players are often at school full-time and younger teams are therefore forced to begin practice when older teams

PASSING THE BALL				
WHAT?	**WHERE?**	**HOW?**	**WHEN?**	**WHY?**
Parts of the body	Space	Manner	Time	Purpose
• Inside of the foot • Inner instep • Outer instep • Outside of the foot • Instep • Toe of the foot • Heel • Thigh • Chest • Head	• Forward pass (vertical) • Diagonal pass • Horizontal pass (to the right – to the left) • Backward pass (to a supporting player) • Man-to-man pass • Zone pass	In relation to the movement of the ball • Ground pass • Drop-pass • Volley pass	• After reading the situation of play and getting information (eye contact)	Maintain ball possession (short- and long-distance play) • Set the offensive build up (cross-field pass) • Gain space (pass in depth – long pass) • Beat one or more opponents (one-two and through pass) • Finish the action (lay-off pass and cross)
PLAYER		**BALL**		
• Standing in a stationary position • Moving (run up)		• Lying in a stationary position • Moving • Direction where the ball comes from (coming ball...) • Direction where the ball is played (ball aimed at...)		
DIRECTION WHERE THE BALL COMES FROM		**DIRECTION WHERE THE BALL IS PLAYED**		
The ball comes from	The path	The ball is played	The path	
• In front Straight in front In front–from the right In front-from the left • The side From the right From the left • Behind Straight from behind Behind-on the right Behind-on the left	• Ground path • Bouncing path • Flat path in the air • Lobbed path in the air	• Forward Straight forward Forward - to the right Forward – to the left • To the side To the right To the left • Backward Straight backward Backward– to the right Backward – to the left	• Ground path • Bouncing path • Flat path in the air • Lobbed path in the air	

Table 1

are also training in the same facilities). Practicing in small training areas and in short periods of time has become a common rule which most coaches now have to deal with every day; this is why it is absolutely fundamental to carefully plan and arrange each training session.

Leave nothing to chance

When a coach begins to plan his soccer activity, he first of all needs to know and test the skill level that his players are starting from – which is possible by carrying out a number of evaluation tests to monitor their abilities – and then sets the technical, tactical and motor goals he intends to achieve during the period of time taken into consideration. While planning his coaching and training activity the coach should carefully consider the physical and psychological features of his players, working out a reasonable sequence of contents (exercises, games and activities in general), moving from simple to increasingly complex situations. This sequence – which will develop in special coaching progressions – favors the learning of basic soccer skills using suitable coaching methods. A well-defined training plan is in contrast with the so-called "culture of improvisation" which often prevails on soccer fields; once the coaching program has been planned, this does not mean it must be implemented literally, but should be adjusted and modified in relation to current needs and requirements.

COACHING UNIT

This coaching unit includes two training sessions. The exercises suggested in square brackets are the activities shown for the second session.

Age: 11 to 13 year olds
Number of players: 16
Primary specific goal: receive (control) and play (pass) the ball
Secondary specific goal: differentiation capacity
Instruments: stopwatch
Equipment: 15 red cones, 24 yellow cones, 8 leather balls, 8 rubber balls, 8 colored training pinnies, 20 x 40 yards playing field
Contents or exercises: exercises in pairs 1 v 1, 2 v 1, 2 v 2, 3 v 3, 4 v 4
Coaching methods: deductive, instructional, inductive, problem solving
Testing: analysis of the conditioned game
Suggestion for the following session: depends on the outcome of the testing
Starting game: 2 v 2 soccer tennis
Analytical exercises: practice the technique of passing the ball from a stationary position, while moving, CLOCK PASS (control the ball and pass) pass the ball in traffic.
Situations of play: 1 v 1 for the final shot on goal, 1 v 1 to dribble the ball up into the goal, 1 v 1 + goalkeeper, 2 v 2 [1 v 1 to control the ball on the goal line, 2 v 1 variations, 2 v 2 variations, 3 v 1]
Conditioned game: 3 v 3 ball played forward to the supporting captain, 3 v 3 + goalkeeper, [3 v 3 ball played backward to the supporting captain, 4 v 4 using four goals]
Final game: unconditioned game with two goalkeepers playing 8 v 8 in one half of the field or in a 20 x 40 yards area.

Mark out the playing areas

In a 20 x 40 yard playing area place 15 red cones (the triangles in the diagrams below) and 24 yellow cones (the small circles in the diagrams below) (see diagrams A – B – C – D) which will be used for the activities of 16 players. The coaching method used for these activities includes different progressive stages. The primary goal of this training session focuses on controlling and passing skills, while the secondary goal deals with the so-called differentiation capacity. This capacity refers to the ability to control muscle tone and therefore measure out the strength needed to carry out the required motor performance in the various contexts of play. It is possible to train and improve this capacity using balls of various weights and sizes.

The 8 small playing fields are marked out using the red cones – bigger than the others - and the yellow cones. The overall portion of the field that is used to develop the two coaching units is 40 yards wide and 20 yards long; the red cones are placed 10 yards apart, while the yellow cones are positioned 4 yards apart at a distance of 3 yards from the red ones. While the session gradually develops, some cones are removed so as to modify the dimensions of the various small playing areas which were 10 x 10 yards at the beginning of the session.

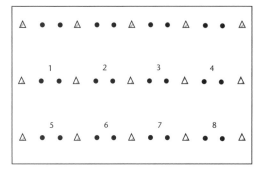

Diagram A - dimensions of the training area and position of the cones

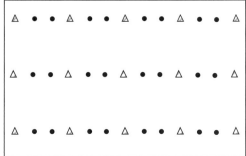

Diagram C - situations of play

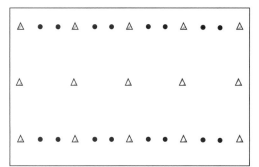

Diagram B - starting game – practice drill

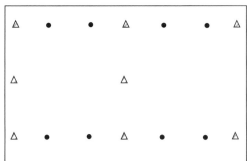

Diagram D - conditioned game

Starting game: 2 v 2 soccer tennis (Use a 10 x 10 yards playing field)

1. The ball can bounce twice in your playing area and the players can all play unconditioned touches of the ball. You must make a pass to your teammate before kicking the ball into the opposing half.

2. The ball can only bounce once in your playing area and every player is allowed three touches of the ball. You must pass the ball to your teammate before kicking it into the opposition's field.

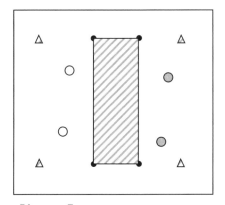

Diagram E

Analytical exercises

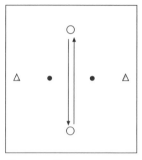 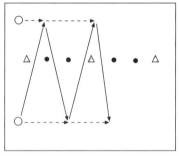 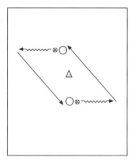

Diagram F **Diagram G** **Diagram H**

Pass the ball while standing in a stationary position
Make a series of passes into the small-sized goal using the instep, the inside of the foot, the outside of the foot, the sole, and suitably adjusting the distance between the players (**diagram F**).

Pass the ball while moving
Exercise in pairs. The two players pass the ball to each other while moving forward. Use the goals made up of cones marking the boundary lines of the playing field.
Variation: Dribble the ball and pass, control the ball and pass, make a first-touch pass (**diagram G**).

Clock pass
The two teammates have one minute to make as many passes around the cone as they can, playing two touches of the ball. For example: control the ball using the inside of the left foot and pass the ball using the inside of the right foot (**diagram H**).
N.B.: These exercises are performed in pairs using one ball; the players can move freely within the playing area marked out by the cones, but cannot touch or knock them down.

Pass the ball while moving in traffic
1. The 8 pairs of players begin to move in the playing area holding the ball in their hands. The ball handler first throws the ball in the air making a pass to himself and then passes the ball to his partner using the various parts of his body. For example: he can make an instep pass or deliver the ball using the inside of the foot, head the ball or throw the ball in. He can choose to make a man-to-man pass if the partner receiving the ball is waiting to meet the ball standing in a stationary position; or give a zone pass if his partner is moving to meet the ball.
   Variation: The ball handler passes the ball to his partner taking a throw-in; the player receiving the ball passes it back to his teammate first time using various parts of the body to make contact with the ball.
2. The player in possession of the ball dribbles it in the playing area, stops it using the sole of the foot and tries to spot his partner to establish eye contact so as to make a zone or man-to-man pass with different trajectories: aerial, bouncing or ground path.

N.B.: The situation is more difficult to handle due to the presence of 8 balls and 16 players crowding together in the same playing area at the same time ("traffic jam"). This will obviously cause obstacles, obstructions, blocks and feints forcing the players in possession of the ball to properly time the pass and choose the best zone to play the ball, and their supporting teammates to accurately spot open spaces to elude the marking and move freely to control the ball.

Situations of play

A pair of players in each of the small playing fields numbered 1 to 8 as in the diagram shown on page 187. Each pair of players compete playing:

1 v 1 games (diagram 1)

1 v 1 for the shot on goal;
1 v 1 to dribble the ball into the goal;
1 v 1 to stop and control the ball on the opposing goal line.

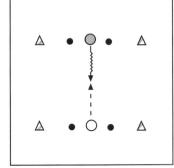

Diagram I

The defender who manages to win the tackle to get possession of the ball and score one point is awarded a penalty kick.

Tournament to designate the winner

Each match lasts 1 minute and 30 seconds.
Winner from field n. 1 v Winner from field n. 5;
Winner from field n. 1–5 v Winner from field n. 2-6;
Winner from field n. 1-2-5-6 v Winner from field n. 3-4-7-8.

Games from 1 v 1 + goalkeeper to 3 v 1

Remove the cones marking the goals shared by playing fields n. 1 and n. 5, n. 2 and n. 6, n. 3 and n. 7, n. 4 and n. 8. You will have four 10 x 20 yard playing fields where several pairs of players will compete playing different games as follows:

1 v 1 + goalkeeper (diagram L)

The goalkeeper is substituted at set intervals of time or every time he gives up a goal. Set the time for the match or the number of goals to be scored to end the competition; for example, decide that five goals must be scored before the game is over.

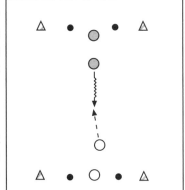

2 v 1 (diagram M)

Each defender defends one half of the field and cannot help his defending partner. The attackers try to reach the target line (the goal line) at the back of the withdrawn defender, preventing the opposition from winning possession of the ball. When the defenders manage to get possession of the ball, the players switch roles.

Diagram L

Variation: The attackers try to make at least five passes in each half of the field in order to score two points, while the defenders try to win possession of the ball and

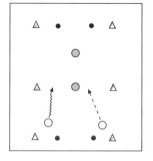
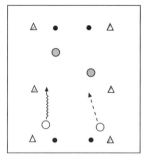
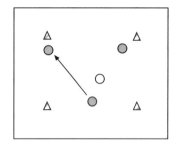

Diagram M   **Diagram N**   **Diagram O**

dribble it playing three touches. If the attackers manage to make three passes in the first end of the field, they can enter the second end to shoot at goal and try to score.

1 v 2 (diagram N)

Play a practice match; each half lasts three minutes.
Variations: Five pass games. Assign set roles and spaces where the players are allowed to play; the defenders on each team play in their own end of the field against the opposing attackers.

3 v 1 (diagram O)

Play monkey in the middle in a 10 x 10 yard playing area or in a 20 x 10 yard field (in relation to the players' skills) setting some particular conditions for the players to handle the ball: play using the less skillful foot; play three touches of the ball; play two touches.

The game develops in a set period of time: how many passes can the "monkey" player intercept in one minute? How many consecutive passes can the players make in one minute?

Conditioned games

Remove some cones so as to form two 20 x 20 yard playing fields where teams of four players compete playing the following conditioned games:

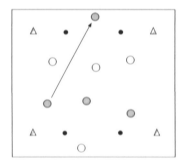

3 v 3 Ball played upward to the supporting captain (diagram P)

3 v 3 conditioned match played in the square playing area. The purpose – and condition – of the game is to pass the ball upward to the supporting captain who is playing behind the opposing goal.
Variation: When the captain receives the ball, he can play it back to his teammates in the playing field and they can shoot at goal playing one touch or two touch.

Diagram P

7 v 3 Ball played backward to the supporting captain (diagram Q)

The purpose – and condition – of this game is to pass the ball backward to the supporting captain who can then support the build up.

Variation: The players must receive the ball played by the supporting captain in order to score a goal.

3 v 3 + Goalkeeper
First time shot on goal.
Shooting at goal from the defensive end of the field.
N.B.: The goalkeeper on the attacking team takes part in the offensive build up in order to outnumber the opposition.

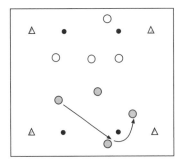

Diagram Q

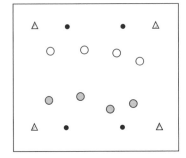

Diagram R

4 v 4 Using 4 goals (diagram R)
Each team defends two goals along their own goal lines.
Play in depth, suitably timing the pass
Use six disc cones to mark out three small goals 4 to 5 yards wide in front of the penalty area: the three small-sized goals are the three access gates A, B and C to the box. After turning around himself while dribbling the ball around the cone, the midfield player n. 8 establishes eye contact with one of the three attacking players n. 7, 9 and 11,

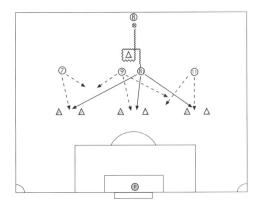

quickly communicates how and where the pass should be made, and sends a pass for the attacker to enter the penalty box through one of the access areas (A, B or C) in order to meet the ball and shoot at goal. The midfield player n. 8 carefully assesses the speed at which his attacking teammate is moving in order to perfectly time the pass so that:

1. the ball crosses the line of the small access goal **before** the attacker gets to the ball to meet the pass;
2. the ball crosses the line of the small access goal **after** the attacker gets to the ball to control the pass;
3. the ball crosses the line of the small access goal **at the same time** the attacker gets to the ball to meet the pass.

The pass made by the midfield player and the attacker's running movement can be suitably combined as follows:

❑ vertical pass (in depth) and diagonal running movement of the attacker
❑ vertical pass (in depth) and vertical running
❑ diagonal pass and vertical running
❑ diagonal pass and diagonal running

Purpose: Carefully time the pass in relation to the concepts of time progression (before and after) and simultaneity (at the same time).

Coaching progression on situations of play
After working on the 1 v 0 situation – that is the pass made by the midfield player for the movement of one single attacking teammate – it is now possible to develop several variations as follows:

3 v 0
The three attacking players move simultaneously when eye contact is established so as to occupy the three different access gates to enter the penalty box, suitably combining their movements in a harmonious manner (cutting diagonal movements, cross-over play and so forth). The midfield player freely chooses a solution to make the pass or follows the coach's directions.

3 v 2
Two of the three attackers are marked closely by their direct opponents. The midfield player passes the ball to the unguarded attacking teammate.

3 v 3
The three attackers are all marked closely by their direct opposing defenders. The midfield player reads the situation of play in order to understand and choose the best solution.

4 v 3
The three attackers are no longer forced to elude the marking to sprint in depth, but can move freely with no restraints to try to score a goal. They can also play unconditionally with their supporting midfield teammate at their backs.
Purpose: Improve communication and cooperation in the attacking phase to choose the right time and space to elude the marking and pass the ball, all this with the final intent of shooting at goal.

x

4.4 FEINTING AND DRIBBLING

Definition of feint: Individual tactical skill which is performed either with or without the ball and does not necessarily involve the player beating his opponent while in possession of the ball.

Definition of dribble: Individual tactical skill which is performed with the ball and involves the player in possession of the ball attempting to beat his marking opponent.

Description: Dribbling, which means the "art of beating the opponent while in possession of the ball", should be considered as the real essence of soccer, since it arouses the enthusiasm of fans, enhances the spectacular nature of play and emotionally involves every single player attracted by the strong desire for competition.

A dribble is usually combined with a feint (a deceiving faking movement) whereby the ball handler can disguise his real intentions, causing his opponent to lose his balance and commit himself in one direction while the dribbler moves in another (intentional movement to beat the opponent).

The offensive player can make a feint pretending to go left by vigorously putting the left foot on the ground so as to upset the balance of the defender in that direction, and strongly pushing the same foot against the ground to move right and past the opponent. What happens if the opponent does not react to the attackers' faking movement and stands motionless? The player in possession of the ball should be able to read the movement and behavior of his marking opponent; in this case, he could continue the movement towards the left, making a prompt change of pace. It is obvious that for a player to dribble the ball past the opponent successfully, he absolutely needs to improve such basic coordination skills as:

- the capacity to "play using his supporting bases", making the right movements of the feet and the body in order to keep, recover or cause the opponent to lose **balance**;
- the ability to read – or better, **anticipate** – the movements of the defender so as to react accordingly, which involves the need to **adjust** and **change** one's moves in relation to the opponent's reaction;
- the capacity to choose the correct distance (**space**) and to suitably **time** one's faking and intentional movements.

Obviously, this should all combine with short time of **reaction** (quick reflexes) and good acceleration capacity.

Players who have improved this important ability – which depends upon maximal force (athletic capacity) – can sometimes dribble past their opponents without making feints, but simply by choosing the right moment ("timing") to make the so-called "change of pace". Feinting technique deserves greater attention; it should be coached and trained in a specific and thorough manner since it is used, combined with most technical moves, in the context of "Soccer Communication" where the soccer player communicates with his teammates by conveying to them precise and unequivocal information, while at the same time communicating with his opponents by giving them false and misleading messages. Faking moves help increase the sense of uncertainty in soccer, taking the opponent's mind off the real situational goal and

forcing him to react with responses that are irrelevant to the current situation. Feints are frequent in any soccer performance and naturally belong to top-class players' technical background; remember for instance such typical actions as:
❑ feinting to shoot and dribbling past the opponent
❑ feinting to shoot and controlling the ball
❑ feinting to cross the ball from the goal line and dribbling inside
❑ feinting to make a long-distance pass and giving a short-distance one or viceversa
❑ feinting to stop in one direction and promptly moving in the opposite direction.

Players who are particularly skillful at dribbling past the opponents standing in front of them, at their side or at their back are obviously effective since they manage to break through well-organized defending lines to gain space forward and clear space on attack, combining the dribbling movement to beat the opposition with the last decisive pass (LAY-OFF PASS) for the final shot on goal.

While performing this technical move every player can express his own personality, creativeness and self-confidence, showing his capacity to take the initiative, risk and assume responsibilities.

The increasing attention that soccer coaches are focusing on the athletic physical aspect of the soccer performance has induced them to optimize the coaching and training plans aimed at enhancing players' power, which means all those conditioning activities allowing them to improve strength and speed. All this, together with the evolution or "regression" of the systems of play that often privilege and exaggerate the concepts of compact short team, pressing, offside and counterattack, has consequently caused the areas of play to reduce dramatically, which means that soccer players have less time at their disposal to:
❑ read and understand the situation of play
❑ choose the best solution in relation to the goal they want to achieve
❑ perform the suitable technical move.

In practice, all this has brought about a significant increase in the rhythm of the performance (i.e. the match), which means the players need to make technical moves at higher speed, not only while performing the gesture (practical performance of the motor act), but also – and specifically - :
❑ in the moment of perception, intended as the capacity to collect information very quickly
❑ in the cognitive and processing phase, intended as the capacity to promptly choose the best solution to the soccer problem.

I do not know if it is right to say that modern soccer players are less skillful at the technical level than the players of the past, but it is undoubtedly clear that it is necessary to revise and further investigate programs and methods to coach and learn soccer technique, specifically to meet modern soccer's features and requirements.

The coaching and learning suggestion shown in the table below specifically concerns the age group from 6 to 12, a period when basic motor training and elementary approach and introduction to sport play a role of critical importance. The learning of soccer technique is only possible starting from the learning of basic motor patterns (**table 1**), on which all the various technical moves are built and from which they can be progressively developed (**table 3**).

SUGGESTION FOR COACHING AND LEARNING SOCCER TECHNIQUE		
PURPOSE	**METHODS**	**CONTENTS**
Basic motor patterns	Play with and without the ball	• Popular traditional games • Games involving elements of various disciplines • Games and exercises with and without small pieces of gymnastic apparatus
Basic technical skills **Coordination skills**	Activities with the ball with no opposition	• Technical exercises in situation of coordination
Individual tactical skills	Practice using the ball playing against one opponent (at least) and with one or more teammate	• Simple play situations (from 1 v 1 to 3 v 3) • Exercises requiring the combination of different technical moves
Team tactical skills	Situations of play involving the participation of both teammates and opponents	• Complex play situations • Conditioned games • Practice matches • Official matches

Table 3

It is possible to learn and improve these primary motor patterns in a purely ludic and spontaneous manner through popular and traditional games played with friends in the street, in the yard, in special playing areas or at school, combining elements of various sports disciplines and under the direction of a competent physical trainer. In case this is not possible for various reasons, the coach should personally take care of the problem, working out a special coaching program to build and consolidate these key motor schemes (see **table 4**), which represent the basis from which children can begin to learn technical skills using the ball. The example shown in **table 2** includes a coaching progression which starts from training such basic movements as walking and running to progressively building the soccer skill "par excellence": dribbling the ball to beat the opposition and shoot at goal.

EXAMPLE OF COACHING PROGRESSION

From walking and running, through dribbling the ball, to feinting to beat the opposition

PURPOSE	METHODS
Walking and running	• Play without the ball: attacker v defender • Play with the ball: 1 v 1 in rugby 1 v 1 in soccer
Dribbling the ball, feinting and dribbling to beat the opposition in condition of space and time perception	• Progression on individual exercises to learn how to dribble the ball and promptly change direction with the ball
Dribbling the ball and feinting with the ball to beat the opposition	• Progression on simple play situations (1 v 1 to beat the opponent)
Feinting, dribbling and shooting at goal	• Conditioned game: play using one goal; the condition is that the players must feint and dribble past their opponents to be allowed to shoot at goal

Table 2

PREREQUISITE ELEMENTS FOR BASIC TECHNIQUE

BASIC MOTOR PATTERNS	TECHNICAL MOVES
Hit – jump Catch – receive – jump Walk – run Fall… Jump – hit Throw Dive – fall - roll	Kick Control Dribble the ball Tackle Head the ball Throw in Goalkeeper's technique

Table 3

PREREQUISITE ELEMENTS FOR BASIC TECHNIQUE

BASIC MOTOR PATTERNS	METHODS - CONTENTS
Walk – run	• Running games: run after the opponent, take the flag, relays • Sports games: all sports intended as play • Individual sports: track and field (speed race, agility race, hurdles)
Jump	• Jumping games: hopscotch, skip, other popular traditional games • Sports games: minivolley • Individual sports: track and field (the high , the long, the triple jump)
Roll - crawl Dive - fall	• Games involving contact with the ground: the snake, the sack, the cylinder or others • Sports games: minirugby • Individual sports: acrobatic and pre-acrobatic gym (roll forward and backward, dive, roll to the right and to the left, fall to the ground)
Throw - catch	• Throwing games: target practice, attack the fortress • Sports games: minibasket, minibaseball, handball • Individual games: track and field (putting the shot, the discuss throw, javelin)
Hit	• Hitting games: hit the ball using your hands, feet, head, a small object • Sports games: minivolley and baseball • Individual sports: tennis, table tennis

After the starting games, our coaching suggestion includes a number of exercises focusing on basic technical skills aimed at developing and enhancing those automatic movements that are necessary to play a soccer; this is possible only through constant repetition of the same exercises so that each move becomes automatic.

In general, the technical automatism that soccer players need to develop cannot be rigid, but absolutely elastic, since they must adjust to the unpredictable nature of any situation of play. These automatic movements can be progressively acquired and developed applying the principle of **MULTILATERALITY OF MOTOR LOAD**, which does not simply mean varying coaching methods and training contents, but specifically means modifying the way that each technical move is performed in relation to various parameters including:

❏ work load – the force applied to the movement (strong – weak, heavy – light)
❏ change of speed, frequency and rhythm (fast – slow)
❏ rapidity and/or accuracy
❏ fatigue, physical well-being (freshness)
❏ combination of simultaneous and consecutive motor acts
❏ coordination skills.

In the example shown in **table 2**, we have suggested a number of exercises in which the soccer player dribbles the ball, feints and beats the opponent in situations requiring balance, kinesthetic sensibility and space and time perception. Planning training sessions and carefully designing suitable coaching progressions means that the coach shall point out each time one of the above-mentioned parameters (in addition to coordination capacity) should be given top priority and prevail over the others.

Our coaching and learning suggestion on basic individual tactical skills continues with simple play situations where the player has to prove he can understand the various contexts of play (perceptive phase of the performance); this means that, in the specific case of a 1 v 1 situation, the player should be able to read the movements of the opposing defender and react accordingly, using the most suitable technical move to beat his opponent, choosing among all those movements that have become automatic in his previous soccer experiences. In short, in the various situations of play important mental processes are activated which help the player learn how to use any technical move as an instrument to achieve a final goal.

When the players play conditioned practice matches (characterized by special technical and tactical conditions, rule variations and various equipment), the coach can direct the players' technical and tactical behavior in relation to specific needs.

In the example shown in **table 2**, feinting and dribbling to beat the opponent are aimed at shooting at goal.

The official match is the best test for a coach to assess the real effectiveness and success of his coaching and learning program; in fact, in official matches players constantly work under psychological pressure in a highly competitive atmosphere and this offers the coach the opportunity to assess his players' skills in feinting and dribbling to support team play and to beat the opposition, gain space upward or make a pass, a cross, take a shot on goal, get free from the opposition's pressure, elude the offside trap and, why not, bring joy to themselves and to their fans as well. The sequence of activities suggested in the following pages can be standardized using suitable variations and applied for coaching and learning any feinting and dribbling move to beat the opposition.

Coaching progression

Game without the ball
Attacker v defender (diagram 1).

The coach calls a number corresponding to a pair of players, made up of a defender and an attacker. The attacker tries to get to and cross the goal line guarded by the defender who opposes the attacking player's movement by touching him on any part of his body.

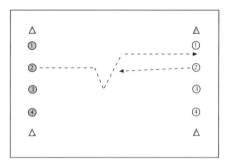

Diagram 1

Variation: The coach calls two pairs of players or the even or uneven numbers at the same time.

Purpose: Walk or run making changes of direction, changes of pace, feints, stopping and promptly restarting to gain space forward.

Games with the ball
The next games are planned and develop in the same way as the exercise without the ball described above.

1 v 1   in rugby: The rugby player holding the ball in his hands tries to get to the opposing goal line, hindered by the opposing defender who will try to touch or tackle him.

1 v 1   in soccer: The soccer player tries to dribble the ball up to the goal line hindered by the opposing defender who will try to touch, deflect, kick the ball outside or win possession.

Purpose: Play a 1 v 1 duel suggested in a ludic form and combining elements of various sports disciplines.

Coaching progression on technical exercises in condition of space and time perception

Dribble the ball freely (diagram 2).

Every player alternates dribbling the ball (unconditionally at first, then following special conditions concerning the number of touches or the body parts to use to make contact with the ball) with changes of direction and pace without losing possession of the ball (feinting and dribbling past the opponent). This means that the player shifts from dribbling the ball with the outside of one foot to using the outside of the opposite

Diagram 2

foot after pivoting, shifting the body weight and pushing on the foot that last touched the ball, recalling in this way the moves performed in the previous games with and without the ball.

Purposes: Improve balance and kinesthetic sensibility.

Dribble the ball in a slalom through cones and poles (diagram 3).

Mark out a slalom track using both cones and poles. Dribble the ball through the cones and make a prompt change of direction and pace through the poles.

Variation: Place cones and poles at set distances at first; then, the distance can be changed.

Diagram 3

Purposes: Balance, kinesthetic sensibility, space perception, enhancing the capacity to assess distances.

Dribble the ball in a slalom with the support of your teammate (diagram 4).

Two players facing each other start simultaneously from the two opposite sides and dribble the ball forward, making a slalom through the cones. When they meet, they promptly make the same change of direction – they both sprint to the left, for example - and go on dribbling the ball. They must make the change of direction at the right distance and at the right moment.

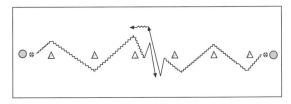

Diagram 4

Purposes: Improve balance, kinesthetic sensibility, space and time perception.

Progression of 1 v 1 simple play situations

1 v 1 along one line (diagram 5). The attacking player dribbles the ball and tries to beat the defender who is only allowed to move along the line between two cones placed at a variable distance from each other according to the skill level of the players involved in the exercise.

Variations: The defender acts as a moving wall and cannot touch the ball; the defender can jump with both feet at the ball, always maintaining his standing position; the defender can touch the ball using his less skillful foot; the defender plays as a goalkeeper and can win possession of the ball using his hands; the attacker must dribble past the opponent making a change of direction; the attacker can dribble past the defender finding personal solutions and freely choosing the best moves.

1 v 1 in the square playing area (diagram 6). The attacker shall dribble the ball up to the goal line beating the defender:
❏ standing inside the square
❏ who is coming from in front
❏ who is coming from the right
❏ who is coming from the left

Variations: The defender can play only inside the square; the defender is allowed to continue the defensive action also outside the square; the attacker must use changes of direction and pace; the attacker is free to dribble the ball to beat the defender with no conditions being set by the coach.

Purposes: Test and apply your individual tactical skills with and without ball possession in situations of play.

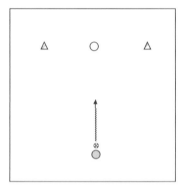

Diagram 5

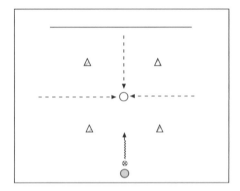

Diagram 6

Conditioned game

Handball-like soccer playing towards one goal (diagram 7).
This match resembles handball:
One team defends their goal inside the penalty box without being allowed to move out of it, while the attacking side plays to maintain possession of the ball outside the penalty area trying to find a cleared lane to break through and dribble the ball to shoot at goal.

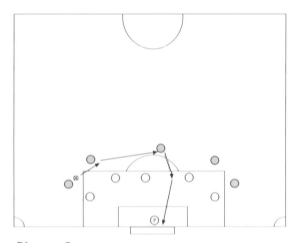

Diagram 7

Variation: If the defending team manages to win possession of the ball, they can promptly counterattack.

Purpose: Use feints and dribbling to beat the opposition and shoot at goal.

4.5 SHOOTING AT GOAL

Definition: Individual tactical skill involving the player striking the ball using his feet towards the goal with the purpose of scoring. Broadly speaking, shooting at goal includes the ability to hit the ball using any part of the body allowed by the rules of the game.

Description: The main purpose of soccer is scoring goals, which is the final, culminating and most exciting moment of the attacking phase. Each individual or team action of play should always be aimed at creating suitable conditions for a successful shot on goal.

Which are the components influencing the quality of shots on goal?

Technical components

Shooting at goal does not differ significantly from kicking technique; the only difference is that the shooting player prepares to make contact with the ball making a less deliberate movement of the shooting foot to approach the ball, which means that the movement of the shooting leg is much shorter and quicker since the player needs to anticipate the opposing defender and goalkeeper by means of a prompt and unpredictable action. In order to deceive and surprise the opposition, the shot should immediately follow a feinting move to disguise one's intention. The parts of the body that soccer players commonly use to shoot at goal are:
❏ the inside of the foot to take accurate shots
❏ the instep to take powerful shots
❏ the inner instep and the head to take first-time shots on goal, kicking balls coming from crosses, corner kicks, free kicks or clearing passes and describing aerial paths.

Athletic components

The power of a shot is determined by such important athletic factors as the player's speed force, explosiveness, the rapidity of the performance and the possibility to repeat and practice maximum intensity movements in time.

Coordination components

Taking a successful shot on goal depends on: - the capacity to maintain a position of balance on the non-shooting foot so as to ensure stability to the whole body; - the capacity to differentiate and control the shooting leg's muscle load in order to ensure accuracy, power and economy of the move; - the ability to anticipate the exact point where the ball is going to arrive or land or anticipate if the ball will bounce on the ground or if it will be deflected or cleared back: these are all necessary conditions for a player to get to the ball and shoot successfully; - the ability to adjust or change the shooting movement in order to handle unexpected events characterizing any situation of play; - the ability to combine movements such as feinting and shooting.

Physical components

The athlete's physical structure determines his predisposition to shoot at goal in a particular manner. Tall players are more inclined to deal with aerial play, while short play-ers are more likely (and prone) to handle situations and moves involving great speed of performance such as dribbling and shooting, turning and shooting, controlling the ball and turning in one single movement to shoot or shooting at goal making acro-batic moves.

Tactical components

In order to score a goal, the player who manages to elude the marking by the oppos-ing defending line and breaks through facing the opposing goalkeeper needs to:

Get close to the goal. If there is plenty of room between the goalkeeper and the attacker, the attacker should sprint at top speed towards the goal, always keeping the ball in front of him so that he can keep his head up and look forward towards the goal.

Read the situation (observe and understand). The attacker should carefully read the position, the speed and the angle of the goalkeeper's movements so that he can assess how much space there is to his sides, in front and behind in relation to the goal. In practice, while the goalkeeper is trying to leave the line to seal off and defend the goal mouth, the attacker should try to open that space by spotting cleared areas where the ball should be aimed and choosing the correct angle for the shot.

Decide. After assessing the rapidity of the goalkeeper's movements, his posi-tion and spotting the unguarded areas of the goal mouth, the attacking player now has all the information he needs to decide what he should do, answering the following questions:

1. Where shall I shoot? The ball should be aimed at the most unguarded area of the goal, considering that it is more difficult for the goalkeeper to save shots on the far post than those on the near one due to the following reasons: - it is more difficult to get into the path of a ball moving away from the goalkeeper; - it is more difficult to catch the ball and hold it; - it is more difficult to deflect or clear the ball far from the goal, and this situation often creates another opportunity for the attacking side to shoot at goal.

2. How shall I shoot? The attacking player can decide to take either an accurate or a powerful shot in relation to the distance of the goal and his own technical skills. For the shot on goal to be successful, the path that the ball will follow plays a role of crucial importance. The goalkeeper finds it more difficult to save ground shots than high ones, both because it is more complex to assess the speed and the path of the coming ball, and because he needs to move his whole body to get to and catch a ground ball, while he is able to save or intercept a high or middle-height shot simply by moving one arm. Diagonal ground shots aimed at the far post are often impossible to save. On the other hand, when the attacking player shoots at goal after controlling a pass or a cross by one of his teammates, he first of all needs to move so as to elude the opposition; in this way, he temporarily gets free from the opponent's marking and is able to beat and anticipate him, sprinting unguarded towards the near post, or running away from him towards the far post or in a withdrawn position to easily control the pass or the cross and shoot at goal. These particular situations clearly stress the player's ability to take advan-tage of a rebound of the ball, of a ball bouncing back or cleared back by another

player. Top-class players also show their skills in taking volley or first-time shots on goal, and the unpredictable nature and speed of performance characterizing these movements often surprise and upset goalkeepers and marking backs. Acrobatic shots on goal – and overhead kicks, in particular – are the best athletic, **COORDINATION** and aesthetic expression of soccer technique and represent the most exciting and spectacular manner of shooting at goal. A statistical study carried out by experts in English soccer on a sample of one hundred and nine matches played by national soccer teams pointed out that players generally shoot at goal 13 to 14 times per match on average and that the average ratio between goals scored and shots on goal is 1 goal per 7 shots. Moreover, that statistical study also showed that a team taking ten shots on goal during the course of a match is 85% more likely to win the game. This information clearly helps us understand how important it is to coach and train shooting technique in youth soccer so that players learn how to create and seize important opportunities. Waiting for the right moment to shoot only when you are inside the penalty box reduces by 50% the chances to score a goal. In fact, it is advisable to encourage players to shoot from outside the area for the following reasons:

❏ the goalkeeper may be screened by your teammates and his own players so that he cannot perfectly see the situation (his field of vision is reduced)
❏ the goalkeeper could be beaten by an accidental touch or deflection by one of your teammates or even one of the goalkeeper's own players.
❏ scrimmages and crowds in front of the goalkeeper favor the attackers who should learn to take advantage of such situations as the ball bouncing on the ground or rebounding off the post or the goalkeeper
❏ the development of many actions of play – specifically those resulting from restart plays – can create secondary opportunities to shoot at goal; this is why attackers should always follow any action of play, moving in strategic positions at the edge or outside the penalty box that would allow them to shoot in case the ball is cleared back by the opposing defensive line
❏ this is often the only manner to beat solid, compact and "unbreakable" defensive lines

3. When shall I avoid shooting at goal? Not only do soccer players need to know when and how to shoot at goal, but they also need to understand when they should avoid shooting; this capacity is part of their soccer competence. In particular, it is better to avoid shooting when:

❏ the goalkeeper or one of the opponents are so close that they could easily intercept the shot
❏ the distance between the shooting player and the goal is too large
❏ the shooting player is standing in a position compared to the goal that considerably reduces the shooting angle.

In the first case, the attacker could decide to dribble the ball past the goalkeeper when the ball is still out of his reach, but at the same time close enough to induce him to lose his balance which consequently prevents him from recovering his position and blocking the shot. The attacker should avoid moving too close to the goalkeeper which would allow him to intercept the ball. Dribbling past the goal-keeper should help widen the area and the angle to shoot at goal from a lateral and slanting position compared to the goal, for example; in this case, the shooting player should dribble the ball inside towards the goal mouth – and not viceversa, as would happen if the attacker starting from the same position dribbled the ball off the goal mouth towards the goal line. In the second case, the attacking player should dribble the ball forward towards the goal, while in the third situation he could decide to cross the ball or give a lay-off pass to one of his teammates who is standing in a better position to shoot.

Shoot. If quick thinking characterizes the perceptive and decision-making phase of the gesture, the speed of motion characterizes the practical performance of shooting at goal; the move should be carried out:
- ❏ focusing on the accuracy of the shot
- ❏ looking at the ball and keeping the head steady when the body makes contact with the ball so as to optimize the impact against the ball itself
- ❏ kicking the ball in the middle or in its upper half to keep it on the ground.

Psychological components

Top-class goal scorers not only have refined physical, technical and tactical skills (which we have been dealing with up to now), but also develop important psychological attributes such as courage and determination that are fundamental to take the risk and responsibility that shooting inevitably involves.

Those players who fear making mistakes or failing and cannot trust their abilities will always lack composure and self-control that are absolutely necessary to be successful when approaching the goal.

It is clear how important it is for a coach to suitably plan special training so as to increase the time dedicated to shooting activities in order to solve those technical and tactical problems which this technique present and specifically to develop in players the right mentality and psychological disposition to handle this important move. In particular, the coach should always try to encourage and motivate his players even when they fail, making constructive remarks and giving them helpful suggestions to enhance in them the sense of confidence they need to take the opportunities they are offered to shoot at goal.

The coach should convince his players that the real effectiveness and success of team play depends on the individual shooting skills of every single player and, among the very few certainties of soccer, he should constantly remind them that: "it is far better to assume full responsibility for missing a goal or having a shot saved by the opposing goalkeeper than to leave the responsibility to one of your teammates for fear of making a mistake".

In the "Decalogue" of top-class goal scorers are synthesized the key concepts pointed out in these paragraphs. In order to improve shooting skills it is first of all fundamental to plan activities and special training to properly combine and integrate all the various factors influencing and determining this critical skill.

The table below should be considered as a guideline to work out a coaching program based on difficulty progression: from simple to complex, from easy to difficult.

PLANNING HOW TO COACH AND TRAIN SHOOTING SKILLS
GRADUALLY INCREASING THE DIFFICULTY LEVEL CONCERNING:

ZONE	Maximum probability		Medium probability		Minimum probability	
DISTANCE	Short		Medium		Long	
PART OF THE FOOT	Inside	Inner instep		Instep	Outside	
SHOOTING SPEED	Low		Medium		High	
SHOOTING METHOD	Accuracy		Power		Power and accuracy	
PATH OF THE BALL	Ground path		Aerial path		Bouncing	
CONDITIONS	Stationary player Stationary ball		Moving player Stationary ball		Stationary player Moving ball	Moving player and ball

TRAINING METHODS

STARTING GAMES	Fixed target		Mobile target		Defending target	
EXERCISES	Coordination load		Athletic load		Psychological load	
SITUATIONS	1 v goalkeeper	1 v 1 + goalkeeper		2 v 1 + goalkeeper	1 v 2 + goalkeeper	
CONDITIONED GAMES	Unguarded goal		Defending goal			
MATCHES	Practice matches		Friendly matches		Season matches	

COACHING UNIT

Age: 13 to 15 year olds
Primary specific goal: improve crossing and shooting skills
Secondary specific goal: read the path of the coming ball (cross) and anticipate the path of the shot on goal
Instruments: stopwatch
Equipment: cones, disc cones, training pinnies, balls
Contents: individual drills and exercises in pairs, situations involving two or three players, games in groups, 8 v 8 team games, unconditioned game
Coaching methods: inductive – deductive
Testing: analysis of the conditioned game
Suggestion for the following session: depends on the outcome of the testing
Starting games:
❏ volley shot ... up to fifteen
❏ the scrimmage
❏ volley shot ... penalty kick, free kick ... up to six
Exercises: cross, shot on goal (3 players + goalkeeper)
Situation of play: coaching progression
Conditioned game: play on the flanks of the field
Final game: unconditioned play with two goalkeepers in one end of the field

Starting games

Volley shot ... up to fifteen

Each player is awarded fifteen points.

Draw lots or count out to decide who will play as goalkeeper among the 8 to 10 players taking part in the game; the goalkeeper stands between the goal posts and starts the game with 16 points (one point more than the other players since he is the first player in charge of defending the goal).

The players freely pass the ball to each other trying to volley or head high balls on goal to score. One point is awarded if the player scores a goal using his feet, two points if he heads the ball into the net, three if he takes a heel shot and four for over-head shots. When the goalkeeper is scored on, one or more points are deducted from the score he was given at the beginning of the game in relation how the goal was scored. For example, if the attacking player scores a goal taking an overhead shot (which is worth four points), the goalkeeper – who was allowed sixteen points to start the game – will continue the game having now twelve points at his disposal and so forth. If the goalkeeper gives up so many goals in the course of the match that his starting score gets to zero, he is excluded from the game.

Any player who is excluded from the game because he has lost all his points can still take part in the match as a "jolly" (all-round player): this means that he can make crosses, passes and act as a supporting player but cannot score.

The attacker shifts his position and plays as a goalkeeper every time he misses a shot as follows:

❏ he takes a wide shot out of the goal mouth
❏ he strikes one of the two posts or the crossbar and the ball bounces out of the playing field
❏ he does not take a volley shot.

The goalkeeper can save himself if he manages to catch a shot and throw the ball into the playing field to strike one of the attacking players; in this case, the player touched by the ball replaces the goalkeeper.

When the goalkeeper is excluded from the game because his score has been set to zero, he is replaced by the attacking player with the fewest points; if several attacking players have the same score at that moment, draw lots to decide who is the new goalkeeper.

The game ends when all but two players are excluded from the competition. The two surviving players take three penalty kicks each to determine the winner.

Purposes: Coach and improve crossing, passing and shooting skills in a ludic situation.

Volley shot ... penalty kick, free kick ... up to six

Draw lots to decide who will play as goalkeeper among the 8 to 10 players taking part in the game; the other players play within the penalty box freely passing the ball to each other with the intent of taking a volley shot on goal to score. However, they have to comply with the following conditions: if they shoot from the goal area, the goal is valid only if they take an overhead shot or head the ball into the net; if they shoot from the penalty box, they can also kick the ball to score.

The player who manages to score a goal taking a volley shot has the right to choose whether to take a penalty kick – if he scores, he is allowed one point – or take a free kick from the edge of the penalty box with two opposing players acting as a wall standing at the two goal posts to help the goalkeeper.

In this case, if the attacker scores a goal, he is awarded two points or can decide to take a free kick from any position outside the box with the opposing players setting the defensive wall; if he scores, he gets three points. An attacking player who misses the volley shot wide of the goal becomes the goalkeeper. If the goalkeeper manages to catch a shot, he can throw the ball into the playing field to hit one of the attacking players. In this case, the goalkeeper has the right to switch his position. The attacking player who first succeeds in scoring six points wins the game.

Purposes: Coach and practice crossing, passing and shooting at goal – taking volley shots and shooting from restart plays – in a ludic situation.

The scrimmage
Eight to ten players pass the ball to each other in the penalty box; they make first-time passes kicking the ball in the air trying to head the ball into the net or take a volley shot at the goalkeeper, who is only allowed to catch the ball in the goal area. The attacking player scoring a goal plays as goalkeeper.

Variation: Two players standing along the perimeter of the penalty box – one is standing along the right short line of the box perpendicular to the goal line and the other along the left one – take turns in crossing the ball towards their teammates playing inside the box, who will move to meet the ball and take volley shots on goal. The attacking player who scores the most goals wins the competition.

Purposes: Coach and improve crossing and shooting skills in a ludic situation.

Analytical exercises

Cross and shoot
Individual exercises to cross the ball while running on the flanks of the field; the ball should be aimed at one of the target zones marked out with cones inside the penalty area at the near post, at the far post and on the penalty spot respectively, where three attacking players are standing to meet the cross and shoot at goal.

Exercises in pairs with the players switching positions in rotation; the players dribble the ball forward along the flanks of the field, pass the ball, make overlapping movements and cross the ball towards the penalty box to the pair of players who had previously played combinations on the flanks of the field and are now playing in the box to meet the cross and shoot at goal – they are allowed to play one touch or two touch – occupying the various positions inside the area.

Purposes: Coach and improve crossing and shooting technique.

Situations of play

Coaching progression: from exercises to situations of play
(diagrams 1a to 1f)

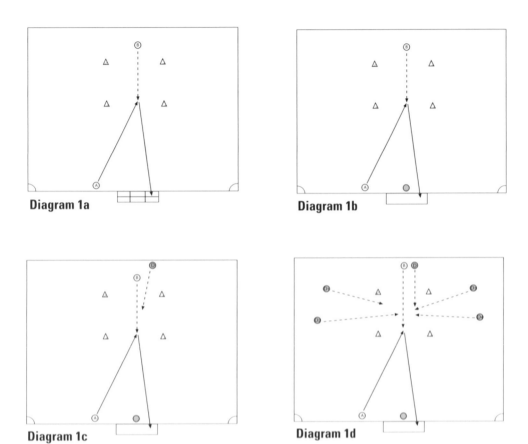

Diagram 1a

Diagram 1b

Diagram 1c

Diagram 1d

The situations of play we now want to focus on involve one of the most common and standard situations of soccer, in which a player crosses the ball from the flank of the field to his attacking teammate who moves to meet the ball to shoot at goal. The difficulty level of the activities suggested gradually increases to shift from simple to increasingly complex situations.

Variations:
1. Change the distance and the position from where the player on the flank of the field crosses the ball to his teammate
2. Change the path of the crossed ball
3. Take a volley shot on goal or control the ball and shoot

Purposes: In this coaching progression the player's attention gradually shifts from the practical movement of shooting (technical concern) to the surrounding environment and situation in order to read and understand the behavior of his direct opponents – the goalkeeper and the defender – who try to prevent him from shooting (tactical concern).

In order to score a goal, the shooting player activates a special mental process to

solve the motor problem; this mental process develops in different phases as follows:
a) collect visual information concerning the target
b) search for the best mental image to solve that problem
c) choose the right move (motor pattern)
d) decide and prepare the movement
e) shoot (performance)
f) test (feedback).

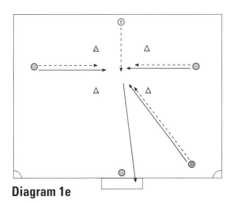

Diagram 1e

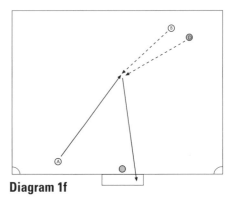

Diagram 1f

Conditioned game

Play on the flanks in one end of the field

Play 7 v 7 + 2 neutral supporting players playing on the 2 opposing flanks of the field between the touch lines and the prolongation of the two short lines marking the penalty box (perpendicular to the goal line) up to the halfway line; the two wide players support the build up of the team in possession of the ball. The players in the field make five passes and then play the ball into the attacking third to their supporting teammate who can easily cross the ball undisturbed by the opposition.

Variations:
❏ the player who passes the ball to the supporting teammate takes his position on the flank of the field (switching positions)
❏ the player who passes the ball to the supporting teammate makes an overlapping movement, sprints forward to meet the pass by his fellow player on the flank of the field and gives a cross towards the penalty box undisturbed by the opposition.

Purposes: Play ball possession to support the offensive build up on the flanks of the field for the cross towards the box and the final shot on goal.

THE "DECALOGUE" OF TOP-CLASS GOAL SCORERS

1. Assume the responsibility to shoot at goal.
2. Don't lose heart when you fail or miss shots.
3. Carefully observe the position of the opposing goalkeeper and decide how and when to shoot accordingly.
4. Determine the zone where the ball should be aimed.
5. Evaluate the technique used to strike the ball in relation to:
   ❏ the position of your head
   ❏ the position of the standing foot
   ❏ the impact of the kicking foot against the ball
6. Vary your shooting technique: take accurate and/or powerful shots, lobs or spin the ball into the net
7. Prefer accuracy to power.
8. Carefully assess when you can shoot and when you should avoid shooting at goal.
9. Verify that the alternative solution you have chosen (pass or dribble the ball past the opponent rather than shoot) is really the best one.
10. Don't miss secondary shooting opportunities resulting from such unexpected situations as a ball deflected or cleared back, the ball bouncing back or free kicks, corner kicks and penalty kicks where the ball can be directly shot at goal.

Diagrams 2 and **3** below show all the various opportunities to score (in percentage) classifying them according to the distance from the goal and the shooting angle.

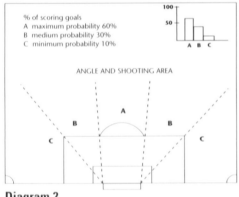

Diagram 2
F. Anzil

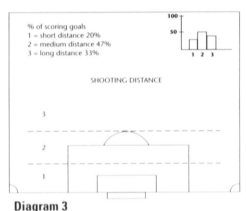

Diagram 3
F. Anzil

INDIVIDUAL TACTICAL SKILLS WITHOUT BALL POSSESSION   5

5.1 TAKING POSITION

Definition: Individual tactical skill allowing a player to hinder and slow down the opposition's build up by taking the best position in relation to the position of the goal, the opponents and the ball.

Description: Individual and team defensive attitudes and strategies are all aimed at reducing both the space and time that the opposition have to develop their offensive maneuver in order to delay their play and prevent them from gaining space forward and to try to win possession of the ball.

When a team loses possession of the ball, the players on that team are generally divided in two groups: the players who are standing in front of the ball and those behind it.

Before trying to regain possession of the ball it is necessary to take position in front of the ball itself; this means that all the players who were cut off from the playing action should promptly recover their positions behind the line of the ball for the following reasons:

❏ their team needs to obstruct the opposition's build up by playing as many players as possible on defense
❏ their team needs to play as many players as possible acting as obstacles for the opposition between the ball and their own goal
❏ in order to make the action of play develop in front of the defensive line since the most serious problems and risks generally develop when the ball is played behind the defensive line.

In order to recover a suitable defensive position in the shortest time possible, the players playing wide on the flanks of the field should move towards the goal, while those playing in central positions should move towards the penalty spot (**see diagram 1**).

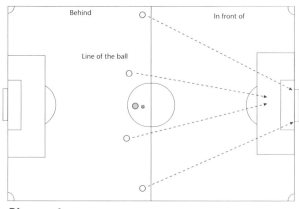

Diagram 1

Those players who do not withdraw to recover a defensive position quickly often force their teammates to defend in a situation of numerical **EQUALITY** or even inferiority; this is why it is fundamental to encourage in players the mentality to make prompt recovery movements on defense and enhance the spirit of sacrifice that this mentality inevitably involves. When the defenders have withdrawn in their defensive positions, they should not lose the concentration they need to decide whether to commit to the player in possession of the ball or the opponents supporting the attacking maneuver without the ball.

Taking the best position to commit the opponent in possession of the ball
The defender nearest to the player in possession of the ball should position his body between the goal and the ball, getting close to the ball at a distance (about 1.5 yards) allowing him to perform the individual defensive action that is commonly known as "pressure" which can be carried out in various forms to attain particular goals:
❏ **space and time pressure**: this form of pressure is aimed at reducing the range of action of the attacking ball handler and the time he has at his disposal to read the situation, decide and play;
❏ **tactical pressure**: it "seals off the ball", which means it prevents the ball handler from playing the ball in depth – forcing him to pass the ball towards the flanks of the field or backward – and make first-time passes, forcing him to delay the build up;
❏ **psychological pressure**: the aggressive attitude of the defender putting pressure on the attacking player in possession of the ball arouses emotional apprehension in the ball handler so that he is much more likely to make mistakes due to the fact that he is forced to decide and play very quickly and has no time to reasonably think of what he should do.

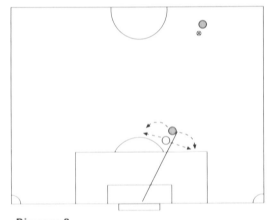

Diagram 2

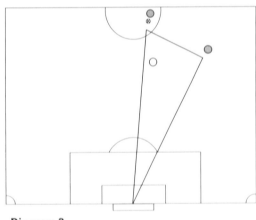

Diagram 3

Taking the best position to commit the opponent playing without the ball
In addition to taking care of the opposing player in possession of the ball, the defenders should also take suitable positions in relation to the attacker's supporting teammates, standing between them and the goal along the imaginary line joining the center of the goal and their immediate opponent; in this way, should the attacking player move in relation to the ball, the defender will stand in the correct position to move on the goal side of the ball (**diagram 2**).

In particular, the defender should move in the triangle whose corners are represented by the ball, the goal and the opponent (**diagram 3**); inside this imaginary triangle he should stand in a slightly diagonal position compared to the attacking player without the ball. Provided that his body and field of vision are suitably oriented in space, this slightly diagonal position inside the triangle will allow the defending player to meet such unavoidable basic conditions of positioning technique as:

1. see the ball;
2. see your opponent;
3. position between your opponent and the goal;
4. see and control the possible upward movement of another attacking player supporting the offensive build up.

Taking the best position to see both the ball and the opponent at the same time

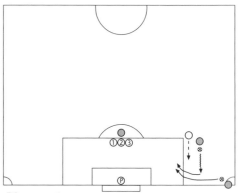

Diagram 4

When an attacking player breaks through the defensive line or the ball is played behind the opposing defense, serious problems are created for the defenders since they find it difficult to satisfy the necessary conditions to take the best position in relation to the opponent without the ball.

Diagram 4 shows an example of a corner kick situation or an offensive build up developing on the flank of the field and ending with a cross made behind the opposing defensive line.

What is the proper position for the defender to take in relation to the opposing attacker standing at the edge of the penalty area?

1. The defender can see the ball but cannot see the opponent. He does not position his body between the goal and his immediate opponent.
2. The defender can see the ball and can see his opponent or, still better, can touch him. He is standing in a position between the goal and his opponent.
3. The defender can see the ball and his opponent. He does not position his body between the goal and the opponent.

From this analysis it emerges that position n. 2 is the one which can satisfy the basic conditions mentioned above, provided that the defender does not orient his body and field of vision in a "closed" direction towards the ball (to which everybody is inevitably attracted); by contrast, the orientation of his body and field of vision should be "wide", which means oriented towards the opposing attacking player in order to perceive his movements and anticipate his decisions.

The goalkeeper taking position

The goalkeeper's performance is strictly connected to "the sense of position" that allows him to move towards the paths of the coming ball, orienting himself inside the imaginary triangle whose corners are the ball and the two goal posts.

In case of central shots he should move slightly forward and stand along the bisecting line of the triangle mentioned earlier; by contrast, when he has to handle shots coming from the right or the left, he should withdraw a little and move slightly off the bisecting line in order to cover the near post. Moreover, he should carefully read the situation of play to understand when he should leave the line and move slightly forward in front of the goal to seal off the goal mouth, or move backward to stand on the goal line between the posts in order to save a lob, for example. What is really difficult for a goalkeeper is that he should constantly change or adjust his position in relation to the position of the ball, of the attacking opponents and, in particular, of his own players standing between the ball and the goal to defend the goal mouth.

It is also fundamental for goalkeepers to take the best position at corner kicks or at free kicks; this also depends on the positions of their own teammates and the defensive wall.

In short, the real success and effectiveness of defensive play first of all depends on the players' ability to position properly, in different roles, which will obviously influence the tactical choices and solutions of the team on defense. Among the various prerequisite elements characterizing "suitable positioning" we would like to remember:

❏ the capacity to orient in space and time, which allows the player to be in the right place at the right time so that he is constantly adjusting or changing his own position – both in static and dynamic situations – in relation to moving points of reference (the ball, his opponents and teammates) and fixed points of reference (the goal, the boundary lines)
❏ anticipation capacity which plays a role of crucial importance in understanding the opponents' intents and the development of the playing action, so that it is possible to decide and prepare suitable defensive countermoves early
❏ simple and complex reaction capacity, which helps avoid being taken by surprise and making up for late perception
❏ perfectly time the defensive action so as to be in the right position at the right time.
❏ rapidity of performance which, all other factors being equal, allows the player to come first on the ball or move first in the ideal space
❏ concentration and rationality, which underline any controlled and reasoned action typical of the defensive line

Starting games

Defend the target
Refer back to the game on kicking technique shown in **diagram 3**, where one or more defending players move in relation to the ball and the target they are defending.
Purpose for the defenders: Take a suitable position between the ball and the target (stationary point of reference).

"Shadow" the captain
Refer back to the game on kicking technique shown in **diagram 4**, where the defenders try "shadow" the captain by taking a suitable position to prevent him from getting possession of the ball.
Variations: Vary the number of defenders and captains involved in the game.
Purpose for the defenders: Take a suitable position between the ball and the captain (moving point of reference).

COACHING UNIT

Age: 13 to 15 year olds
Primary specific goal: taking position
Secondary specific goal: space and time orientation
Instruments: stopwatch
Equipment: disc cones, training pinnies, balls
Contents: exercises in pairs, in groups of three and four players, complex situations 5 v 4, team and conditioned games
Coaching methods: inductive – deductive
Testing: analysis of the conditioned game
Suggestion for the following session: depends on the outcome of the testing
Starting games: defend the target, "shadow" the captain
Analytical exercises: stand on the line – between the ball and the goal – between the ball, the goal and the opponent
Situations of play: 5 v 4 to take position
Conditioned game: take position and play
Final game: unconditioned game playing two goalkeepers in one end of the field

Analytical exercises

Stand on the line (diagram 5)

Several groups of three players each - A and B are the attacking players, while D is the defender in each group – move in a playing area previously marked out with cones. The attackers can move freely within the playing area, reducing and increasing the distance between themselves, while the defender must always move along the imaginary line joining the two attackers A and B.

Do the defenders find it easier to stand midway between the two attacking players or closer to one of them?

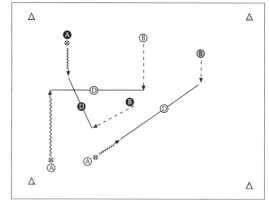

Diagram 5

1) A, B and D move without the ball
Purposes for the defender:
❏ Enhance peripheral vision since the defender needs to see and control the two attacking players at the same time
❏ Take the suitable position between the two opponents without the ball.

2) A and B dribble the ball while D plays without the ball
Purposes for the defender:
❏ Enhance peripheral vision
❏ Take the suitable position between the two attackers playing with the ball

3) A dribbles the ball, while B and D move without the ball
Variation: When the defender does not cover the imaginary line joining the two opponents, the attackers can pass the ball to each other.
Purposes for the defender:
❑ Enhance peripheral vision
❑ Take the suitable position between the opponent in possession of the ball and one of his teammates without the ball (indirect challenge)
❑ Intercept any possible pass made by the two attackers.

Between the ball and the goal (diagram 6)

Game in pairs with the two players divided by the halfway line. Three or more attack-ing players, each in possession of the ball in one end of the field: they move freely in their playing area dribbling the ball, changing pace, direction and turning.

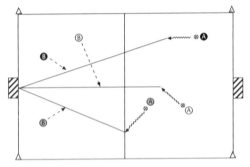

The corresponding defenders playing in the opposite end of the field try to stand and move along the imaginary line joining their teammates in possession of the ball (facing them) and the center of the goal (at their backs).

Diagram 6

Variation: The attacking players only use and pass one ball inside their own playing area, while the defenders try to position in relation to the movements of their own attack-ing partners.
Purposes for the defender:
❑ Enhance peripheral vision
❑ Take the suitable position between the player in possession of the ball and the center of the goal.

Between the ball, the goal and the opponent (diagram 7)

Play 8 v 4 divided in two groups in two ends of the field. In one end of the field there are 4 mid-field players who practice making passes from the right cone to the left one and viceversa. In the other end four attackers are standing in stationary positions; the corresponding four defenders try to position in rela-tion to the position of the attacking players, always considering the ball, the center of the goal and their opponent.

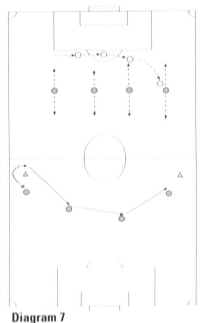

Purposes for the defenders:
❑ Enhance peripheral vision
❑ Orient in space
❑ Take the suitable position in relation to the ball, the center of the goal and the static opponent.

Diagram 7

Variations:
❏ The attackers can move (forward and backward)
   getting closer to or further off the ball
❏ The attackers can move freely inside their playing area and the defenders follow
   them very closely in their movements, playing man-to-man marking.
Purposes for the defenders:
❏ Enhance peripheral vision
❏ Orient in space and time
❏ Take the suitable position compared to the ball, the goal and the moving
   opponent.

Situations of play

Take position (diagram 8)
Play 5 v 4 with the players divided as follows: two midfield players (4 and 8) versus the opposing half back (6), playing just beyond the halfway line, who try to pass the ball to the attackers (7, 9 and 11) marked by their corresponding defenders (3, 5 and 2) to shoot at goal.

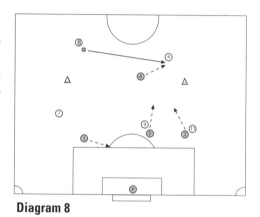

Diagram 8

Variations:
❏ The defensive line play man-to-man
   marking
❏ The defensive line play man-to-man
   marking + the sweeper
❏ The defensive line play zone marking.

Take position and play on "free ball" or "sealed off ball"
Suitable positioning should allow defender 2 (**diagram 8a**) both to intercept a forward pass played by 4 over a short distance (1) to his teammate standing in front of the opposing defensive line, and to "SEAL OFF" a long pass (2) played by 4 behind the defenders.

If the half back 6 manages to put pressure on the ball (SEALED OFF BALL) played by the midfield players (**diagram 8b**), 2 should position to anticipate a possible pass made over a short distance – which is most likely the case; by contrast, if the half back cannot put pressure on the opponent in possession of the ball (free ball), the ball is more likely to be played over a long distance and 2 should position to SEAL OFF a long pass.

Being taken by surprise with the ball played over a long distance behind the defensive line means allowing the opposing attacker to easily meet the pass and control the ball in the direction of the goal while facing it.

Purposes for the defenders:
❏ Enhance peripheral vision
❏ Orient in space and time
❏ Take the suitable position in particular situations of play on a "free ball" and on
   a "SEALED OFF BALL".

Conditioned game

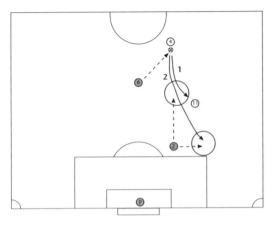

Diagram 8a

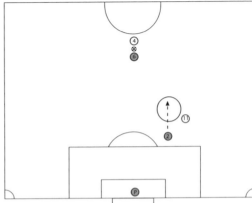

Diagram 8b

Take position and play

Play a small-sided practice match in a small playing area, or in one end of the field, dividing the group in two teams with two goalkeepers. Positioning is the only condition at restart plays or in dead-ball situations; this means that the defending team decides when the match can restart after taking suitable positions on the playing area. The team who is not in possession of the ball will never be taken by surprise with their players "out of position" at restart plays or when the ball is played by the goalkeeper after a save.

Purposes for the defensive line: Pre-arranged positioning.

Purposes for the attackers:

❑ Understand how difficult it is to beat well-arranged defensive lines

❑ Express the need and understand the importance of counterattacking in order to take by surprise an unbalanced defensive line who have lost equilibrium and are out of position.

5.2 MARKING

Definition: Individual tactical skill involving putting pressure on the opponent so that he cannot enjoy complete freedom to move as he pleases, standing at a suitable distance (space) and in the best position (orientation in space and time) to prevent him from building the action of play or controlling the development of a possibly dangerous offensive maneuver.

Description: When a team loses possession of the ball, the distinction between roles and positions no longer exists, so that as many players on that team as possible should take part in the defensive phase, withdrawing towards their own goal behind the line of the ball or getting closer to the ball in order to build a strong and compact defensive wall that can seal off spaces and defend the goal in order to:
❏ delay and slow down the opposition's build up to prevent them from moving forward
❏ prevent the opposition from shooting at goal
❏ win possession of the ball.

Every defender should be able to "read the starting defensive situation" when his team loses possession; in particular, when assessing the situation of play defenders should answer the following questions:

Where is the ball, or better, where is the player in possession of the ball?

Taking a suitable position on the playing area and orienting in relation to the ball is the first important stage.

If the defender is standing in a position behind the ball, he should promptly sprint in front of it between the ball and his own goal; on the other hand, if he is already in front of the ball he can choose among the following possible solutions:
❏ challenge the opponent in possession of the ball
❏ mark an opponent playing without the ball
❏ cover a space.

The defender who is standing closest to the ball should "put pressure on the ball", while those who are off the ball should position near the opponents without the ball and mark them, making suitable defensive diagonal movements.

Another important aspect to consider concerns the physical, technical and tactical features of the opponent in possession of the ball, so that the defender can avoid being overcome by his "possible moves". Is he slow or fast? Can he dribble past the opponent and beat him? Can he make short or long passes? Does he prefer to play the ball in depth? Does he attack spaces with or without the ball?

Where are the opponents?

The relationship between the position of the ball (and the ball handler, consequently) and the position of the opponents without the ball determines the potential lines for the ball to be passed along and through which could develop the offensive build up (**diagram 1**). The defenders should properly understand and anticipate the attackers' options if they want to prevent the attacking maneuver from moving forward.

The dynamic nature of play, with both the ball and the opposition constantly moving in the playing area, forces the defender to frequently re-set this relation of   positions and also requires careful perception, great attention and constant information processing.

Where are my teammates?

For defensive play to be effective and successful, the whole team should take an active part in supporting the defending phase. The reference is often made to the concept of "search for defensive balance", which underlines the need while in a situation of numerical superiority to exploit the advantage through position

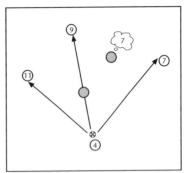

Diagram 1

ing and movement. In fact, 1 v 2 situations – with a defender putting pressure on the ball handler and another defender covering the space at his back – offer the ideal psychological and tactical conditions to carry out an aggressive defensive action, while in situations involving numerical equality (1 v 1) or even inferiority (2 v 1) it is advisable to play more cautiously on defense, trying to delay the opposition to gain time.

In synthesis, the defender should be able to collect and select as many pieces of information as possible and understand the starting situation in order to choose the most suitable defending strategy; at first, he will take the best position as we have explained earlier and then decide to mark either the opponent in possession of the ball or his supporting teammates.

Modern training includes the development of tactical thinking (see – understand – choose) through special activities and coaching-learning methods based on high cognitive involvement, stimulating soccer players to make decisions by themselves and solve problems independently without coaches playing a "vicarious role" deciding on behalf of them, as is too often the case.

Mark the player in possession of the ball

We have already explained above that, after reading the starting situation of play, the defender closest to the ball should mark the opponent holding ball possession, putting pressure on him in order to prevent him from playing first time or playing the ball in depth.

For this to be possible, the defender should approach the ball handler in the appropriate manner, standing in the ideal marking position allowing him to "SEAL OFF THE BALL" and consequently force the attacking opponent to play the ball to the right or to the left or to make back passes.

Moreover, this defensive action could be used for the following purposes according to the circumstances:
❏ delay and gain time
❏ force the opponent in possession of the ball to move in a certain direction
❏ win ball possession.

Get close to the ball handler

The defender should get close to the opponent in possession of the ball as quickly as possible (**diagram 2**) to prevent him from gaining space forward and gaining speed.

The defender should take care to reduce his running speed when approaching the attacking opponent, gradually slowing down at the right distance, in order to take a position of balance and react quickly (this is a fundamental position for marking players) to avoid being easily beaten by the opponent in possession of the ball if he makes a change of pace and direction.

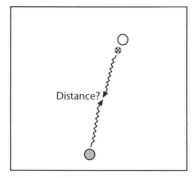

Diagram 2

The defender should constantly look at the ball and focus his attention on it and avoid being deceived by the opponent's faking movements.

For a more detailed analysis of this posture you can refer back to "the basic position of the player without the ball" carefully described in the chapter focusing on eluding the marking.

At this point, after reading the situation of play, the marking defender should choose one of the following defensive strategies:

Delay

Delaying literally means "gaining time", slowing down the defensive action and waiting for the right moment to act.

When?

The defender decides to react and "play on the ball" only when he is sure that his defensive move is likely to be successful, otherwise he should adopt a delaying tactical attitude specifically in some particular situations including:

❏ in situations of numerical inferiority

❏ in conditions of psychological and physical fatigue

❏ when he is dealing with a fast and/or powerful opponent

❏ when he is playing against an opponent who is particularly skillful at dribbling the ball, specifically if the attacker is "dribbling straight towards him" while perfectly handling the ball

❏ when the attacking opponent is standing at an ideal distance to shoot at goal or cross the ball, which would create serious problems if the defensive action were not successful.

How?

Starting from the basic defensive position, the defender always tries to maintain a certain distance from the ball handler and begins to draw back, moving the left leg first if the attacker dribbles the ball forward to the left and viceversa.

If the player in possession of the ball dribbles the ball straight forward in very short spaces and moves at a slow speed, the defender should make the so-called "**DEFENSIVE SLIDE**", which means he should draw back without crossing or joining his legs but slide backward moving his feet on the ground without

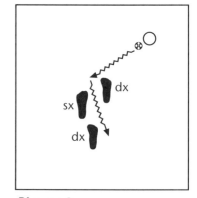

Diagram 3

hopping backward.

In case the attacker suddenly changes direction while dribbling the ball from the right to the left or vice-
versa, the defender should orient his body differently in space, moving the leg that is now in front of him backward so as to avoid turning his back to the ball handler and losing sight of the ball (**diagram 3**).

By contrast, if the attacking player in possession of the ball dribbles the ball straight forward in much wider spaces and at top speed or simply changes pace, the marking defender should twist his trunk, shifting from defensive sliding to standard running (keeping pace with the ball handler) which would allow him to move at the side of the opponent and react to his changing pace and direction.

Why?
This defensive strategy is specifically intended to slow down the speed at which the opposition are developing the offensive build up and allows the players on the defending team to recover their covering positions and restore the condition of numerical superiority on defense (defensive balance). At this point, this would allow the defensive line to carry out a more active defensive action like putting aggressive pressure on the ball handler or double teaming.

Force the ball handler to move in a certain direction
Carefully "reading the match" could allow the defender to force play to develop in a certain direction, which means forcing the attacking player in possession of the ball to move:

Where and why?
❏ towards the flanks of the playing field, so that the two sidelines become an additional obstacle to the ball handler since they limit the possibilities and solutions for playing the ball and also prevent him from dribbling the ball centrally towards the goal.
❏ towards another defender – who is standing in a strategic position – in order to favor the defensive action performed by the defender or double teaming
❏ towards the "less skillful foot" of the attacker in possession of the ball, forcing a left-footed player to dribble the ball using his right foot, for example, to induce him to make mistakes.

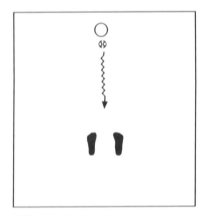

Diagram 4a

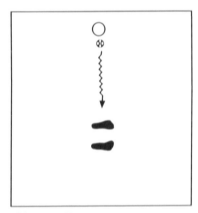

Diagram 4b

How?

The possibilities mentioned above depend on how the defender positions and orients his feet – and consequently his body - on the ground, which means that the various solutions of play depend on the position of the marking player's feet compared to the direction in which the attacking opponent is dribbling the ball.

If the defender marked the ball handler by directly facing him like in **diagram 4a**, he would be allowed wide range of motion on the frontal plane (i.e. he could easily move to the right and to the left), but would be particularly vulnerable when moving on the **SAGITTAL** plane (forward and backward). By contrast, if the defender challenged the ball handler standing on the side, like in **diagram 4b**, he could move very rapidly forward and backward, but would be handicapped when moving sideways. The correct position for the marking defender to challenge the attacking opponent in possession of the ball could be the one shown in **diagram 4c** (the boxer position) which combines the need to stand in a posture that offers balance and stability with the possibility to make rapid movements both on the frontal and the sagittal plane.

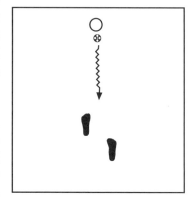

Diagram 4c

The concepts of weak and strong (favorite) side clearly emerge from the analysis of this position (**diagram 5**); the former concerns the part of the foot put forward, while the latter corresponds to the back foot. The defender who is beaten on the weak side by the dribbling opponent finds it very difficult to recover since, in order to follow the ball handler, he must turn his back and lose sight of the ball, or make a 270° twisting movement to keep his eyes on the ball. On the other hand, if the defender is beaten on the strong side, he is already standing in the most natural position to sprint to follow the attacker since his feet are already oriented in the direction of the ball handler's motion.

Consequently, the defender should always try to prevent the opponent in possession of the ball from dribbling straight towards his advanced foot so as to avoid being beaten on his weak side or having the ball pass directly between his feet. For this to be possible, the defender should stand in a position so that the path of the ball handler coincides with his withdrawn foot or even develops on the external side of that foot (see **diagram 6**).

Only in this way can the defender force play to develop on his strong side or, in general, force the opponent in possession of the ball to move in a strategically favorable direction.

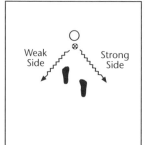

Diagram 5

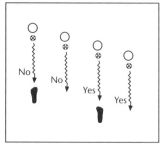

Diagram 6

Win possession of the ball

When the defensive line are suitably positioned compared to their attacking opponents, the defender marking the attacker in possession of the ball can accelerate the defensive action, putting greater pressure on the ball handler and adopting a much more aggressive behavior in order to:

❑ force him to move in an unfavorable direction
❑ induce him to turn his back to the defender
❑ force him to make a move (play the ball off his feet, for example)
❑ create a situation of emotional stress

All this is aimed at winning possession of the ball by tackling the opponent or intercepting the ball; for further details, the reader can refer back to the paragraphs specifically focusing on the main phases of this defensive action:

❑ Get close to the ball to seal off spaces
❑ Slow down and delay at a suitable distance to avoid being beaten easily
❑ Take the basic defensive position
❑ Concentrate on the ball to avoid being deceived by the body feints made by the attacker in possession of the ball
❑ Be patient because time generally favors the defender
❑ Always try to stand in an upright position because you are cut off from play if you fall down
❑ Take the initiative by faking to tackle or intercept the ball
❑ Choose the right moment (time your movement) to try to gain possession of the ball when it is moving off the feet of the ball handler
❑ Sprint rapidly to counterattack if you manage to win possession of the ball
❑ Be ready and willing to follow the ball handler, drawing back in a defensive position in case your challenge or tackle is not successful.

Mark the opponent without the ball

In order to defend successfully it is not enough to put pressure on the opponent in possession of the ball, it is also necessary to carefully guard the attacking players moving without the ball. The defenders who are marking the opponents supporting the ball handler – both forward and backward – should carry out a strategy of accurate observation of the opposition's offensive build up, which allows them to constantly "keep under control" both the ball and their immediate opponents. Since the field of vision of a player is 120° to 130° wide – but can even be up to 170° to 180° wide if we also consider blurred images (peripheral vision) – and playing a soccer match requires players to have 360° total vision, it is necessary to learn how to move and direct one's eyes in relation to the situation of play, always being aware of the fact that if one is focusing his eyes on the ball, he may lose sight of the opponent and viceversa.

The defensive action performed on the attacking opponents playing without the ball is successful only if the marking defender is standing at a suitable distance from his direct opponent, and this depends on: (**diagram 7**)

❑ **The ability of the ball handler**

It is fundamental to consider the technical and tactical skills of the player holding possession of the ball, since he is the real source of play.

Can he play the ball in depth? Can he dribble past his opponents? Can he make accurate crosses? Can he give long passes to his teammates?

Is he A FINISHING PLAYER?

This information allows the marking defender not to be caught unprepared and be beaten if the opponent in possession of the ball makes his favorite and best move to

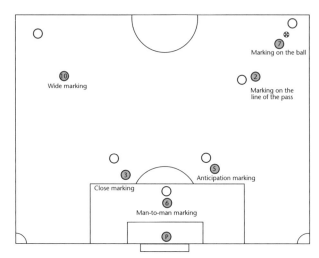

Diagram 7 This artificial situation of play - created for a purely didactic purpose - shows the various possibilities for marking.

play the ball to one of his supporting teammates either forward or backward.

❑ **The distance of the ball from the direct opponent**

The larger the distance between the ball and the direct opponent, the more the marking defender can stand off his opponent (wide marking) and viceversa (close marking – man-to-man marking).

❑ **The distance between the ball and the goal in relation to the direct opponent**

The closer the action of play gets to the goal, the closer the defender should mark his direct opponent.

❑ **The direct opponent's technical skill**

If the attacking opponent is particularly skillful at the technical level and at dribbling the ball past his opponents, the defender should approach him to try to anticipate him, preventing him from receiving the ball.

❑ **The direct opponent's physical and athletic capacities**

If the attacking opponent is faster and more powerful than the defender, it would be advisable to release marking pressure to cover space in depth. On the other hand, the defender could endeavor to anticipate the attacker to win possession of the ball: however, if his action were not successful, he would be beaten and irreparably cut off from play.

❑ **Situation of free ball or "SEALED OFF BALL"**

In a situation of play where the ball is free from any defensive pressure and can be played in depth, the defender should release marking pressure in order to cover the space at his back. By contrast, should the ball be SEALED OFF due to the defensive pressure carried out by the marking player, the defender can reduce the distance between his direct opponent and himself in order to anticipate the attacking player.

❑ **Positions of one's fellow players**

If the defensive line are properly positioned on the field to maintain defensive balance (numerical superiority to outnumber the opposing attacking line) and rationally occupy space, the marking defender can approach his direct opponent with a more aggressive defensive behavior and be prepared to take reasonable risks.

❏ Defensive strategy of the team

In those teams playing zone defense and using pressing strategy players gradually get accustomed not only to pressuring the opposition and double teaming the opponent in possession of the ball, but also to moving close to the opponents supporting the ball handler and on the lines of the pass as well, so that they are more likely to anticipate their opponents and intercept the ball.

In synthesis, after the defender has read the situation of play and decided who he is going to mark, he needs to assess at what distance he should stand compared to his opponent (the ideal distance that allows him to handle the balls played both in front of the defensive line – anticipation action – and behind the defenders trying to cover any space. See diagram 8a, the paragraph focusing on taking position).

In short, the defender should decide whether to move off his direct opponent or get close to him, thus carrying out the real defensive action.

Move close to the opponent who is about to receive the ball.

In the situation shown in **diagram 8**, the defender must decide the speed, the path and the angle of his movement to get close to his opponent n. 7 who is about to receive the pass made by his teammate n. 4; in relation to the circumstances, the defender can choose among:

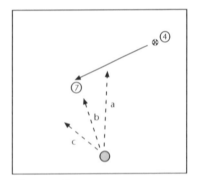

Diagram 8

❏ **Path a)**, the longest path of motion which would cross the path of the ball forming an angle larger than 90°. This path of motion allows the defender to intercept the pass if he is able to accurately assess both the speed at which the ball is played and the distance between himself and the line along which the pass is given (line of the pass), or better the distance from the "point in space where he is going to intercept the ball". This "defensive anticipation" action, whereby the defender manages to get first on the ball, involves great skill.

❏ **Path b)**, of middle distance, which would cross the path of the ball to form an angle of 90°. This path of motion allows the defender to directly challenge and tackle the opposing attacker if he accurately assesses both the speed at which the pass is made and the distance separating him from the exact point where the challenge occurs. This challenging action, whereby the defender and the opponent receiving the pass both get to the ball simultaneously, requires the defender to perfectly time his movement towards the ball (timing ability) in order to avoid being cut off from play – specifically if he is late on the ball – if the opponent n. 7 plays the ball first time.

❏ **Path c)**, this is the shortest path of motion which would cross the path of the ball to form an angle smaller than 90°. It allows the defender to SEAL OFF the ball and create the ideal conditions to handle a 1 v 1 situation. This SEALING OFF action, in which the defender gets on the ball after his attacking opponent has controlled the pass, requires the defender to understand that he is arriving late on the ball and consequently needs to carry out a delaying defensive strategy.

We would like to conclude this subject showing you the table below which summarizes the main concepts and principles of marking and the coaching unit table on the next page: frontal marking of the player in possession of the ball in conditions of

MARKING				
WHERE?	HOW?	WHERE?	WHEN?	WHY?
• The opponent in possession of the ball (ball handler) • The opponent without the ball (supporting player forward or backward)	Compared to the opponent with the ball: • with no pressure to slow down defensive play (delay – force the opponent to move in a given direction) • pressing the opponent to accelerate the defensive action (challenge – tackle – intercept) Compared to the opponent without the ball: • on the path of the ball (intercept - anticipate)	Compared to the opponent: • Forward – Backward • Right - Left	• The opponent is in possession of the ball • The opponent is about to receive the ball	• Prevent the opponent from playing the ball (pass – shoot – dribble the ball) • Prevent the opponent from receiving and touching the ball • Win possession of the ball

COACHING UNIT

Age: 13 to 15 year olds
Primary specific goal: marking technique
Secondary specific goal: enhance space and time orientation
Instruments: stopwatch
Equipment: disc cones, training vests, balls
Contents: exercises in pairs, situations of play involving two or three players, team games 8 v 8, 6 v 6, unconditioned game
Coaching methods: inductive – deductive
Testing: analysis of the conditioned game
Suggestion for the following session: depends on the outcome of the testing
Starting games: ten passes throwing the ball, duels, the boxer
Analytical exercises: defensive sliding
Situations of play: 1 v 1 + goalkeeper, 1 v 1 played in a long and narrow lane, 1 v 1 played in a large and short playing area
Conditioned game: play with the captain
Final game: unconditioned game with two goalkeepers in one end of the field

Starting game

Ten passes throwing the ball
Refer back to the coaching unit focusing on eluding the marking.
Purpose: gradually become familiar and learn basic marking movements

Fencing duel
Two players compete facing each other in a long and narrow playing area simulating a fencing duel in which they try to touch the opponent's chest using their hands and lunging at each other (i.e. making sudden attacking and defending movements)
Variation: Touch any other part of the body of the opponent standing in front of you – his thighs, for example.
Purposes: Touch and dodge, suitably moving your feet on the sagittal plane (forward and backward)

The boxer
In a ring-like playing area, simulate the performance of a boxer who practices punching the palms of the open hands of his sparring partner who is moving forward and backward.
Purpose: touch the opponent moving your feet on the frontal plane (forward and backward).

Analytical exercises

Defensive sliding
Work in pairs with the two partners standing in the playing area facing each other. The player in possession of the ball zigzags dribbling the ball forward, while the defender presses him standing about one yard apart in the basic position of marking players, slightly sliding to the right and to the left. The marking defender should get accustomed to constantly looking at the ball, taking care that the path of the ball corresponds to his withdrawn foot so that he can easily force the opponent to move towards his strong side.
Variation: the attacking player in possession of the ball makes sudden changes of direction and pace while dribbling the ball – which the defender should adjust to – in order to cross the finishing line at a distance of 20 to 30 yards earlier than the defender.
Purpose: the defender needs to adjust his defensive sliding movements to the speed at which the attacker is dribbling the ball.

Situations of play

Soccer duel
Refer back to the situation of play shown in table 2 concerning the scouting reports and tests on particular situations explained in the first chapter of this book.
Variation 1: ask the marking defender to SEAL OFF the ball and delay in order to

wait for his supporting teammate who has started 20 yards behind the attacking player and is moving forward to take a covering position.

Variation 2: ask the marking defender to force the ball handler towards the sweeper (right or left) in order to try to challenge, tackle or intercept the ball after deliberately directing play towards a certain area of the field.

Variation 3: ask the marking defender to increase pressure on the ball handler and be more aggressive since the sweeper is standing behind in a covering position.

Purposes for the defender: mark the opposition in a situation of numerical superiority (1 v 2) and learn how to delay, force play to develop in a given direction and increase pressure on the opponent.

1 v 1 played in a long and narrow lane

Purpose for the defender: suitably handle defensive movements on the sagittal plane (moving forward and backward).

1 v 1 played in a large and small playing area

Purpose for the defender: suitably handle defensive movements on the frontal plane (moving to the right and to the left).

Conditioned game

Play with the captain

Refer back to the coaching unit and activities focusing on eluding the marking.
Purpose: mark the opposition in real situations of play.

5.3 TACKLING

Definition: Individual tactical skill whereby a defending player tries to kick the ball off his attacking opponent or win possession of the ball.

Description: Tackling and intercepting the ball are the two basic moves characterizing the transition phase in soccer, a very rapid situation of play occurring frequently in soccer that allows a team to shift from non possession of the ball to gaining and holding ball possession.

The ability to break the opposition's offensive build up by tackling the ball handler to take the ball away from him plays a role of crucial importance in the defending phase and is a fundamental skill for those teams who base their strategy of play on defensive organization (keep the team short and compact, pressing strategy, double teaming) with the clear intent of winning possession of the ball and promptly counterattacking to restart the new offensive build up in the opposite direction.

This particular manner of interpreting soccer is possible and successful only if a team has players who are particularly skillful at winning possession of the ball by directly tackling the opponent in possession of the ball or challenging him in an indirect manner, which means preventing him from controlling the pass made by one of his teammates and forcing him to stand in a shadow area (the defending player positions himself between the opponent who is ready to control the pass and the ball).

There are various types of direct tackles which can be classified in relation to the positions of both the attacker and the defender.

Front block tackle

This tackle is often used by midfield players who challenge and tackle their opponents using the inside of the foot which offers a large body surface to make contact with the ball and allows the defender to measure the pressure and power of the foot against the ball.

The player slightly bends his knees so that his center of gravity is low: this position allows him to maintain steady balance, convey suitable power to the ball and better absorb the force of the impact with the opponent and the ball.

When the inside parts of the feet of the two contending players have made impact against the ball, pushing the ball in two opposite directions so as to hold it as if in a vice, the defending player can try to win possession of the ball in the following ways:

❏ he can raise or make the ball roll on his opponent's foot;
❏ he can strongly push the ball "through" his opponent's feet or legs;
❏ he can kick the ball sideways, out of the contest;
❏ he can cause his opponent to lose balance pushing him with his shoulder.

Sideways tackle

This tackling technique is generally used when the defending player is forced to run after the attacking opponent as happens, for example, when an attacker pursues an opposing defender dribbling the ball forward; the attacker needs to accurately assess his running speed so as to reach the defender from behind, run at his side to challenge him and finally tackle him as follows:

❏ he needs to place his standing foot (the foot closest to his direct opponent in possession of the ball) slightly beyond the ball and pivot on that supporting foot to allow the whole body to make a twisting movement to turn almost in front of the ball handler and face him and tackle the opponent using the inside of the non-standing foot.

Sideways tackle pushing the opponent with the shoulder

The tackling technique described above can become still more successful and effective if the defending player first pushes his opponent with his shoulder before tackling in order to cause him to lose his balance; however, the tackling player should always take care to comply with the rules of the game to avoid committing a foul.

Sliding tackle

"The player lying with his bottom on the ground can no longer fight!", this is a typical saying in soccer that underlines the disadvantages of this technical move in case the tackling player fails to win possession of the ball; in fact, that player forces his team to play in numerical inferiority – even though only temporarily – while the opponent can dribble ahead unguarded. Moreover, this technique also implies considerable expense of energy due to the great effort made to perform such a move and also because it forces the player to promptly stand up and react to make up for his mistake, regaining ground and recovering the position he has lost.

All this helps us understand that this tackling technique should be used with great attention and prudence, only as an emergency solution, for example when this is the last opportunity to stop an opponent in possession of the ball from sprinting forward towards the goal.

When the defensive line move late to break the opposition's build up, they may find it necessary to slide and stretch their bodies to make the last desperate effort to try to tackle the opponent and take the ball away, always taking care to avoid committing fouls which may have unpropicious consequences: for example, a free kick could be awarded at the edge of the penalty box, or the tackling player could be sent off because of an unfair charge as the last defender standing in front of his own goalkeeper.

The defenders playing on the flanks of the field often use sliding tackles to try to take the ball away from their opponents.

At a theoretical level, it is therefore advisable to endeavor to "stand on one's feet" as much as possible while defending, sliding on the ground and using this risky tackling technique only in case of need.

Performing successful sliding tackles requires the player to enhance and refine pre-acrobatic abilities and coordination skills. The defending player can tackle the opposing ball handler using the inside of his right foot, for instance, when he slides on the ground supporting on his bent left leg (for example, he can challenge the ball handler who is dribbling straight at the goal sliding from his right side, using the leg farthest from his opponent) (**diagram 1**). Or he can tackle using his right outer instep when he slides on the ground supporting on his stretched right leg (the defending player can tackle the ball handler dribbling straight at the goal challenging him on the left, using the leg closest to his opponent, for example) (**diagram 2**).

In general, this technical move results in the ball being sent over the touch line or the goal line (which means out of play) and allows the defense to break the opposition's offensive build up. By contrast, if the defender manages to tackle the ball handler successfully, stop the ball and win possession of it, he can promptly start a new attacking maneuver in the opposite direction (positive transition), which is a positive and constructive manner for interpreting the defensive phase.

Prevent the attacking opponent from turning with the ball

It often happens in soccer that the players on the defending team need to mark the ball handler who stands with his back to the goal and tries to turn to face the goal and "dribble straight at it" or " break through the defensive line".

In order to prevent the attacker from turning with the ball and achieving the offensive maneuver successfully, the defending player should behave as follows:

Diagram 1   **Diagram 2**

❏ take the basic position for marking defenders, slightly bending his knees so as to maintain the center of gravity low, a position that allows him to look at the ball from a suitable distance (1 to 1.5 yards behind the attacking opponent in possession of the ball);

❏ delay patiently in order to perfectly time his movements and tackle his opponent at the right moment, that is when the attacker has just started his twisting movement and is standing half turned. In fact, in this position the defender can see the ball lying sideways compared to the attacker and the attacker cannot screen it since he is not standing in perfect balance, but is putting the weight of his body on his pivot foot.

❏ perfectly time his tackling move; the defender should move rapidly and with great determination, always trying to avoid committing a foul.
The performance of any tackling move is obviously influenced by some particular conditions and is possible only when:

❏ one or more defending teammates are standing in covering positions so that they can promptly move to make up for any possible mistake or failure while tackling;

❏ the attacking opponent can dribble and handle the ball in a restricted range of action;

❏ the defender can choose the best moment to tackle his opponent so that he is sure he can intercept the ball.

In conclusion, we now want to summarize all the various phases, principles and skills on which the success of any tackling move depends:

❏ gradually get close to the opponent in possession of the ball, carefully assessing his running speed and the direction of his movement;

❏ take a suitable "waiting position" that ensures good balance and stability and allows you to make quick and agile movements;

❏ concentrate on the ball in order to react to its movements, without being deceived by the opponent's body feints;

❏ take the initiative when it is possible, faking to tackle the opponent so as to deceive him, forcing him to make a backward pass, for example, or to pass the ball too quickly or to kick the ball too far from his feet or even have a poor control of the ball;

❏ choose the right time to tackle the opponent (time your performance) in relation to some particular moments, for example when the ball handler kicks the ball too far from his feet while dribbling or when he tries to dribble the ball past you , or when he is about to receive the ball or make a pass;

❏ tackle your opponent in possession of the ball, always remembering the following principles conditioning such a move:

a) the performance must be quick and decisive

b) keep your ankle and the leg making contact with the ball very rigid

c) the point where your tackling foot conveys power to the ball should pass through the center of the ball

d) when you are tackling your opponent you should distribute the weight of your body equally on your standing foot and the foot of your tackling leg;

❏ be determined and firm when tackling, but don't forget self-control which helps you avoid committing fouls and prevents injuries;

❏ you need courage to overcome the fear of getting hurt in man-to-man challenge (body contact with your direct opponent) or when falling to the ground (impact

---

COACHING UNIT

Age: 13 to 15 year olds
Primary specific goal: front block tackling
Secondary specific goal: improve time perception
Instruments: stopwatch
Equipment: disc cones, training vests, 8 balls
Contents: exercises in pairs, situations of play in pairs, games played in groups, 4 v 4 and 8 v 8 team games, unconditioned game
Coaching methods: inductive – deductive
Testing: analysis of the conditioned game
Suggestion for the following session: depends on the outcome of the testing
Starting game: sandwich, take the ball away, the sparrow-hawk, preys and hunters
Exercises: duel exercises in pairs
Situations of play: tackle to shoot at goal in pairs
Conditioned game: tackle and play
Final game: unconditioned game played with two goalkeepers in one end of the field

Starting games

Sandwich

In a 10 x 10 yard playing area two players tackle their opponents frontally starting from a stationary position with the ball already placed between the inside parts of the feet of the two contending players (sandwich). When the coach gives the starting signal, the players challenge each other and the one who manages to push harder while tackling, win possession of the ball and take it out of the square playing area wins the game.

Purpose: Improve front block tackling technique with both the ball and the players standing motionless.

Take the ball away

Two teams line up along two opposite lines 20 yards apart facing each other, and are divided in several pairs of players. Each pair is given a number and when the coach calls their number in rapid sequence one after the other, they promptly sprint towards the middle of the playing area and challenge each other to win possession of the ball and take it back behind their own starting lines.

After each go, the coach places the ball in a stationary position in the middle of the playing area between the two formations.

Purpose: Practice and improve front block tackling with the ball lying in a stationary position and the players moving in the playing area.

The sparrow-hawk

16 players take part in the game, each one in possession of a ball, while the "sparrow-hawk" plays without the ball in the central zone (5 x 12 yards) of a rectangular playing area (20 x 12 yards) which the prey players try to cross longitudinally, dribbling the ball from one side up to the opposite one. The sparrow-hawk tries to tackle the prey players dribbling the balls through the playing field to win possession. Each time the hunter tackles his opponent successfully and the prey loses possession of the ball, that prey player immediately becomes another sparrow-hawk. The game ends when there are only four prey players left playing against all the other sparrow-hawks. The sparrow-hawk winning possession of the largest number of balls wins the game.

Purpose for the sparrow-hawk: Improve front block tackling with the ball moving and the defender standing in a stationary position.

Prey and hunters

In a 20 x 20 yard playing area, 12 prey players – each in possession of a ball – dribble the ball around and try to screen it from the attack of the 4 hunters playing without the ball. The hunters struggle to win possession of the ball by tackling their opponents: only in this way are they allowed to switch positions.

Purpose for the hunters: Practice and improve tackling with both the ball and the players moving in the playing area.

Analytical exercises

Duel exercises in pairs

The exercises in pairs suggested below should not be considered as duels and competitions that one necessarily needs to win, but should be seen as basic technical activities through which one can understand and practice why, how, when and where front block tackles should be performed with the coach constantly giving helpful suggestions.

1. The ball is tossed up vertically in the air (like a jump ball in basketball) between the two players A and B standing one yard apart in a square 10 x 10 yard playing area. The two players make contact with the ball simultaneously to block it between the inside parts of their feet.
   Variation: The player who manages to dribble the ball out of the square – i.e. the one who wins possession of the ball while tackling his opponent – wins the "duel" (**diagram 1**).
2. Players A and B tackle each other frontally on a stationary ball, both making the tackling movement simultaneously (**diagram 2**).
3. Player A dribbles the ball towards his opponent B who accurately times his front block tackle to win possession of the ball (**diagram 3**).
4. Player A dribbles the ball and then voluntarily kicks it far from his feet. At that point, his opponent B - who was delaying to time his action – chooses the right moment to make a front block tackle to win possession of the ball (**diagram 4**).
   Purposes: Practice and improve front block tackling in condition of time perception, specifically focusing on the principle of contemporaneity (now) and succession (before and after).

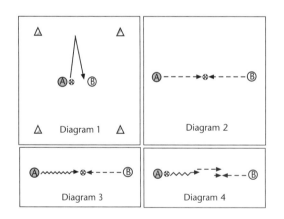

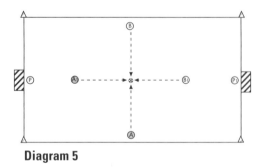

Diagram 5

Situations of play

1. Tackle to shoot at goal

Mark out a 30 x 15 yard playing area with two goals defended by the two goalkeepers at the two opposite goal lines. In the middle of this playing field the players perform the "duel exercises" along the longitudinal axis suggested in the previous phase. The player who manages to tackle his opponent successfully and win possession of the ball shoots at goal (**diagram 5**).

Variations:
❏ Shoot at the goal opposite to the player who has tackled his opponent successfully
❏ Shoot at the goal behind the player who has tackled his opponent successfully
❏ The players start from the two opposite touch lines crossing the field in its width (sideways compared to the goals) and repeat the same duel exercises described above, shooting at goal from a sideways position towards the right or the left.
Purpose: Improve front block tackling aimed at shooting at goal.

Conditioned game

Tackle and play
Play a 4 v 4 or 8 v 8 practice match following special conditions: each time play restarts (in dead ball situations) with a front block tackle suitably studied, suggested and controlled by the coach who can decide to place the ball in a stationary position, make it bounce on the ground or make it describe an aerial path and suggests to his players the tackling technique they must use every time.

5.4 INTERCEPTING

Definition: Individual tactical movement whereby the defending player breaks the passing lane touching the ball played by one of his opponents.

Description: In the context of a soccer match, the players on the team playing on defense should take suitable covering positions and mark their attacking opponents in order to prevent them from shooting at goal and scoring, but specifically to try to win possession of the ball. Intercepting the ball is one of the typical actions of soccer that specifically aims at this purpose; intercepting consists of anticipating the opponent who is about to receive the pass made by one of his teammates. This requires the player to enhance and refine his "sense of positioning", the ability to anticipate his opponents' moves, as well as his sprinting skill and timing capacity. The quality of this defensive action is clearly expressed in the need to break the opposition's offensive build up through a clearing shot or a deflecting movement, and in a much more complete sense, in the ability to promptly start the offensive counterattack (following the principle of transition).

Any intercepting technique or movement is successful only if the defending player can understand his opponent's intentions – how, where and when he wants to pass the ball, for example, so as to anticipate his movements, acting before he touches the ball and avoiding being taken by surprise and cut off from play as often happens if the defender reacts when the pass has already been made. All this is strictly connected and subordinated to the player's capacity to perceive and read the situation of play, which means being able to collect all the necessary information concerning:
❑ the orientation and posture of the opponent in possession of the ball
❑ the position of the ball
❑ the position of his own teammates and his opponents.

All the information collected must be quickly analyzed and processed to choose the best solution in relation to how, where and when the defending player should sprint towards the ball with quick resolution and to perform the technical move that best suits that situation.

In the defensive phase, any player should learn how to take suitable covering positions and play man-to-man marking (positioning between the attacking opponent and his own goal) but should also improve the so-called "anticipation marking technique", which requires the player to position himself between the opponent and the ball, i.e. along the possible passing lanes with the intent of breaking them. When the defender intercepts the pass halfway between the ball handler and his teammate who was supposed to receive the ball, this is called **LONG ANTICIPATION**, while we speak of **SHORT ANTICIPATION** when the defender intercepts the ball closer to the player to whom the pass was made. A competent defender should understand when it is necessary to mark the opponent and when it is better to "mark" the passing lane to anticipate the receiving player.

COACHING UNIT

Age: 13 to 15 year olds
Primary specific goal: practice and improve intercepting technique
Secondary specific goal: motor anticipation
Instruments: stopwatch
Contents: exercises in pairs or in groups of three; six player situations; restart play situations; team games and conditioned games
Coaching methods: inductive – deductive
Testing: analysis of the conditioned game
Suggestion for the following session: depends on the outcome of the testing
Starting games: pass through the defensive line; ball at the corner
Analytical exercises: intercept the pass; intercept the shot
Situations of play: 4 v 2 for ball possession; intercept the free kick; intercept the corner kick
Conditioned game: intercept and play
Final game: unconditioned game played with two goalkeepers in one half of the regular playing field

Starting games

Pass through the defensive line (diagram 1)

Three different teams made up of three to four players each position in the three different playing areas A, B and C. The team in zone A play the ball to the group positioned in zone C, making ground passes through zone B where the players try to intercept the ball and prevent it from reaching the team in zone C. The team who manage to intercept the largest number of passes in a set period of time win the game.

Variations:

❏ Play using two balls
❏ The defending team in zone B play in numerical inferiority in order to make the attackers' task much easier
❏ The attackers can dribble the ball into zone B, but the defenders in that playing area can challenge and tackle them. The attackers are also allowed to make aerial passes over zone B, which the defenders can intercept using their hands.

Purpose for the defenders: Improve team play and cooperation to try to intercept the ball.

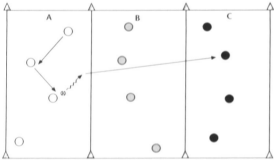

Diagram 1

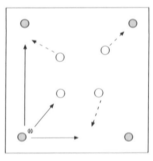

Diagram 2

Ball at the corner (diagram 2)

Mark out the corners of a square playing area (10 to 15 x 10 to 15 yards - diagram 2) using four hoops inside which stand for four players in possession of the ball. The players standing at the four corners throw the ball to each other making the ball describe any kind of path, but without moving out of their hoops. The four opponents are free to move inside the playing area and try to intercept those passes. After they manage to intercept the ball ten times, the players standing at the four corners and those moving in the playing area switch their positions. Who manages to intercept the largest number of passes?

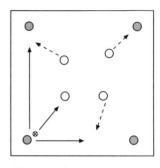

Diagram 2

Variation: Mark out larger corner zones (3 x 3 yards) and make passes from one player to another.

Purposes: Cover/occupy predetermined passing lanes.

Analytical exercises

Intercept the pass (diagram 3)

In a set period of time, the two players A and B pass the ball to each other as many times as possible, disturbed by the opposing defender D who plays alone moving in the area he has been assigned (a 10 x 10 yard square zone) trying to intercept his opponents' passes and win possession of the ball.

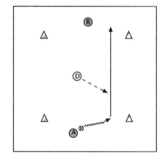

Diagram 3

Variations: The two players passing the ball to each other from the two opposite sides of the square can make ground or mid-height aerial passes.

Purpose for the defender: Practice and improve intercepting technique and peripheral vision.

Intercept the shot (diagram 4)

Attacker A shoots at one of the two small-sized goals placed along the same line, taking ground shots. Both goals are defended by one defender who tries to intercept the attacker's shots.

Variation: Two attackers play together against one defender passing the ball to each other horizontally.

Purpose for the defender: Intercept the ball anticipating the attacker's intentions and movements.

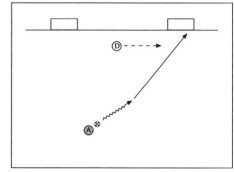

Diagram 4

Situations of play

4 v 2 for ball possession (diagram 5)

In a 10 x 10 yard playing area are two defenders who are free to move around to intercept as many passes made by the opposing attackers as possible in a set period of time. Four attacking players (two pairs) are standing behind the four sides of the square playing the ball to each other with ground passes so that the ball always rolls through the playing area guarded by the two defenders.

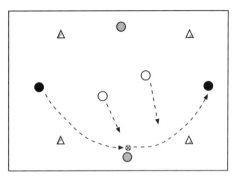

Diagram 5

Purpose for the defenders: Cooperate and work in pairs to intercept the ball.

Intercept the free kick

Take free kicks from a vertical or a slightly diagonal position in the attacking third of the field, kicking the ball towards the attacker standing in the penalty box and marked by the opposing defender who tries to intercept the ball.
Variations:
❏ Vary the path of the ball
❏ Vary the distance from the penalty box (long, middle or short distance)
❏ Vary the number of attackers and defenders taking part in the situation of play and also play a sweeper.
Purposes: Intercept the ball at restart plays while also applying the offside rule when the ball is cleared back.

Intercept the corner kick

Take a number of corner kicks – also kicking the ball over a short distance – towards the three attacking players marked by the three opposing defenders (who try to intercept the ball).
Variations:
❏ Increase the number of players taking part in this situation of play. Practice and test special attacking schemes and positions as well as defensive countermeasures and solutions.
❏ The defensive line play man-to-man marking
❏ The defensive line play zone marking (so as to cover mark all the various paths that the ball could follow).
Purposes: Intercept the ball at restart plays and promptly restart to build the offensive counterattack moving towards the attacking third of the field if the ball has been intercepted successfully.

Conditioned game

Intercept and play

Play a 4 v 4 or 8 v 8 practice match with two goalkeepers using a small-sized playing field. The players on defense cannot directly tackle the attacking opponent in possession of the ball, but can only win possession of the ball by intercepting their opponents' passes.

Variations: The defensive line play in situations of numerical superiority or inferiority.

Purposes:
❏ Cover and defend the passing lanes
❏ Encourage cooperation and team play on defense in order to anticipate the passes made by the opposition.

5.5 DEFENDING THE GOAL

Definition: Individual tactical skill whereby the defending player protects his own goal by interposing his body between the ball and the goal itself.

Description: Every team should try to stay short and compact while defending, which means they should reduce both the vertical distance between attackers and defenders, and the horizontal distance between the players playing wide on the flanks of the field so as to form one single block protecting all the various approaches to the penalty box. In the highly dangerous playing zone in particular – i.e. the shooting area from about 20 to 25 yards from the goal – the position and behavior of every single player should primarily be aimed at defending the goal.

The defender should position between the ball and his own goal, challenging the opposing attacker in possession of the ball with courage. If the defending player fears his opponent, he often takes a wrong position turning his back to him and running the risk of:

❏ scoring an own goal because of an accidental deflection of the ball;
❏ being beaten by the ball handler making a feint or dribbling the ball past him; this is due to the fact that he is standing in a position of unstable balance and cannot see his opponent's moves;
❏ getting injured: the ball may strike him accidentally since he has lost sight of it.

In case the attacking player is going to shoot, the defender should be able to cover and screen a part of the goal, using his body as a shield and his dominant leg as a mobile barrier, in particular. However, this action should not prevent the goalkeeper from seeing and constantly keeping the situation of play under control, which depends on his position, as well as on his cooperation and mutual understanding with his defenders. If the attacker's shot breaks through the defensive line, the defender should sprint rapidly towards his goal in order to gain possession of the ball in case the goalkeeper gives up a rebound.

Starting games

Defend the goal (diagram 1)
The defending team – made up of 4 to 5 players – are all positioned along the goal line, while the attacking team – consisting of the same number of players – position in the playing area between the edge of the penalty box and the attacking third of the field.

Diagram 1

The defenders alternate in kicking the ball lying stationary on the goal line into the opposition's playing field. When the defender kicks the ball, all his defending teammates sprint forward to touch the line marking the edge of the box and immediately drop back to defend their goal from the attackers' shots. The attackers control the ball kicked by the defender and shoot at goal from outside the penalty area.

The defenders try to prevent their opponents from scoring by intercepting the ball using any part of their bodies – with the sole exception of the hands. If they manage to gain possession of the ball, they can counterattack by passing the ball to each other to move up to the attacking third of the field defended by the opposing attack-

---

COACHING UNIT

Age: 10 to 13 year olds
Primary specific goal: learn and improve how to defend the goal
Secondary specific goal: enhance simple and complex reaction capacity
Instruments: stopwatch
Equipment: disc cones, training pinnies, balls
Contents: exercises in pairs, situations of play in pairs and in groups of three; team games, unconditioned game
Coaching methods: deductive – inductive
Testing: analysis of the conditioned game
Suggestion for the following session: depends on the outcome of the testing
Starting game: let's defend the goal all together – defend the goal
Analytical exercises: techniques to clear the ball back and prevent shots on goal
Situations of play: 1 v 1 - attacker v defender
1 v 1 + goalkeeper - attacker v defender + goalkeeper
Conditioned game: defend the small-sized goals
Final game: unconditioned play with two goalkeepers using one end of the regular playing field

---

Variations:

❏ The defenders can kick the ball into the attackers' playing area after juggling the ball or playing the ball to each other or after playing one-touch in the goal area
❏ The players can use their hands; in this case the game involves the players using typical goalkeeper techniques.

Purposes for the defenders:

❏ Kick the ball and sprint
❏ Drop back and defend the goal using your body
❏ Build the offensive counterattack.

Defend the goal (diagram 2)

The four players standing outside the square (one at each side) first throw and then kick the ball to each other, trying to strike the ball lying in the middle of the square. Player E inside the square must screen the target ball using any part of his body with the sole exception of his hands.

Variation: The ball in the middle of the square can be

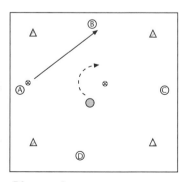

Diagram 2

replaced by a two-sided goal – triangle- or square-shaped – at which the players can shoot from either side.

Purposes for the defender:

❏ Take position

❏ Defend the goal using your body as a "shield".

Analytical exercises

Techniques to clear the ball back

1) Play in pairs. The attacker takes a penalty kick, while the defender standing on the goal line tries to prevent the shot from entering the goal using his body to deflect the ball.

Variations: Take a ground shot or an aerial shot so as to make the ball fly at different heights, carefully measuring the speed of the shot and the shooting angle in order to favor the defender's movement.

Purposes for the defender: Defend the goal, opposing the shot frontally using the various parts of your body.

2) Play in pairs. The attacker standing at the edge of the penalty box takes a number of free kicks aiming the ball at the near or the far post. He first kicks the ball slowly and softly and then takes rapid fire shots with the intent of scoring a goal; the defender starts from the far post and sprints to intercept the shot and prevent the ball from entering the goal (**diagram 3**).

Purposes for the defender: Defend the goal moving sideways, also deflecting the shot by sliding on the ground.

Diagram 3

3) Play in pairs. The attacker juggles the ball undisturbed at the edge of the penalty box and suddenly lobs the ball towards the net with the intent of scoring a goal. When the attacker shoots, the defender standing on the penalty spot should withdraw towards the goal line to try to clear the ball back.

Variations: The defender can start from a position facing or turning his back to the goal.

Purposes for the defender: Defend the goal from the opponent's shot while dropping back using your body as a shield to deflect the ball.

Situations of play

Attacker v defender

❏ A defender standing inside the goal area "obscures" and disturbs the attacker in possession of the ball moving to and fro at the edge of the same area, from right to left and viceversa with the final intent of scoring a goal. The two contending players are divided by the line marking the boundary of the goal area and cannot come into contact with each other (**diagram 4**).

Variation: The same duel described above develops along the two lines joining the short sides of the goal area and the boundary line of the penalty box, from right and left (**diagram 5**).

Purposes for the defender: Defend the goal trying to deflect the opponent's shot using the leg or arm nearest to the ball handler as a moving shield.

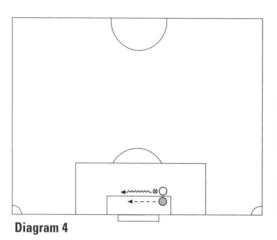

Diagram 4

Diagram 5

Attacker v defender + goalkeeper (diagram 6)

Use some disc cones to mark a semicircle including the goal area and up to the penalty spot. An attacking player in possession of the ball starts from the goal line and dribbles the ball around with the final intent of shooting at goal and is disturbed by the opposing defender playing inside the semicircle; the goalkeeper supports the defender's play.

Variations:

❏ Play 3 attackers v 2 defenders + the
  goalkeeper
❏ The defender can also move and
  dribble the ball in the semicircle; in this
  case the defender can tackle him.

Purposes for the defender:
Defend the goal with support from the goalkeeper in order to prevent the attacking opponent from scoring a goal.

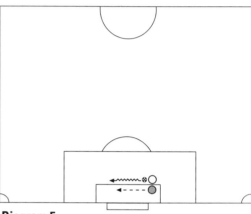

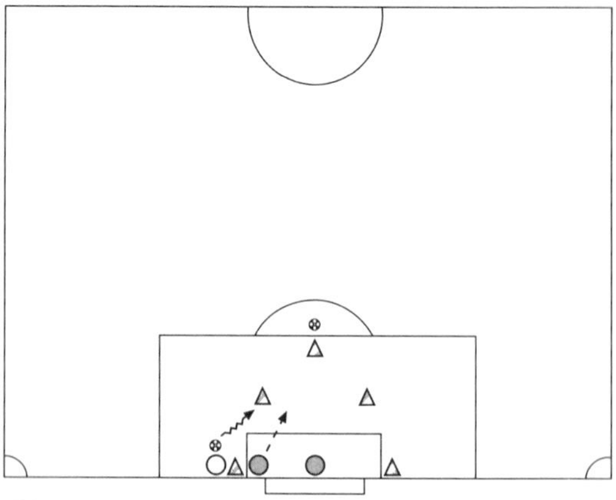

Conditioned game

Diagram 6

Defend small-sized goals

Play 6 v 6 in a 40 x 30 yard playing field with four small-sized goals (1 x 1 yard), two on each goal line at the two opposite sides (in the zones of the four hypothetical corner flag posts).

The intent of the play is to widen the attacking front line: for example, the action of play can start on the right flank of the field and suddenly shift to the left wing (through a cross-field pass, for instance) so as to create a situation of numerical superiority in front of the goal. If the defenders are caught by surprise, they must withdraw quickly to screen the goal.

Purposes for the defenders: In particular emergency situations – like when the defensive line are outnumbered by the opposition's attacking front line, it is advisable to delay dropping back towards the center of the goal in order to screen the goal mouth.

REEDSWAIN BOOKS

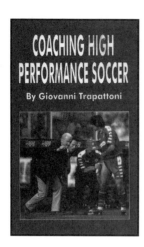

#242
Coaching High
Performance Soccer
by Giovanni Trapattoni
$12.95

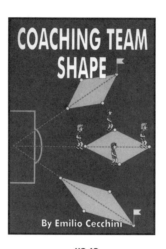

#243
Coaching Team Shape
by Emilio Cecchini
$12.95

#290
Soccer Practice Plans
for Effective Training
by Kenneth Sherry
$14.95

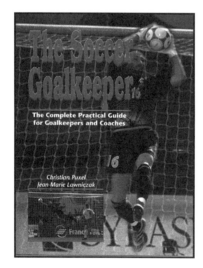

#160
The Soccer Goalkeeper
The Complete Practical Guide for
Goalkeepers and Coaches
$14.95

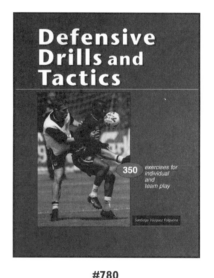

#780
Defensive Drills and Tactics
350 Exercises for Individual
and Team Play
by Santiago Vazquez Folgueira,
Barcelona FC
$14.95

1-800-331-5191 • www.reedswain.com

REEDSWAIN BOOKS

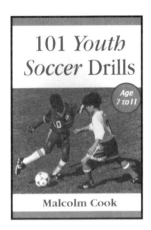

#254
101 Youth Soccer Drills
Ages 7-11
by Malcolm Cook
$14.95

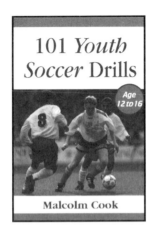

#255
101 Youth Soccer Drills
Ages 12-16
by Malcolm Cook
$14.95

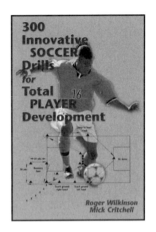

#188
300 Innovative
SOCCER DRILLS
for Total PLAYER
Development
by Roger Wilkinson
and Mick Critchell
$14.95

#266
24 Easy to Follow
Training Sessions
for 5-7 Year Olds
by Peter Schreiner
$12.95

#297
24 Easy to Follow
Practice Sessions
for 8-11 Year Olds
by Peter Schreiner
$12.95

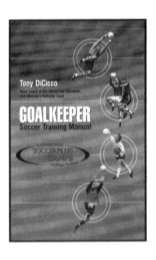

#164
Tony DiCicco
Goalkeeper Training
Manual
Edited by Mick Darcy
$12.95

1-800-331-5191 • www.reedswain.com

REEDSWAIN BOOKS

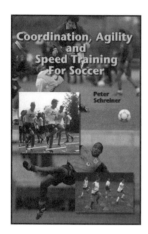

#265
Coordination, Agility
and Speed Training
for Soccer
by Peter Schreiner
$14.95

#256
The Creative Dribbler
by Peter Schreiner
$14.95

#195
Dutch Soccer Drills
Vol. 3
by Henny Kormelink
$12.95

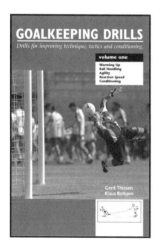

#161
Goalkeeping Drills
Volume One
by Gerd Thissen
Klaus Röllgen
$12.95

#161
Goalkeeping Drills
Volume Two
by Gerd Thissen
Klaus Röllgen
$12.95

#249:
Coaching the 3-4-3
by Massimos Lucchesi
$12.95

1-800-331-5191 • www.reedswain.com

REEDSWAIN BOOKS

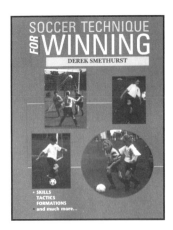

#155
Soccer Technique
for Winning
by Derek Smethurst
$14.95

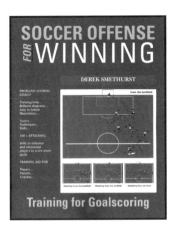

#156
Soccer Offense for
Winning
by Derek Smethurst
$14.95

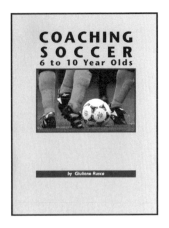

#264
Coaching Soccer
6 to 10 year Olds
by Giuliano Rusca
$14.95

#167
Soccer Training
Games, Drills, and
Fitness Exercises
by Malcolm Cook
$14.95

#149
SOCCER TACTICS
An Analysis of Attack and
Defense
by Massimo Lucchesi
$12.95

#950
SOCCER:
How to Play the Game:
The Official Playing and
Coaching Manual for
Youth Soccer of the USSF
$29.95

1-800-331-5191 • www.reedswain.com

NOTES